The Nine Standards

Ancient Cairns or Modern Folly?

Stephen Walker

HAYLOFT PUBLISHING LTD.
STAINMORE

First published by Hayloft 2008

Hayloft Publishing Ltd, South Stainmore, Kirkby Stephen,
Cumbria, CA17 4DJ

tel: 017683 42300
e-mail: books@hayloft.eu
web: www.hayloft.eu

ISBN 1 904524 60 5 (paperback)
ISBN 1 904524 64 8 (hardback)

A catalogue record for this book is available from the British Library

Printed and bound in the EU

Papers used by Hayloft are natural, recyclable products made from wood grown in
sustainable forests. The manufacturing processes conform to the environmental regulations
of the country of origin.

This book is dedicated to my wife Marie without whose understanding and support it could not have been researched and written. *Dengan segenap hatiku.*

Nine Standards from Hartley, near Kirkby Stephen.
Photograph courtesy of Peter Koronka.

Contents

List of Figures and Plates

FIGURES:

PLATES:

Foreword

Actually I never intended to write a book about the Nine Standards: I simply wanted to find one somewhere, to buy it and read it, so that I could find out more about these old friends on the Westmorland skyline of my childhood. But it wasn't as easy as that, and the more I looked, the more puzzling it became. So I gave up the search for a book, and started to look around to find out what was really known about them, which turned out – as others have already found – to be very little indeed.

I had always thought that they were 'ancient cairns', but it didn't take long to discover that the recognised antiquarians do not even mention them, and that in the absence of any solid information about them, the Nine Standards have often been dismissed as a recent 'folly', built by someone with more money than sense, or as the work of a few locals, drystone wallers perhaps, coal miners, shepherds or lead miners, with time on their hands and nothing better to do. So before wasting a lot of time, I walked up there and had another look, to reassure myself that my childhood memories of them, reinforced over the years by repeated visits, had not exaggerated their size or their dominating presence in the landscape of my youth.

My parents (grandparents, and great-grandparents) were Kirkby people and we lived by the waterfall down Mill Lane, now called Riverside. The stones of the old weir that had once diverted the Eden to power the High Mill were still visible in our lower garden and then they crossed the river diagonally, pointing towards Hartley Castle up on the hill, and beyond that towards the Nine Standards on the distant skyline. The layers of history were all around, taken for granted, and absorbed unconsciously to become the roots of life. Even as children, we understood that our landscape had been lived in and used in changing ways for centuries. The old mill was now a house, but it still had thick flagstones on the roof, and an arched front door high enough for a horse and cart to pass through. Floods had broken the weir, and the mill race was now a rose garden, but the foundations still stuck up and you could paddle across the river on them to drink cool water at the spring on the far side. Sir Andrew's castle, built on an earlier fort, had long been dismantled, taken away stone by stone to Edenhall, and was now a working farm; and the Nine Standards – well, they were just the Nine Standards, on guard above the town, as they always had been.

Coming back to them after almost fifty years, and seeing them from a different perspective, they were even more impressive than when I first visited them around 1949. But now the lack of facts about them was puzzling, even irritating. After all, we knew our house was once a mill: we had the builders' drawings to prove it, as well as Grandpa's stories. We guessed the town was 'a nest of traitors' in a violent past because we played in the underground tunnels as children. We knew about the famous Lords of Hartley Castle and Wharton Hall: their tombs were in our Church. But the Nine Standards remained a mystery: so, ancient cairns or a modern folly?

After a career that began at the Directorate of Overseas Surveys, like the Ordnance Survey but tasked with mapping the Colonies and Commonwealth, my first instinct was to look at the Ordnance Survey's First Edition maps of Westmorland from 1867, and I was duly reassured to find the Nine Standards clearly shown. So they are at least 150 years old. Some of the earlier maps of Westmorland also showed them – and some didn't – but this still pushed their age back into the early 18th or late 17th century. Perhaps they were not so young after all. I started to make a few notes.

The next major class of material was the many surviving parish, township and manorial 'perambulations', traditionally carried out in Rogation Week, five weeks or so after Easter, and known as 'beating the bounds.' Originally this involved a circuit of the various way-points around the boundary, a series of memorable landmarks, recited or perhaps chanted, by the asssembled worthies from both sides of the border as they rode or tramped around the mutually agreed limits. Memorised by every succeeding generation in a pre-literate society, these landmarks eventually came to be written down, and now form a treasure trove of early place names in sometimes very remote areas, written down using what for us is strange grammar and spelled in an amazing variety of early forms. Place names themselves can tell us a good deal about the people who coined them, and if used with care may indicate the dates at which the places appear to have been named. Occasionally the hint of an old and very early charter emerged from the shadows, and this book – for that is what my accumulated notes were now coming to resemble – could well have been sub-titled 'The search for Gilbert's Charter.'

But often the limits of recorded local and national history are reached around the time of the Norman Conquest in 1066, and the search for information about the Nine Standards becomes more diffuse, entering many diverse and complex fields of specialist knowledge where rash amateurs intrude at their peril. There are hints from pre-history or proto-history of many possibilities: here, there is scope for speculation and an absence of certainty as we reach those very margins where the map-makers of old would write, 'Here be dragons.' And then there is archaeology. Or would be, if any archaeological evidence were available for the Nine Standards. That remains for the future, perhaps.

In brief, the present book seeks to establish that the Nine Standards are ancient cairns, not a modern folly, and to present in detail some of the material that is available to suggest their existence over at least a thousand years, and thereby convince the sceptical that the Nine Standards are a legitimate subject for properly funded archaeological research. The hope is that the book may also stimulate others to bring forward, or to unearth, material of which they are aware or may have heard whispers. Research is always a communal endeavour, building on what has gone before, correcting previous errors – and making a few more – but above all, presenting information to those who will come later. In the meantime, material and leads for the thousand years preceding the Norman Conquest are accumulating, and the various loose ends in the present book are being pursued. So it is very much a record of work in progress. But this seems a good time to pause and reflect.

Stephen Walker
Candi Dasa, Bali
4 June 2008

List of Abbreviations

AD	Anno Domini, in other words After Christ
BC	Before Christ or Before the Christian Era
BL	The British Library
Bodleian	The Bodleian Library at Oxford
CRO	County Record Office
CROC	County Record Office at Carlisle
CROK	County Record Office at Kendal
DRO	Durham Record Office
D/HH	Durham County Record Office archive of Hanby Holmes papers
ECCP	East Cumbria Countryside Project
HER	Historical Environment Record data base at the Council Offices, Kendal
HH	Hanby Holmes archive of papers at DRO
Kew	Location of The National Archives in Surrey
n.d.	not dated, no date, undated
NYCRO	North Yorkshire County Record Office, at Northallerton
OAN	Oxford Archaeology North (fomerly Lancaster University Archaeology Unit)
OS	The Ordnance Survey, at Southampton
PRO	Public Record Office
RCHME	Royal Commission on Historical Monuments Evaluation
RCHMW	Royal Commission on Historical Monuments Report for Westmorland
SAL	Society of Antiquaries of London
St. Pancras	Location of The British Library in London
TCWAAS	Transactions of the Cumberland and Westmorland Antiquarian and Archaeological Society
TNA	The National Archives, at Kew
WD/HOTH	Westmorland Deposit of the Hothfield family, held at CROK

Acknowledgements

I make no apologies for including in the text quotations from named individuals who have given me the benefit of their time and knowledge in writing this book. I hope that their inclusion will be seen and understood as an acknowledgement of my gratitude to them, and my recognition that they are indeed joint authors of this book. I have transcribed their views from letters, phone conversations and emails as accurately as I can, and I have made every effort to present a balanced account of what they said. I apologise unreservedly to them for any errors I may unwittingly have made in understanding or interpreting what they said. I hope by including their names in the text that their generous contributions to this book will be recognised and appreciated by all its readers, as much as they have been by me.

I also want to thank anybody I may have inadvertently missed off this list. Finally I acknowledge the inputs made by the many people with whom I have discussed the Nine Standards over the last few years: they are too numerous to mention individually but their knowledge and views are greatly valued. I have tried my best to reflect them accurately in the text that follows.

Steven Allen, master waller, Drystone Walling Association Central Committee, at Tebay, Cumbria; Lawrence and Sheila Barker, local historians at Healaugh, Swaledale; Geoffrey W S Barrow, DLitt., FBA, FRSE, Professor Emeritus, University of Edinburgh; Rev. Gillian Bobbett, retired Minister and local historian at Muker, Swaledale; Margaret J Bousted, Senior Archivist (collections), and staff at NYCRO; David M Bowcock, Assistant County Archivist, and staff at CROC; Claire Breay, Curator at the British Library; Janet Burton, BA, DPhil., FSA, FRHist. S, Professor of Medieval History, University of Wales at Lampeter.

Dick Capel, Project Manager at the East Cumbria Countryside Project, at Kirkby Stephen; Helen Clifford, PhD, Curator at Swaledale Museum, Reeth, Swaledale; Greg Colley, Reference Librarian, Special Collections and Manuscripts, Bodleian Library, Oxford; William R Cooper, MA, PhD, ThD at Portsmouth; Sean Cunningham, PhD, Medieval Records, at The National Archives, Kew; Peter Eyre, Assistant County Archivist, and staff at CROK;

Margaret Gelling OBE, DLitt., FBA, at Birmingham; Jennifer Gill, MA, County Archivist at DRO; Adrian James at the Society of Antiquaries of London Library; Emilia Jamroziak, PhD, Senior Lecturer in Medieval History, University of Leeds.

Simon Ledingham, Gyrocopter Pilot and Photographer, at Carlisle Airport, Cumbria, working in collaboration with www/visitcumbria.com; Eric Jones, Hon. Sec. TCWAAS and independent researcher; Barry Stacey, Manager, Tourist Information Centre at Kirkby Stephen; Jo Mackintosh, Historic Environment Records Officer, Economy, Culture and Environment, Cumbria County Council, Kendal; Keith O'Sullivan, Cathedral Librarian at Canterbury Cathedral Library and Archives; Charles V. Phythian-Adams, Professor Emeritus and University Research Fellow, Department of English Local History, University of Leicester, Dr John B A Hamilton, Mallerstang, local historian, Alan H Bell, Nateby, local historian.

ONE

Introduction

The Nine Standards are a group of drystone cairns on the skyline on the Pennine watershed east of Kirkby Stephen, on the border between the present counties of Cumbria and Yorkshire in northern England. From the Pennines rivers flow west into the Irish Sea and east into the North Sea, as shown in Figure 1 (see page 66). The cairns are built from slabs of gritstone, flagstone or sandstone dug from nearby quarry sites, and laid to form a line of tall cairns on a deliberately chosen site. They are emphatically not 'clearance cairns'; they were not created by digging out and piling up rough stones in random piles to make cultivation easier. They are made of flat slabs, generally larger at the bottom of each cairn, and becoming smaller towards the top, constructed without any mortar or cement and shaped to withstand the harsh environment of the fell tops.

Each cairn is roughly circular in plan; diameters at the ground vary from 1.7m to 3.7m and they taper to blunt summits between 2.5 and 3.5 metres above the ground. The largest is the central cairn, which has two intermediate 'steps' enabling the intrepid to gain access to the very top. The nine cairns are spread out across the skyline at irregular intervals, in a slightly curved line some 75 metres from end to end. The northernmost cairn is an exception; reconstructed as a former Ordnance Survey Bench Mark, it is roughly square in plan, about 1.4m on each side, and is slightly offset from the main line, as shown in the author's sketch map in Figure 1 (page 66), and the digital aerial photograph in Plate 1 (page 65).

The whole group is aligned on a roughly north-north-east to south-south-west axis, and hence faces towards the west-north-west, to Kirkby Stephen, and on down the Eden Valley. It is not possible to say whether they were originally built precisely in a straight line. Periodic collapse and re-building may have slightly altered the original alignment, but as a group it is clear that they were deliberately placed along the crest of the watershed at this point, and on the skyline as viewed from the lowlands of the Eden Valley to the west. To the east and south-east, they are practically invisible until hikers are within a few hundred yards.

Over the years, like the drystone walls that are such a feature of the local farming landscape, wind and rain, frost and ice, all take their toll in these very exposed situations. Periodically, they have needed maintenance and re-building, and the unspoken tradition in earlier times, as elsewhere in the mountains, was that those who passed by would add a stone to each cairn, and ensure that these landmark aids to navigation and the survival of travellers in what can be rapidly changing weather conditions would survive down through the generations.

As a native of Kirkby Stephen, I first visited the Nine Standards in the 1940s as a small child, the last bit of the return journey on my father's back! I have returned very frequently since, to recharge batteries run down by too much urban living. In those days, everybody who passed by added a stone to each of the cairns, and in that way they were constantly maintained with very little effort. I can't recall anybody ever saying that this had to be done; but everybody did it. It was a tradition. Occasionally, during a particularly severe winter, one or other of the cairns would collapse and then some of the older men from the town or from local farms would go up and repair it. Most locals still look up to them several times each day, but the habit of adding a stone on each visit seems sadly to have lapsed.

In the summer of 2005, the five northernmost cairns were made safer for public access and greatly improved by the foresight and generosity of the East Cumbria Countryside Project (ECCP) under Dick Capel. Great care was taken to re-build the cairns in the same shapes and sizes, by comparison with earlier photographs and postcards of various dates, and in exactly the same places as before. The work was carried out over three days by Steve Allen, a master waller, and two of his assistants.

Oblique aerial photographs of the cairns taken by gyrocopter pilot Simon Ledingham in May and September 2005, before and after the reconstruction, are given in plates 2 and 3 (page 67). Photographs were also taken during the reconstruction – see plates 4 and 5 (page 68), kindly supplied by Barry Stacey.

During the reconstruction, all the stones for each of the five cairns were removed right down to and including the lowest layer of flat slabs, which was just one round below grass level. The ground surface below the lowest round was gravel and stone. These were the only footings - there were no foundations as such, and the wallers did not notice any signs that there might be anything buried underneath. Nor did they notice any initials, inscriptions or other markings on the individual flagstones. There were no large boulders in the middle of any cairn – it has been suggested that a number of large single stones, possibly the type of rounded ice-worn boulders known as 'glacial erratics', may once have stood on this ridge, each forming a central core around which a cairn might have evolved, but there is no evidence for it. The expert wallers noted that the last cairn at the northern end was of much more recent construction than the rest – this is the one the OS used as a Bench Mark, as mentioned above.

Folk memory

We do not know when the Nine Standards were built, by whom or why, so the question has often been asked by people new to the area and its traditions: are they ancient cairns or some modern folly? The dictionary defines a 'folly' as a costly structure, considered by most people as useless, and often linked with the builder's name. With such a prominent landmark as the Nine Standards, it is highly likely that the builder, the event and/or the date would have been recorded in some form in the place name, and that it would be remembered locally. If they had been built in the last 300 or 400 years, a local memory of the event would have persisted.

One such folly in the area, the Fox Tower on the Hellbeck estate above Brough, has attracted speculation about its origins. But it is known (Robertson and Koronka, 1992), that it was built by John Metcalfe Carleton in 1775 as an addition to Helbeck Hall, the fine mansion he also built. Mr Carleton enjoyed fox-hunting but tradition has it that he was somehow disabled, and built the tower so he could follow the hunt. However, the tower commands fine views over the surrounding countryside, and is said to occupy the site of a beacon formerly used to warn of Scottish invasions, so it is just as likely that it was built so that the owner and his family could enjoy the wonderful vista in comfort. The point here is that its origin is known.

There are several other good examples in the area where much older and far less prominent features of the landscape are specifically associated with named historical individuals: a few cases are given below. They bear witness to the very strong persistence of local folk memory throughout the ages when literacy was rare, and oral tradition was the norm.

For example, on Mallerstang Edge there is a drystone cairn some 1.5 metres high, roughly square and tapering from perhaps a metre wide at the base to about half a metre at the top, with the initials AP and the date 1664 on one of the larger stones half way up on the south side. This is known to be a manorial boundary marker placed there by Anne Pembroke, better known locally as Lady Anne Clifford, Duchess of Pembroke, Dorset and Montgomery. Less than a kilometre away, what some call Gregory Chapel on Mallerstang Edge is also called 'The Lady's Building' in a perambulation of 1811. After 350 years, Lady Anne's association with the cairn is as well-known as her long residence and reconstruction at Pendragon Castle in the valley below and along the high road over to Skipton, as well as elsewhere in the Eden Valley.

The Lord's Stone above Fell House on the boundary between the civil parishes of Winton and Hartley, an impressive rock almost two metres high, four metres long and over three metres wide, is probably another Clifford manorial boundary marker for Winton, or possibly a Musgrave marker for Hartley. There are various sets of initials and enigmatic signs on the sides and top, but none are easily legible today.

On Kirkby Stephen Common a long series of manorial perambulations, in 1651, 1684, 1749, 1808 and 1842 all record as a boundary marker, "a stone [that] had formerly stood with the Clifford's name on it, it being in Asse Fell end." These parish boundaries however do not pass anywhere near the Nine Standards and so only the earliest and most complete are reproduced in the relevant section below, but again the association with the Clifford family is remembered after more than 350 years.

Similarly, in Mallerstang the second boundary marker listed by John Hamilton (1993) reads: "2. Thence through Sopkeld, otherwise Killing Close, to a place where a crab tree formerly stood which was marked by Henry Lord Clifford, great grandfather to George, late Earl of Cumberland, as his boundary mark; near which place in the year of our Lord 1651, when the said boundary was ridden for the Right Honourable Anne, Countess Dowager of Pembroke, stood an ash tree which upon that occasion was marked AP as a boundary mark."

This appears to be an amalgamation of material from Rev. W. Nicholls (1883) and Mary Thompson (1965) dating to around 1906. A very much older perambulation of Mallerstang which long precedes the Clifford association is given in a later section on types of early charters. The 1906 perambulation of Mallerstang is not included in this book because the boundary goes nowhere near the Nine Standards, but the above quotation from John Hamilton reinforces the point about the very strong persistence of local memory in a rural society with limited literacy. Similarly, High and Low Dolphinsty on the Mallerstang manorial boundary recall one of several locals named Dolphin or more correctly Torphin, minor lords in the area, all of whom flourished before 1400, a folk memory exceeding six hundred years.

Perhaps the most convincing examples are the names of two places cited in several manorial boundary rolls which record their association with Hugh de Morville (1105-1162), who was given the lordship of Appleby in 1136, or perhaps with his more famous son Hugh, Lord of Westmorland (who died in 1174). The two places, on the boundary of Swaledale with Bowes and with Mallerstang, are now known as Hugh Seat on Mallerstang Edge and Hugh Seat Nab near Tan Hill (see OS Explorer Map OL19 at 1:25,000 scale). In manorial boundary rolls, or 'perambulations', at the dates shown they are variously referred to as:

12th/13th century	He Seat
1199x1377	the Heighte of Morvill
1199x1377	Hugh Seate
1617	the hew Seat
1651	Hugh seat Nabb
1684	Hugh seat Nabb
1735 a	Hudeseat Morvill
1735 b	Hudeseat Moracle [misreading for Morvill!]
1811	Hew Seat Morvile is Sir Hugh Morvill's Sear or Hugh's Seat
1812 a	The Hugh Seat
1812 b	Hugh Seat
1812	Hewseat Nab
Late 18th/early 19th	Hewset Nab
1882	Hugh Seat Nab

In some cases, such folk memories may combine two historical individuals as for example in the 1812 perambulation which records, "the great Hurrock of Hugh Seat by some called Lady's Pillar," recalling the successive associations of both Sir Hugh de Morville and Lady Anne Clifford with one and the same place. Lady Anne rode the bounds herself: no doubt Sir Hugh, Lord of Westmorland, was also a competent horseman. As can be seen from the titles of the perambulations quoted below, the Lord or Lady of the Manor rode the bounds with their bailiffs, agents and other local worthies as witnesses; hence the folk memories and strong associations.

Other local landmarks with long CVs attached include the Brandreth Stone at Tebay, a red sandstone slab, inscribed with two St. Andrew's crosses, that was lost during the vandalism of building the M6 motorway; Hollow Mill Cross, an ancient inscribed stone that stood on the pass over Tailbrigg up to about 1800; and of course the most famous of all, the Rey Cross on the pass over Stainmore, which has particularly exotic associations including William the Conqueror, Malcolm Canmore, and even Marius.

The pass of Stainmore itself is well known as the place where Eric Bloodaxe, the last Viking king of York, met his death in AD954; less well known is that William Harrison, Canon of Windsor, in *An historical description of the Islande of Britayne* in the first volume of Holinshed's Chronicles, 1577, calls it "Athelstane moore" after King Athelstan, AD895–939, the first to bear the title King of all Britain. Like Machell, Harrison considered that Stainmore extended from upper Teesdale right down the high fells to Uredale and Wensleydale. He describes the Eden as, "a water coming from the Morevill hills" and goes on, "The Eden well fraught with salmon descendeth (as I heare) from the hills in Athelstane moore at the foot of Hussiat Morvel hil, where Swale also riseth, and south east of Mallerstang forest. From thence it goeth to Mallerstang towne, Pendragon castell, Wharton Hall, Netbie, Hartleie castell, Kirkebie Stephan and yer it come to Musgrave it receiveth three waters..." We might now add, "1577 the Morevill hills" and, "1577 Hussiat Morvel hil" to the above list as well.

All these examples demonstrate unambiguously the strength and persistence of local memory about important landmarks or boundaries and prominent people associated with them, stretching back over more than a thousand years. But there are no such hints, indications or associations in the case of the Nine Standards. These prominent drystone cairns, on a skyline that dominates the whole of the Upper Eden Valley, are a far more outstanding landmark than any of those mentioned above that are associated strongly and persistently with known historical individuals. But the origins, builders and purpose of the Nine Standards are so far unknown. This in itself argues that they were not built in the last thousand years.

What do the locals say?

William Whelan in his *History and Topography of Cumberland and Westmorland* (1860) is quite clear at least about their purpose: "About two and a half miles East of the village [of Nateby] is the lofty mountain, Nine Standards, so called on account of some stones set up there to mark the boundary of Westmorland and Yorkshire."

On the Westmorland side, my maternal great-grandfather J W Braithwaite, in his 1884 *Guide to Kirkby Stephen, Appleby, Brough, Warcop, Ravenstonedale and Mallerstang*, on page 90 in the section on Mallerstang, has the following: "Nine Standards, a place where nine pillars are erected on the summit of the adjoining Hartley Fell, is about three miles from Nateby. There is a tradition that Oliver Cromwell blew down Hartley Castle from Nine Standards, but there is probably nothing further remarkable about the Pillars than the fact that they mark the boundary between Westmorland and Yorkshire."

The range of 17th century cannon was far less than the three miles, or four and a half kilometres, between the Nine Standards and Hartley Castle, but if the castle was to be attacked in that or indeed any other way, it should certainly be from the east so that the aggressors would be attacking downhill! To the south, west and north, the land falls steeply away from Hartley Castle, making it an excellent defensive site, probably the best in the upper Eden valley. However, J W Braithwaite offers no view on their history or age.

In his 1924 *Guide*, on page 26, giving directions for a walk to the Nine Standards from Kirkby Stephen, J W Braithwaite says: "Past Fell House, beyond old lead workings, past a shooting box, and taking an old coal road to the right, not very easy to find, go right to Nine Standards, which will be found to be nine pillars loosely built of such rubble stones as lay about, and which, tradition says, once served to scare off a military force approaching Westmorland from Swaledale which is immediately east of the Nine Standards. A more prosaic fact is that they mark the boundary between Westmorland and Yorkshire."

Equally prosaic is the fact that the Nine Standards are invisible from Swaledale; they cannot be seen from any point on the present road from Birkdale in Yorkshire to Nateby in Westmorland, and anybody climbing up to them directly on foot or by horse from the east or south-east by any likely route cannot see them until they are within two or three hundred metres. Whoever evolved this particular tradition was clearly not blessed with fine weather for their visits, unhappily an all too common experience for us all!

In both versions of his guidebook, though, J W Braithwaite states unequivocally that the Nine Standards form the boundary between Westmorland and Yorkshire, and this is repeated in all the perambulations, and on all maps prior to the Ordnance Survey. As a pillar of the local establishment, he was a regular participant in the perambulations of the manorial and parish boundaries of his time. On such occasions, any prevalent knowledge or traditions about each waypoint and landmark would certainly have been repeated; and he would equally certainly have recorded them.

On the Yorkshire side, Ella Pontefract and Marie Hartley, in *Swaledale* (5th edition, 1944), approach the Nine Standards and the rigg they occupy by climbing up from the Swaledale valley to the east. "The nine pillars which give their name to the hill are misleading. Having seen them from various points, the Mallerstang road and the road from Tan Hill to Kirkby Stephen, you expect them to rise as a guide to the summit, but instead they seem to hide themselves. From the top of the Rigg you can see miles of moor, and hardly dare to peer into the distance lest they should be seen leering from another hill. The land dips quickly at the north end to a lower ridge, and on this the nine stones stand.

"If the nine standards are illusive they are astounding when they do appear. They stand in an uneven row, built firmly – not in the haphazard manner of a currack – of small stones, and of various shapes and sizes, some a high dome, others on huge square bases with a pillar narrowing toward the top. Nobody seems to know just why they were put there. Some say they were built by prehistoric men, others that they marked an old boundary, others that they were placed to represent soldiers, and frighten the raiding Scots by making them think that an army was marching over the Rigg. But a more prosaic theory is that they were built by shepherds as a landmark, and to occupy the long hours they had to spend on the ridge when there were several sheep-folds there; the ruins of these sheep-folds still remain... The view from Nine Standards Rigg has again that contrast of the green Eden Valley and the bleak fells behind."

Apart from pointing out that the Nine Standards are not simply 'nine stones' – and our task might be much easier if they were – but nine drystone cairns, as they say in the next paragraph, constructed from a multitude of small flat flagstones of sandstone and gritstone, this is a suggestive description. They are not on the highest point, and you cannot see them on an approach from the east or south-east until you are right on top of them, which draws attention to their unique location, of which more later.

The legendary Alfred Wainwright has perceptively remarked in his *Coast to Coast Walk* (1973): "there are many theories about the origin of the group of cairns long known as the Nine Standards, as is usually the case when the truth is not known. Certainly they are very old, appearing on 18th century maps and giving their name to the hill they adorn. They have multiplied slowly, visitors in recent years having added a few more. They occupy a commanding position overlooking the Eden Valley, this giving rise to the legend that they were built to give the marauding Scots the impression that an English army was encamped here. More likely they were boundary cairns (the county boundary formerly passed through them), or beacons. Harder to believe is the theory that the builders were local lads with nothing better to do to pass the time. Whatever their purpose, they were made to endure, having suffered little from the storms of centuries,"

And again Wainwright says in *An Eden Sketchbook* (1980): "The Nine Standards are massive drystone cairns of uncertain age, built so well that they have withstood Pennine gales for centuries. Their remoteness too, on the crest of a hill at 2,250 feet, has been a factor in preserving them from wilful damage. They are conspicuously seen from afar and an impressive sight at close quarters. There is no authentic documented explanation of the cause of their existence, and in the absence of facts, many legends are attributed to them... That they are of considerable age is undoubted."

In *Secrets and Legends of Old Westmorland* (1992), Dawn Robertson records numerous versions of their origin and purpose. Amongst others, the following: "One story is that they were built to fool the Scots into thinking that there was an English Army encamped on the fell tops. An elaboration of the camping army story was that the cairns were supposed to be individual soldiers of gigantic stature who were about to stride down the fellside and fight off marauding Scots. A more recent theory is that Nine Standards has a religious significance and was somehow associated with Ninekirks Church near Brougham, said to have been founded by St Ninian, one of the first Christian visitors to the Eden Valley. One explanation of the name Standards is that it may be derived from standers left by miners in underground workings. The name may have been used because the cairns resembled standers which were pillars of rock left to support the mine roof. One final explanation of Nine Standards was suggested by Mr Sullivan [1857] who thought that they were very ancient memorial stones, possibly erected to commemorate some event which has since been lost in history. Another angle on the memorial theory can be related back to Aristotle who said it was customary to erect as many obelisks around a hero's monument as he had slain enemies. Perhaps some heroic Cumbrian warrior lies buried at Nine Standards and nine cairns represent his vanquished foes."

The theme continues in Douglas Birkbeck (2000): "Were they boundary stones between Westmorland and Yorkshire, or were they a memorial to some event now forgotten? One theory that has often been put forward, though with no evidence to support it, is that the cairns were placed on the fell to fool the invading Scots into thinking that an English army was positioned there, ready to descend and engage with the raiders. Although the nine would perhaps give the impression of giants on the distant fell top, it would have needed more than that number to have fought off an invading horde. Perhaps the enemy might have been deluded into thinking they were merely the vanguard of a host coming up the eastern slope of the Pennines."

What is clear is the status that the Nine Standards enjoy in the locality. It is a place to visit on the occasion of eclipses of the sun and moon, coronations, jubilees and other occasions of great moment, and they are a waypoint on both axes of the North of England, the east-west Coast-to-Coast walking route and the north-south long distance Pennine Way. More mundanely, it is a regular and traditional meeting place for the shepherds of Upper Eden and Upper Swaledale to exchange sheep that have strayed off their heafs.

And the scope of the traditions expands each year. The

Mallerstang Horseshoe and Nine Standards Yomp is now in its 26th year and attracts hundreds of participants, from dedicated professionals, semi-professionals and the armed forces to family groups and fancy-dress oddballs raising money for worthy causes.   The 23 mile/37 kilometre route goes from Kirkby Stephen up Wild Boar Fell, down into the Eden Valley and up onto Mallerstang Edge, down onto Tailbrigg, up again to the Nine Standards, and then back down to Kirkby.   The New Year's Day Nine Standards fell race is now in its 20th year, and is run on an eight mile/thirteen kilometre course from the Market Square in Kirkby to the Nine Standards and back.   There is even a recently inaugurated Nine Standards music festival which uses the name, but not the venue!

Whatever the origins of the Nine Standards, then, there is no clear and unequivocal local memory of who built them, when and why. There are strong and clear associations of known people and events with other and much less prominent landmarks going back almost a thousand years; if the Nine Standards had been built within that time, we would almost certainly have a local memory of it. So if we wish to make progress in resolving this enigma, we have to approach these questions indirectly. We can look at the name itself, and see what clues that might offer us. We can look at the archaeological record and at documentary evidence in the historical period, where it exists. Finally we can examine the monuments themselves and their setting within the lansdcape, perhaps drawing our own conclusions from what we see. It may then be possible to consider their likely origin and possible subsequent roles in what we might term the proto-history and pre-history of the area in which they are found. The definitive answers to these and many other questions may only be unearthed, literally, by a careful and detailed excavation. I hope this book may persuade some brave soul that this would be a worthwhile project.

What does Nine Standards mean?

The received authority on local place names in the former county of Westmorland is the English Place Name Society, Volume XLIII, *The Place Names of Westmorland* by A H Smith, 1967. In Part Two, Westmorland Barony, the entry for Nine Standards on page 29 reads as follows:

"NINE STANDARDS, 1777 M, *the Nine standares* 1636 BdyR
(M.3), *ye Nine standers* 1687 ib (Miss 1), a set of boundary marks
on the hill between Winton and Hartley, from e.ModE *stander*
'upright pillar', possibly adopted from its use as a mining term for
a column of mineral left to support the ceiling of a mine (cf. NED
s.v. §6), cf. Tackan Tan (ii, 7 supra)."

Unpacking the abbreviations in sequence, '1777 M' means that
they are shown on the Kitchin map in Nicolson and Burn *History and
Antiquities of Westmorland and Cumberland*; this is not the earliest
map on which the Nine Standards are shown – see below – but they
are shown on it. '1636 BdyR' means that Smith says they are mentioned in a Boundary Roll dating from 1636, and '(M.3)' should indicate the third boundary roll in the Musgrave deeds at Carlisle County
Record Office.   I contacted CROC and was assured by David
Bowcock, the assistant county archivist, that the early Musgrave
papers, although not yet fully catalogued, do not include any boundary rolls.

Similarly, '1687 ib (Miss 1)' evidently refers us to the same (*ibi-
dem*) boundary roll source, but the meaning of 'Miss 1' is unclear as
there is no corresponding entry in Smith's list of abbreviations. The
abbreviation 'BdyR' by itself would refer to, 'Boundary Rolls in the
care of Miss Rosemary Heelis, Solicitor, Appleby,' and 'Miss 1' perhaps to the first item in Miss Heelis' collection? I contacted the
offices of Heelis Solicitors at Appleby and no such papers are kept
there at present so far as Bob Earnshaw, the present solicitor, is aware.
Nottingham University, current home of the English Place Name
Society archive and some of Smith's original notes, was also contacted without shedding any light. No boundary rolls for either 1636 or
1687 are quoted below, as none has so far been found for those dates;
one assumes that Smith had seen them, or at least something from the
17th century, but he left us such opaque references to them that they
remain a mystery. However, since the dates he cited do not coincide
with any items in my listings, they may still turn up.

Moving on, 'e.ModE' simply means early Modern English, an
attribution repeated on page 289: "*stander* e.ModE (noun) = 'upright
pillar' eg Nine Standards, Jack Standards, Standerstone etc." In the
Introduction to Part One, page xlvii, Smith says: "in a few instances,
the names provide evidence of earlier use as with... *stander* 'pillar' in

Standerstane (part ii, page 50) from 1379." Most of Smith's examples of early usage he ascribes to *A New English Dictionary*, Oxford, 1888-1933.

It is worth noting here that Edmund Cooper, a local historian from Swaledale, wrote in an exchange of letters with Alec Swailes, the history teacher at Kirkby Stephen Grammar School for many years after the new school opened in 1955, that he recalled being shown a document in which the Nine Standards were named as *neun standen* which appears to be in a different language again. Unhappily Edmund Cooper could not recall when this had occurred, nor the document in which he had seen it, but it likely still exists somewhere in Swaledale. Copies of these letters include one from Alec Swailes to Tom Clare, the then archaeologist at Kendal, and are currently held at the Historic Environment Record database, with a file link to the Sites and Monuments Register. Margaret Gelling (personal communication 2008) offers: "if it really was seen in a document, it was probably an attempt to reproduce a rustic pronunciation."

An interesting sidelight is that in the twenty volume *Oxford English Dictionary*, (J A Simpson and E S C Weiner, Clarendon Press Oxford, 1989, Vol. 16) under the entry for 'standard' there are some thirty different meanings or usages of that word as a noun, none of which is even remotely related to drystone cairns. Similarly with the adjectival uses. However, one of the earliest forms of the name is 'stander', and here we find the following definition under item 6: "an upright support, a supporting pillar, stem and the like; also a candlestick." The earliest example of this usage drawn to my notice by Margaret Gelling is 1459, from the Pasten Letters (*Compact Edition of the Oxford English Dictionary*, 1979). The earliest use that I could find of 'stander' was 1548 "a tree left standing for timber, also as standel, standard," but not in a mining sense. And also 1552 about Berkshire Church goods, "A payre of grete candylstyckes called Standers."

The oldest use in a mining sense dates from 1605, and is cited in R Welford's *Historical Newcastle* (1885), Volume III, page 170, thus: "He shall so work the mines as he leave standers for the upholding of the grounds thereof." This definition corroborates several local authors who declare it to be a term used by miners. It implies that in order to support the roof, they left pillars or columns of the bedrock undisturbed while excavating the surrounding material; and this echoes the latter part of Smith's explanation of the name. While there are no tunnels – so far as we know – under Nine Standards Rigg, the comparison is easily understood, especially as the area has numerous defunct coal mines as well as lead and copper mines, and a local memory at least in Swaledale of the mining techniques in common use. However, it is undeniable that the surface of the ridge has been extensively disturbed and modified, as discussed towards the end of the book.

The Nine Standards are a conspicuous feature seen from almost everywhere in the upper Eden Valley, and at close quarters they are a very impressive sight in all weathers, yet they have such a simple and obvious name. There is no mystery: it is a straightforward description of a striking feature of the area, apparently invented by newcomers and strangers unaware of any folk memory of who built them and why, with no romantic, mythical or legendary associations to stimulate the imagination, or to recall events long past: just a highly strategic landmark that they found on arrival, and for which they needed a memorable name that they could use. The form in which that name has been handed down to us dates according to the place-name scientists to the middle of the 15th century at the earliest.

So much for the word 'Standards.' It appears to be a straightforward description, agreeing with what we can observe for ourselves, and we can therefore accept it at face value. It is less easy to decide why there are nine of these Standards. To demarcate a boundary or to emphasise a particularly important place, one substantial cairn would be sufficient, and even two would seem an unnecessary exuberance. To build not just one or two, but nine huge cairns, all of which dwarf Lady Anne's modest pillar on nearby Mallerstang Edge, requires a considerable and sustained effort; to build them in the first instance, and then to maintain them over succeeding centuries. It therefore demands some explanation. This is dealt with in a later section; we first need to examine the archaeological and historical records and to collate whatever information can be gleaned from those sources.

The archaeological and antiquarian record

The first of these is easy to deal with: there is no archaeological record. The Nine Standards were not mentioned in the Royal

Commission on Historical Monuments inventory volume on Westmorland, published in 1936. I have not found any reference to them in the Old, New or Record Series of the Transactions of the Cumberland and Westmorland Antiquarian and Archaeological Society, starting in 1874; I have not yet exhausted the full range of their publications, but I am confident that any such paper would have been mentioned in one of the many sources that I have fully searched.

There are a number of other sources, published and unpublished, where I thought useful material might be found. The antiquarian John Hill, a native of Appleby, eleven miles from Kirkby Stephen, who died in 1861, left seven volumes of notes on the history and antiquities of Westmorland without any mention of the Nine Standards. Celebrated local historians Nicolson and Burn who published their two volumes on the *History and Antiquities of Westmorland and Cumberland* in 1777 make no mention of them, in spite of the fact that Burn was a native of Winton, a mile from Kirkby Stephen, and for part of his career was headmaster of the local grammar school, he must therefore have seen the Nine Standards on the skyline every fine day. Nicolson and Burn is the standard work on the two counties, and its existence may explain why there is no Westmorland volume in the otherwise excellent Victoria County History series.

Similarly, the Rev. Thomas Machel (1647-1698), a village priest at Kirkby Thore, near Appleby, left over 3,000 pages of manuscript notes in six volumes on the history of Westmorland, but he has nothing to say about the Nine Standards. They appear twice in his manuscripts, as described below; but he does not mention them as an ancient landmark, nor does he draw attention to them as a special feature. Indeed, from the context it is clear that their inclusion in his text was almost incidental, and not a deliberate and conscious decision by him. This apparent lack of interest from the antiquarian and archaeological community is astonishing, and one has to wonder why it should be so. It is almost as though the cairns were not there.

In fact, the only study of the Nine Standards that I have been able to trace is the report commissioned by Dick Capel for the East Cumbria Countryside Project in 2005 as a statutory requirement prior to the reconstruction of five of the nine cairns already mentioned above to make them safe for public access. One had collapsed and others were deemed to be dangerous, as can be seen from the various plates. This review paper by Oxford Archaeology North (formerly the

Lancaster University Archaeology Unit) was mainly a brief desk study, and it summarised available map and documentary references to the Nine Standards from official sources, principally in the County Record Offices at Kendal, Carlisle and Northallerton. With a very modest budget, it could not be a fully comprehensive study, but it provides an excellent starting point for further, more detailed, research. In fact, having read it, I was surprised that we apparently knew so little about the Nine Standards, and so I decided to find out more about these intriguing old friends on the Westmerian skyline. I felt that the OAN paper did not do them justice, and that it raised more questions than it answered.

My initial purpose was to look for sufficient concrete historical evidence to persuade myself – and an apparently indifferent archaeological community – that the Nine Standards are of legitimate interest. They were not built to give invading Scots the impression that an English army was camped up there; it is hard to imagine a worse camp site, or one less strategically placed to control the main marching routes through the hills over Stainmore or Tailbrigg. Nor were they a job creation scheme for indigent lead miners by some eighteenth or nineteenth century philanthropist, still less a 'folly' built by one of the more deranged landed gentry, as some have suggested. They are in fact ancient and demonstrably so. But until now they have resembled the proverbial elephant in a crowded room, because the professionals have deliberately chosen to ignore them.

TWO

The Historical Record

Are the Nine Standards mentioned anywhere in the historical record? The surprising answer is: yes, they are. Unambiguous and specific documentary references to them by name can be found almost as far back as the Norman Conquest.

Maps, perambulations and related documents

Starting with the 1862 Ordnance Survey Six Inch (1:10,560) First Edition maps of Westmorland and working backwards in time, the Nine Standards are shown and mentioned by name on various tithe, enclosure, estate and county maps dating back to at least 1738, and on more than twenty manorial boundary rolls from Westmorland and the North Riding of Yorkshire from much earlier dates. Material of relevance, as well as direct references to them, are also found in various documents written by manorial agents or estate bailiffs and others, and these are also quoted here for the light they shed on the subject.

The oldest of these boundary definitions, or 'perambulations' as they were termed, appears to date from the late 12th or early 13th centuries, but just possibly from the early 12th century, within a hundred years of the Norman Conquest. The references and extracts from other documents that follow are by no means exhaustive; the search is ongoing, and there are many leads still to be chased up. But they demonstrate that the Nine Standards have been recognised and used as important markers in the landscape by those living there, as the boundary between adjacent medieval manors and ecclesiastical parishes, but also as the border between the ancient counties of Westmorland and Yorkshire, and in very early recorded times as the limits between what were only then becoming known as Scotland and England.

The following excerpts are presented in reverse chronological order, starting from 1900. To anticipate readers' queries, I should mention that it includes a small number of well-known maps and documents in which the Nine Standards are not mentioned, though other contemporary sources do record their existence at that date. These sources are listed here for completeness, because they are obvious places to look in such a search. The archive reference and date (if known) are given. Often, the date of the original material is not precisely known, and we know of its existence only because it has been transcribed or selectively quoted in a later document that has survived.

The convention adopted here lists such items according to my best estimate of the date of the original material, not the date of the often much later document in which the original material is quoted, and which may be the only place it appears to have survived. Where the date is believed to fall somewhere between two dates, the start and end years are separated by an 'x', thus 1220x1240, to avoid confusion with the convention 1220-1240 to indicate continuity, such as a king's reign, the hyphenation meaning 'from... to...' This gives a clearer indication of the degree of uncertainty than saying about 1220 or circa 1240.

The title of the source document and the full section of text in which the name Nine Standards appears are given in quotation marks word for word from the original text, including the original – sometimes highly original – spelling and grammar, which are not to be mistaken for 'typos', or poor proof-reading (which of course has been impeccable!) In a limited number of cases, where these are of particular interest, the full text from the original document is given, for reasons which I hope are apparent in each case. In other cases, the full text is presented in Appendix C. My interpretations or additions throughout are in square brackets. Words that are illegible or missing in the original text are indicated by '...' Text continuations are also indicated by '...' where superfluous or repetitious words are omitted to save space. Where the original text is difficult to read, or readable but not understood, such queries are followed by a question mark, thus [?].

It may be objected that such a listing makes for tedious reading; it makes for tedious typing too. However, it has the undeniable merits that in reproducing faithfully the original text, it records the original place names; it establishes authenticity, thereby indicating the degree of reliability; and it also allows the document under mention to be readily and unambiguously identified. In so doing, it provides a quick and clear means for the sceptical to check for themselves the actual wording and indeed spelling in the original material that might not otherwise be easily available to the reader. It is a notable feature of the original texts that the spelling of place names varies considerably, providing much material for future onomastic enquiry. It will save the future researcher much valuable time, and reward the present reader with an occasional smile or raised eyebrow. In many cases, the quotations are limited to those sections that mention the cairns by name, and only sufficient text is included to retain the sense and identity of the original document. Full transcriptions of each document were made, and where they are of particular interest as the earliest or fullest versions, or otherwise unique, the complete texts are given.

The perambulations were made at varying intervals, perhaps in some places every year, elsewhere maybe only every ten years, but they were certainly held once in every generation so that each succeeding generation knew – and, more importantly, agreed – the boundaries between themselves and their adjacent manorial neighbours. Usually no written record was made; the metes and bounds were part of an oral tradition strictly preserved by the numerous local witnesses attending on each occasion, originally 24 but later twelve on both sides, essential in a pre-literate society with a high mortality rate. The boundary rolls gradually came to be written down only when literate agents or bailiffs were charged with defending the interests of their manorial lords, in the 17th and 18th centuries. The boundaries are mostly of the parishes and townships of Kirkby Stephen and of Brough in the upper Eden Valley and of upper Swaledale; see Figure 3 (page 69). The major features in the immediate area around the Nine Standards are illustrated in Figure 4 (page 70) to assist the reader in locating the major places that are constantly mentioned in the texts.

As an aside, one might imagine the perambulations would be discontinued as an unnecessary periodic nuisance once the Ordnance Survey maps had been surveyed, printed and made available as an allegedly objective version of the boundaries. But perambulations continued, because the boundaries depicted on the OS maps were not universally accepted as the correct traditional manorial limits. There were specific and persistent disagreements for example in the areas of Stainmore and the Nine Standards, as in the 1896 perambulation quoted below. These disagreements had persisted for centuries, reflecting both the age-old desire to establish and if possible extend pasture rights, and also the more recent and even more lucrative pursuit of mineral exploitation, particularly lead and coal, but also copper, millstones and flagstones for roofing. The full sequence of references to the Nine Standards is as follows.

1700-1899

1899: The Ordnance Survey Six Inch Second Edition at a scale of 1:10,560 plots the position of each cairn, showing them as a line. Curiously, the north-north-west to south-south-east orientation of the line of cairns shown on their map is wrong by some 45 degrees, an error repeated on the Third Edition in 1920. The correct orientation of the nine cairns is roughly in a line from south-south-west to north-north-east, as already stated above, and shown in Figure 2 (opposite) and Plate 1 (page 65).

1896: Dated 19 September 1896. (DRO D/HH 6/2/283)
   "To: Sir Richard Musgrave Bart. Lord of the Manor of Hartley in the County of Westmoreland, and to James Parkinson Shepherd of Penrith in the said County of Westmoreland Steward of the said Manor of Hartley.
   "Take Notice that the Boundaries of the Manors of Healaugh Old Land, Healaugh New Land and Muker in Swaledale in the County of York as against the County of Westmoreland and as against the Manor of Hartley are as follows, namely:
   "From Nine Standards (where the manor of Swaledale adjoins the Manor of Hartley) as Heaven Water deals to White Mossey Hill and thence leaving Colber Scar on the left as Heaven Water deals to the head of Duckerdale where begins the Lordship or Manor of Nateby.
   "And on behalf of Captain Francis Horner Lyell Lord of the said Manors of Healaugh old Land, Healaugh New Land and Muker I hereby protest against your claim that the manor of Hartley extends within the aforesaid Boundaries And I do hereby discharge you from riding in or including any moors lands grounds and hereditaments by and such Boundaries in your Riding and perambulation

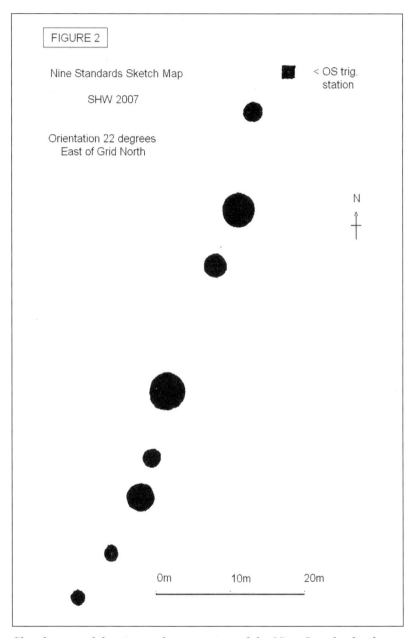

FIGURE 2

Nine Standards Sketch Map

SHW 2007

Orientation 22 degrees
East of Grid North

< OS trig.
station

N

0m   10m   20m

*Sketch map of the size and orientation of the Nine Standards, drawn
by the author.*

of the Boundaries of the aforesaid manor of Hartley.

Dated this 19th day of September 1896.

A Bernard Hudson, Steward of the said Manors of Healaugh Old Lands, Healaugh New Land and Muker."

Marginal note: "Received a copy of the within written Notice the 17th day of September 1896. [signed] J. P. Shepherd."

1882: Footnote dated 12 September 1882. (DRO D/HH 6/2/256)
"By a tracing of Lord Hothfields Boundary... Mr Oliver [?] by his Agent the line seems to go from Tack an Tan along Cock Lake Rigg to Hew Seat Nab then in line to Beck Meetings, then by Davy Mea to White Mossy [?] Hill then to Buston Gill Head – then to 9 Standards Rigg."

1862: The Ordnance Survey Six Inch First Edition at a scale of 1:10,560 Westmorland Tile 031 of 1862 shows Nine Standards Quarries on Nine Standards Rigg, and also Standards Haggs, Standards Mire and Standards Well, but not the actual cairns called Nine Standards, nor the spatial arrangement of the cairns, though curiously the Bench Mark where the parish boundary line bends at the northernmost cairn is shown.

1844: Tithe map of Hartley Township, (CROK WDRC/8/35): the Nine Standards are shown by a composite symbol (two rows of four dots each) in a roughly north-eastern orientation at the flexure of the parish boundary; they are not actually named though it is evident what they represent.

1841: Plan of disputed boundaries between Winton and Kaber, Westmorland and Muker in Yorkshire. (CROK WD/HAL/26) The Nine Standards are shown as a collection of about thirteen dots (again, the dots do not show the actual arrangement of the cairns).

1836: Notice of Perambulation on 15 July 1836 of the Boundary of the Common and Waste Lands in the Manor of Hartley in the County of Westmorland, (DRO D/HH 6/2/216) and the Plan of the Boundary as ridden, (DRO D/HH 6/9/3) both show Nine Standards Rigg. The text reads as follows:

"Notice is hereby given that the Boundary of the Common and

Waste Lands in the Manor of Hartley in the County of Westmorland will be ridden and perambulated by the Agents and Tenants of Sir George Musgrave Baronet the Lord of the said Manor on Friday the fifteenth July next and that they will commence the said riding and Perambulation at a Place called the Nick of Longrigg where the Gate leading into Hartley Common formerly stood at ten o'clock in the Forenoon of the same Day when and where all Lords of the several adjoining Manors or Lordships and all other Persons concerned may attend if they think proper. Dated this fifteenth Day of June 1836."

An appended manuscript note reads: "To the Lord or Lords Lady or Ladies of the Manor of Swaledale & his or her Agents or whom else it may concern. Mr. ... [D.Abasnine?] Agent to the said Sir George Musgrave Bart."

1812: Riding of the Boundaries of Healaugh and Muker 29 and 30 June 1812, (DRO D/HH 6/2/211). An extract from Tackan Tan to Hollowmill Cross, which reads as follows (the full text is given as Appendix C, item 1):

"On Tuesday the 30th day of June 1812 we whose names are hereunto subscribed with sundry other persons proceeded further [for a second day] riding and perambulating the Boundaries of the said Manors of Healaugh and Muker the like Notice in writing having been first given to all the adjoining Lords who met and attended as hereinafter mentioned that is to say beginning at Tackan Tan aforesaid where we were joined by the said Mr Briggs and Mr Dickinson Mining Agent of the Earl of Thanet and others Tenants and Farmers of the said Earl for his Manor of Brough or Stainmore Dale and from thence as Heaven Water Deals to Hewseat Nab, from thence as Heaven Water deals to Tarn or pool of Water above the Head of Wyth Gill called Brownbery Tarn from thence as Heaven Water deals to the height of Brownbery Edge and from thence along the said Edge between the Head of Buxton Gill and Blobery Gill as Heaven Water deals to the nine Standards where comes in the Lordship or Manor of Hartley We were joined by Mr Lancelot Dixon, Thomas Hamilton and others Agents Stewards or Tenants to Sir Philip Musgrave for the said Manor of Hartley and from there as Heaven Water deals to a large Hurrock of Stones called Rawlinson Hurock and from thence as Heaven Water deals to the Head of Duckerdale where begins the Lordship or Manor of Nateby and here we were joined by Mr Lamb Agent to the Earl of Lonsdale for the said Manor or Lordship and from thence as Heaven Water deals to the bounder stone West from Hollowmill Cross where we ended for this day."

1812: The Boundary of Swaledale rode [Wednesday] July 1st 1812 By Ottiwell Tomlin Gentleman Steward and Edmund Alderson Knowles Deputy and the inhabitants of Swaledale, (DRO D/HH 6/2/212). Details of the Swaledale boundary from Tack and Tan to Shunner Fell; repetitious wording has been omitted for brevity and is indicated by ...

"1. As Heaven water deals from Tack and Tan to Cocklakerigg.

2. As Heaven water deals from Cocklake rigg to a stone in Little Maya

3. ... to the SE end of Hugh Seat edge.

4. ... to Brownber Tarn.

5. ... to Brownber Stake.

6th As Heaven Water deals from Brownber Stake to the East end of Nine Standards Rigg.

7th As Heaven water deals from the East end of Nine Standards Rigg to a Gill on the East end of Rollison Hurrisy.

8th As Heaven Water deals from a gill on the East end of Rollison hurrisy to the Grey Yode at the far end of Coldber.

9th ... to Duccoy Beck head.

10th ... to a stone west of hollow mill cross.

11th ... to the Grey stone in Fellsend.

12th ... to the height of Fells end.

13th ... to the Height of High Pike Hill.

14th ... to the height of High seat.

15th ... to the height of Gregory chapel.

16th ... to Long gill head in Little Sleddle.

17th ... to the height of Hugh seat.

18th ... to Long gill head in Mickle Sleddle.

19th ... to shortengill head.

20th As Heaven Water deals from Shorten gill to the height of Shunner Fell..."   [subsequent pages not copied]

Note the repeated use of the curious word hurrisy in 7 and 8 above to indicate a 'hurrock', that is, a cairn of loose stones, from the Old

Norse/Icelandic *hreysi*. The variety of words used to designate cairns is discussed further at the end of this section. Pontefract and Hartley contrast the "haphazard manner of a currack" with the massive form of the Nine Standards.

1812: 3 February, 1812. Letter of Thomas Fothergill, Slater at Nateby to Thomas Buston at Thwaite, Swaledale, concerning manorial boundaries, quoting in full the Boundary. Thomas Slater had from Thomas Robson of Wharton Hall from its meeting with Mallerstang to the Nine Standards, where a large area is in dispute between Lord Smith and Lord Musgrave's Liberties. (DRO D/HH 6/2/210). This extract is from the full text in Appendix C, item 2.

> "I know the boundry Markes betwixt the Huse Seat and The Nine Standards as well as the Garth be hind My own House which is a vallowabel part of The Comon which Is Eaten by the adjoinin Lords for want of Lord Smith Looking to his Right of former Tenants...
>
> From Your Humble Servant, Thos. Fothergill Slater at Nateby. Feb. 3 1812."

1811: Copy of a paper lent by Mr Edmund Alderson of Wharton in Westmorland to E. A. Knowles of Low Row, Oct 28, 1811 (DRO D/HH 6/2/209). Elsewhere Edmund Alderson is referred to as Knowles' Deputy i.e. Deputy Agent – see D/HH 6/2/212. This may have been copied from "a beter boundry book of a allder standing", described in the DRO D/HH 6/2/210 letter quoted above; the older source has not yet been identified; it may have been the "Russendale Book" discussed elsewhere. This extract is from the perambulation of the boundary of Swaledale as a whole, full text in Appendix C, item 3.

> "The Boundary of Swaledale beginning at Stollerton Stile.
> 1. From Stollerton Stile to the head of Cogden...
> [Waypoints 2 to 12 omitted]
> 13. Thence as heaven water deals to the Grey Yaud in Cowdbright or Coedber.
> 14. Thence as heaven water parts to the Nine Standarts
> 15. Thence as heaven water parts to the hart Horn Cragg
> 16. Thence as heaven water deals to Brownbergh Edge
> 17 Thence down the White Gill
> 18 Thence as heaven water [deals] to the Tann* Tarn – viz.

Brownber tarn to Hugh's Seat Nab (Seat any thing to Sit on)
19 Thence as Heaven water deals to Taggon and Tann...
[Waypoints 20 to 34 omitted]
35. Thence down Swale to Stollerton Stile."
* In the Original 'Tann' is erased and the remainder of that line and
the following Line inserted.

Not later than 1811: Copy of description of the boundary of Birkdale
in Swaledale taken by Edmund Alderson from papers in possession of
his father. One paper. No date. (DRO D/HH 6/2/251)
    "A Boundary of Birkdale in Swaledale in Yorkshire taken and
    copied from a Copy of my Father's, Richard Alderson; Edmund
    Alderson." One Richard Alderson of Muker died in 1838; see
    NYCRO ZQT Alderson family papers. This perambulation may
    be part of the same batch as D/HH 6/2/209 dated 28 October 1811
    quoted above.
    "Birkdale-Bounder-Marks As Below, Namely:
    From Humble-Pool in the River-Swale To the Head of the River-
    Whitsundale, And Then to Brownber-Stake, Namely Which is a
    Long Stone upon Brownber And so on the Height of Brownber on
    the North of Brownber-Tarn to the Nine-Standards. And so on by
    Lush-Water-Deals to Rowlandson-Beacon, And thence to the
    White-Stone in Cold-Burn And then to Lady-Bogg And then to the
    Gray-Stone on Tailbrigg to the Gray Stone on the Side of Fells-
    End to the Top of Fellsend And Then by Lush-Water-Deal to the
    Lady's-Building, And then down by Sleddale-Close-Side And
    Then to Heilton-Gill-Foot And Then by Great-Sleddale-Back to
    the Head of the River-Swale & Then Down to Humble-Pool. Edm.
    Alderson."

19th Century? Map of Muker, Arkengarthdale and Romaldkirk,
undated (YRO MIC 2002/31 n.d.). Nine Standards appear to be
shown as a group of dark dots, though these may be symbols for
rocks.

Late 18th or early 19th century? Definition of the border between
Yorkshire and Westmorland (DRO D/HH 6/2/259). There is no author
or date, but it is later than Nicolson and Burn 1777, and was probably
written during John Caley's career as Keeper of Documents at the

Public Record Office in London, 1777-1832, as he is mentioned as a correspondent. Concerning a dispute over mines, it is quoted in full:-
"Healaugh and Arkengarthdale N.R. Yorkshire.

Information has been desired as to these Manors which belong to Mr Smith and the Manors of Mallerstang and Stainmore in Westmorland belonging to the Earl of Thanet but the principal Object of Inquiry is the establishment of the boundary between Westmorland and the North Riding of Yorkshire.

"The names of the boundaries in dispute between Mr Smith and the Earl of Thanet are as follows: "From Tacken Tan west to Hewset Nab from thence to a Tarn or Pool of Water above the Head of Wyth Gill from thence to the height of Broomber Edge from thence along the said edge between the head of Baxton Gill and Bleaberry Gill to the 9 Standards" all those as Heaven Water deals from boundary to boundary.

"Mr Smith now adjoins to the Musgrave Family for a length of Ground [from the Nine Standards to Hollow Mill Cross and up to the Grey Stone in Fells End], and the Earl of Thanet begins again at Fells End which is also in dispute and where the Colliery in question is situate. "From Grey Stone in Fells End to High Pike, High Seat, Gregory Chappel; from thence to the Hurrock of Stones in Stony Band, from thence above the Head of long Gill, from thence to the Great Hurrock or High Seat, all these from boundary to boundary as Heaven Water dealeth."

It seems evident from the language of this boundary, "*ut aquae celi descendit*/as Heaven Water deals" [note: the writer's original boundary roll was therefore in Latin] that it had been taken from some ancient survey or Inquisition [pity he did not quote his source...], and Mr Caley [=John Caley at the Augmentations Office: see note below] has therefore endeavoured to discover such a record as yet however unsuccessfully. Such records as he has hitherto been able to find seem unlikely to yield the information required. Neither Healaugh nor Arkengarthdale are to be found in Domesday Book and it is well known that no part of the Barony of Westmorland is discoverable in that venerable record...

"With repect to the boundary of the County of Westmorland it is apprehended it has never as a whole County been defined by matter of record..."

"The County it is well known was divided into two great

Baronies viz. Kendal and Westmorland the latter is that which is connected with the present inquiry.

"The Barony of Westmorland consists of the Honours or Seignories of Appleby and Burgh which contain under them all the Subordinate Manors holden of the Lords of Westmorland, and indeed all that seems anciently to have been deemed within the County of Westmorland. The Descent of this Barony from the Veteriponts, Cliffords and Tuftons to the present Earl of Thanet is fully stated in Nicholson and Burn's History of the County Vol. 1. P. 265 & co... In the same book it is said that in the Domesday Survey an Account is taken of many Places within the Barony of Kendal together with the adjoining Places in Lancashire and Yorkshire. Whereas of Westmorland properly so called no survey was made being all wasted and destroyed and worth nothing.

"Of Mallerstang and Stainmore many particulars are recorded in the History of Nicholson and Burn above referred to and other particulars may be found in Inquisitions & co. not there cited but none of these go to the length of ascertaining boundaries especially of so minute a Description as that which is now sought for.

"It is by Perambulation chiefly and Historical Tradition that boundaries of this nature are known and they but rarely are corroborated by written Testimony unless in Cases when Legal Controversy has previously arisen."

Smith bought the Wharton Manors in 1738; there was a court case by 1742; see DRO D/HH 6/2/268-279 and 6/2/263 and 6/2/254. John Caley was Keeper of Documents at the Augmentations Office 1777-1832 according to Index of Entries of the British Library Manuscripts Catalogue. So this was probably written in the late 18th or early 19th century. There is no "h" in Nicolson, a common error that may make this standard work difficult to find by on-line searching.

1777 Kitchin's Map shows Nine Standards as a named group of nine dots.

1770 Jeffrey's Map shows Nine Standards as a named irregular group of six or possibly nine dots, hard to discern amongst the cartographic formlines.

1738 Map of Swaledale (YRO MIC 2062 327 1738); this is a parchment map in the NYCRO collection at Northallerton. It shows Nine Standards as a waypoint on the northern boundary of Swaledale, between Harthorn Cragg and the "Gray Yawd in Cawdburneth," on the descent to "Holy Milne Cross" on the Tailbrigg road. Apart from these very distinctive place names, the map itself has several features that suggest a much earlier date than 1738, in my view an attribution given solely because the inscription on the reverse side of the parchment states that it changed hands in that year. On the back, in the centre, is the word "MINING" in modern pencil script; above in ink is the title "Mapp or Survey of Swaledale" and below also in ink is the note: "8th June 1738. Received from Mr Thos.[?] Swales [or Smales] and gave him a receipt for same" followed by some illegible initials.

This is a good but crude sketch map on parchment, such as might have been produced by a competent estate bailiff or agent, drawn on what could be the hide of an old Swaledale tup, whereas Jeffrey's 1770 paper map is recognisably modern in its cartography, with correct distances and proportions. On this enigmatic sketch, the symbols more ressemble Saxton's 16th century maps, but unlike Saxton, distance and proportion are incorrect. There are at least two distinct fonts or styles of writing, the script which labels mining features is noticeably more modern than the script naming landscape features and the landmarks around the perimeter already familiar from the boundary rolls. It is understood (Margaret Bousted, personal communication) that NYCRO received this map from the Laing Art Gallery, in Newcastle-upon-Tyne, who in turn had it from the estate office at Snape Castle; with this provenance it should be possible to secure an accurate history for it. The several bridges and the various mining features might also help to verify the date. It is probably late 17th century at the latest, and possibly very much earlier in my view.

1735: DRO Catalogue entry reads, "Boundary of the Honour of Richmond n.d., c. 1900" but it is actually dated March 1910, (DRO D/HH 6/2/244, 2 pages). Transcription by James Iveson of Angram, dated March 1910, who gives the date of the original source as 1735. Full text in Appendix C.4.

"Copy of the Boundary of the South and Western portion of Swaledale from Stollerton Stile to Hollow Mill Cross From Hollow Mill Cross To Stollerton Stile (vice versa).

"From Hollow Mill Cross as Heaven Water deals – to the Grey Yawd in Cawdburgh and from the Grey Yawd in Cawdburgh as Heaven Water parts – to the Nine Standards – & from the Nine Standards as Heaven water parts – to the Harthorne Cragg & from the Harthorne Cragg as Heaven water deals to Brownbergh Edge from Brownbergh Edge down the White Gill as Heaven water deals to the ..... Tanne (or Tarn perhaps) from the Tanne as Heaven water deals to Taggon – Tanne (or Tarne) & from Taggon Tanne as Heaven water deals to Thomas Gill Head...

"P.S. In copying the Boundary It is found that the names are altered or differently called then unless an Error has been made by the former copyist, and some places that are mentioned cannot be found – namely the Tanne or Taggon Tanne – approximate to Brownber Edge – & some other places. Coppied C March 1910. Previous copyist 1735, 175 years of difference. James Iveson Angram. Mch. 1910."

The punctuation and underlining are as in the original; repetitions have deliberately been left in for once, to avoid confusion.

1710: Summerlodge Boundary Dispute. Copies of Mr J[ohn] Davies's Minutes (DRO D/HH 6/2/260). Page 2 begins:
"which Copy the said William Chaytor wrote from the brief, which being in his possession. By virtue of an order hereunto annexed for Riding the Boundaries of the Maners of Healaugh and Muker in Swaledale from Windygates to nine Standards."

For future reference, the witness list includes five Fryers (Anthony, Ralph, Cornelius, George and James), and one Christopher Smales. There should also be a second part of this document somewhere, which will include the places between Fell's End and Nine Standards.

1710: 19th June (DRO D/HH 6/2/256, pages 3 and 4 of four). This extract is taken from the full text in Appendix C.5.
"By virtue of an ... annexed for riding the Bounder of the Manner of Healaugh and Meucar in Swaledale from Wynd Gate to Nine Standards wee whose names are hereunder inscribed together with several other persons Did upon Monday the nineteenth day of June 1710 instant ride the same."

Undated: 1710? 'The Bounder of the North side of Swaledale from Hollow Mill Cross to the Lordship of Marrick.' Another Bounder mentioning the same Boundaries.

"From Hollow Mill Cross as Heaven Water deals to the Gray Yaud in Cawd berge from the Gray Yaud in Caud berge as Heaven Water parts to the Nine Standards, from the Nine Standards as Heaven Water parts to the Harthone Cragg, from the Harthorne Cragg as Heaven Water deals to Brownebergh Edge, from Brownebergh Edge down the Whittgill as Heaven Water deals to the Tenn [=Tarn?] from the Tann as Heaven Water deals to Tagon Tann, from Tagon Tann as Heaven Water deals to Thomas Gill Head, from Thomas Gill Head as Heaven Water deals to East Stonesdale Grove Head, from East Stonedale Head, etc..." [next page not copied]

1710: 18th August (DRO D/HH 6/2/256, 1-4 of four) Chaytor 1710? Transcription:

"Pursuant to the within written authority for riding the within men- tioned boundary, we whose names are hereunto inscribed together with several other persons did upon Wednesday the 18th day of this instant August ride ye same, Notice in writing having been first of all given to ye severall adjoining Lords or their respective Agents who all of them attended and meet att the said Rideing where the said Boundaries adjoined to their respective Manners or Lordships which bdy. was [then] rid or gone in manner following:

"Viz. Beginning at the Moor Hen Nest in Water Cragg where wee were joined by Mr Arthur Farmer [?], Mr George Cowpland also all other Agents and Tenants to Charles Bathurst Esq for his manner and Lordship of Arkengarthdale And from thence as Heaven Water deales to Mirke Fell Standard where begins the lordship and Manner of Bowes from thence as Heaven Water deals to ye Great Stone... called ye Grove Sat [?Seat?] att Tann Hills near unto ye Meare Stone where we were joined by Mr Charles Whyeth [?] Mr Peter Hammond and other Agents or Stewards to Tho. Pulleise [?] Esq. and from thence as Heaven Water deals between two large stones marked one LW ye other CH with Figures 1676 upon... [the two inscriptions actually read 'LW 1676' and 'WPE B1759' – see plates 6 and 7 (page 71), and note below] from thence by Fryer Shaft as Heaven Water deals to Tackan Tann where wee were joyned by Mr. John Hall, Mr. Thomas Carleton and severall others Stewards Agents and Tenants to the Earl of Thanet for the Estate of Stain Moor Dale and from thence as Heaven Water deals to a Tarne or poole of water above ye head of Wyth Gill from thence as Heaven Water deals to ye Height of Brownber Edge and from thence along ye Edge between ye Heads of Baxton Gill and Blobery [?] Gill as ye Heaven Water deals to ye Nine Standards, where comes in ye Lordship and Manner of Hartley where we were joyned by William Bell, Thomas Mellons [?Nelson?] James Rogers [?] and others Agents and Tenants to Sir Christopher Musgrave for ye said Manner of Hartley and from thence as Heaven Water deals to a large heape of stones called Rawlinson's Hurrock and from thence as Heaven Water deals to ye Head of Duckerdale where begins ye Lordship or Manner of Nateby and from thence as Heaven Water deals to the Bounder Stone next [?West?] from Hollow Mill Cross."

These two inscriptions on the flat rocks just west of the Tan Hill pub are also quoted in the Appendix C.1 document, where the second date is wrongly given as WPE B1756. The curious and distinctive shape of the W in each case is the same and can be seen in plates 6 and 7 (page 71); it is thought to be a double vee, with overlapping limbs, and to stand for 'Virgin of Virgins'. These signs have also been found in some of the very old farmhouses on Stainmore, such as Great Skerrygill, where they are found above doors, fires and staircases. They have also been found in caves; one such example from Somerset is the Goatchurch Cavern (itself surely a place name redolent of dark practices) written up by Binding and Wilson (2004). A useful summary is found on the Apotropaios website at: http://www.apotropaios. co.uk/goatchurch_cavern_marks.htm with underline marks between the words 'goatchurch,' 'cavern' and 'marks.'

They have often been called 'witch marks' but have more recently been given the less misleading name of 'ritual protection marks.' Witch marks are usually understood to indicate real or imaginary marks on an alleged witch's body, often an additional or unnatural teat where the witch is thought to feed a 'familiar,' an imp, or the devil. Witch marks therefore have pejorative associations, indicating a person alleged to indulge in evil practices. Ritual protection marks, on the other hand, are intended to ward off evil influences, and have been found in many places; here someone has seen fit to mark them indelibly on an ancient land division, a watershed, and more recently a parish and township boundary.

1709: MS dated 19th August 1709. (CROK WD/HOTH). The outer sheet carries the title: "19 August 1709. Stopps then made to Sir Christopher Musgrave and his Officers, and Tenants riding their pretended bounder of Hartley adjoyning to ye Manor of Winton & Winton South Stainmoore. 3 September 1709 Copy St [?] to My [?] .. [??]" Initialled JK or JC? The text reads:

"Meme [?] that Sir Christopher Musgrave of Eden Hall baronet beinge that day about to begin to ride the bounder or pretended bounder of Hartley, Mr John Hall, Mr Thomas Jackson, Richard Waller, John Shaw, John Nicholson [?] and Thomas Rudd officers and servants to the Rt. Honourable Thomas Earle of Thanet did meet the said Sir Christopher Musgrave at ye Grey Stone within Hartley yeat being the bounder Marke [?] herein named [?], and then and their [sic!] the said Mr Carleton Steward to ye said Earle defied ye said Sir Christopher Musgrave to heare ye bounder Roll of ye said Earle Red [= read], whereon ye said Mr Carleton red over ye said Earle's pretended bounder Roll so far as ye bounder Meir Pott [?] to ride ye said Earle's Manner or Lordship of Winton & Winton South Stainmore from ye said Sir Christopher's Mannor of Hartley in these words:

"1. beginning at Winton brigg stones

2. from thence up ye sike neare ye south end of Winton Mill and to Fletcher Close nooke

3. from thence up Whingill beck to Whingill head

4. from thence along A wall called Winton ring dike to Stainbank head

5. from thence to A grey stone near ye east end of Coat Garth house

6. from thence along Langrigg Scar to A gray stone within Hartley Yeat

7. from thence to Raven Scarr [?]

8th. from thence up Harngill beck to Harnegill side

9th. thence to A gray stone on Low Grayrigg

10th. thence to A great stone on high Grayrigg

11th. thence up the north end of Greene Side by ye Magor [=

Major?] Potte

12th. from thence to an hurrock of stones on Basson Fell Side

13th. from thence to a Mare Stone on ye south side of Nine Standards

14th. from thence to an hurrock of stones on ye middle of Benty Batts

"and then told the said Sir Christopher that ye bounder Marks above named were the true ancient immemorial & only bounder Markes dividing ye said Mannors of Winton & Winton South Stainmore from ye said Mannor of Hartley... [deletions] & had been soe always ridd by ye said Earle and his ancestors [?] and their tennants... [deletion] but ye said Sir Christopher Musgrave being led by his tennants of Hartley began to ride his bounder or pretended bounder at A place called ye Nick of Langrigg to A swallow or hole on Harnegill, & from thence by severall pretended bounder Markes to ye place called Nine Standards within... where ye Said Earle's officers again meet ye said Sir Christopher & then told him he and his company had rid quite wrong, from the said Nick of Langrigg to ye place called ye Nine Standards, by which riddings of ye said Sir Christopher and his Company, they included or surrounded above eighty acres of coarse common belonging to ye said Earle, & his tennants agree beside [?], and we do further certifie that ye said Mr Carleton at ye Nick of Langrigg Skar when ye said Sir Christopher begin to ride his bounder from thence to ye said Swallow or hole told ye said Sir Christopher that he and ye rest of ye said Earle & officers in ye said Earle's Name, made stoppe to ye said Sir Christopher & his company & told them they ridd wronge & desired him to show their bounder book but ye said Sir Christopher only provided A loose paper, but did not read ye bounder markes therein mentioned. All which we are redy to Attest when required. Witness our hands ye 19th day of Aug anno Domini 1709."

Witnessed by five 'Tennents' Thomas Scaife, John Bland, Richard Monkhouse, Thomas Blinklin [?] and Thomas Morland, and ten 'Not interested' [i.e. impartial, with no vested interest either way] Jo Hall, Tho. Carleton, Richard Waller, John Wharton, John Nicholson, Michael Wharton, Henry Satterthwaite [?], Tho. Carleton Jnr., Robt. Dennison, Tho. Rudd.

1708 [Title page] "Stops made on the Lord Wharton's officers riding their bounds of Swaildail adjoining to Stainmoore. EAH" [initials of E A Heelis, Agent]. (CROK WD/HOTH) August 18 1708. The preface, in a different script, reads:

> "A Particular of the Bounder Marke between Stainmore and my Lord Wharton's bounder of Swaildale where my steward read to his steward and Tenants my Bounder for they had none, and when they entered within my Bounders my steward stoped them and showed them there mistakes which they rode the 18 August 1708."

This extract is taken from the full text in Appendix C.6.

> "...and from ye two becks meeting on Whitsondale, ye said Earle of Thanet's bounder marke was to a hurrock of stones of ye South end of benty batts, from thence to an Hurrock of Stones on ye midle of Benty battes, from thence to a Mare Stone on ye South Side of Nine Standards, but ye said Lord Whartons officers or tennants carryed their bounder flagg on ye ridge or topp of ye hills and did not go by ye said two hurrocks of Stones on benty batts, whereby they included above one hundred acres of waist ground from ye said Earle Thanetts waist grounds (as we believe) to ye said Lord Wharton's waist grounds."

1400-1699

1695 On Morden's map, the Nine Standards are not shown; "Hoomill Cross" is shown on the border between Westmorland and Yorkshire.

1687: A H Smith in Part Two of his EPNS volumes on Westmorland refers to a Musgrave boundary roll at this date. As noted elsewhere, this was checked with Bob Earnshaw at Heelis Solicitors in Appleby, and with CROC where David Bowcock stated that although the early Musgrave papers have not yet been fully catalogued, there are no boundary rolls at that date; see also 1636 below.

1684: Machell MSS *History of Westmorland,* Volume 3 page 95, on paper. CROC.

> "The Bounder of Stainmoor ridd by the right honourable Thomas Earl of Thanet Island, Lord Tufton of Tufton, Lord

Clifford Westmorland and born [?] Lord of the Honour of Skipton in Craven, and hereditary Sherriffe of the County of Westmorland in his owne person ye 11th and 12th dayes of September in the thirtieth year of the reigne of our Sovraine Lord Charles the Second by the Grace of God of England Scotland France and Ireland King, Defender of the Faith, AD 1684."

This dating recognises the Commonwealth of Oliver Cromwell 1649-58, and Richard Cromwell 1658-59, whereas the dating of the WD/HOTH version below does not.
"1. Beginning at Winton Briggstones.
[Waypoints 2–11 omitted; the full text is given in Appendix C.7]
12. From thence to an Hurrock of Stones on Bassen/Baxen Fell Side
13. From thence to a meare stone on the South side of the nine Standers
14. From thence to an Hurrock of Stones on ye midle of Benty Batts. [Waypoints 15-50 omitted]
This Bounder was ridd in the presence of us (the undersigned)."

The texts in the two versions from CROK/WD/HOTH and CROC Machell MSS Volume 3 are virtually identical; the only difference at waypoint 12 is separated by a forward slash / above.

1684: "No 3 Stainmoore Bounder" on parchment: the text is virtually identical to the above; but this copy is much harder to read. (CROK WD/HOTH) "11/12 September The Boundary of Stainmoor ridd by the Right Honourable Thomas Earl of Thanet in his own person... in 35 Charles II."   This dating ignores the Commonwealth, Oliver Cromwell 1649-58, Richard Cromwell 1658-59; Charles II actually 1660-1685: Machell says 30th year of Charles II's reign.

1664x1698: undated Machell MSS Vol. 3 page 181 but it must be later than 1664 as it cites Lady Anne's pillar, built in 1664; and other dates in the text range from 1673 to 1697: Machell died 1698. Deletions are as in the original. Note that this is the boundary of the entire Kirkby Stephen parish, not the much smaller Kirkby Stephen township within it.
"KS Parish – The perambulation of which goeth thus:

Begin at the foot of the River Below [= Belah] (called Rezen or Clovet [?] Stoneshot by the Enquiry of Robert Moss of Heggarscale) where it enters Eden thence to Blands house which is in Little Musgrave and a quarter of a mile above ye Church. Thence East up the river till you come at the Head of Henning Wood where Brough parish comes in. Thence up hill you come at the foote of ye water which runs under Buckle Bridge; thence south up the said water till you conme at Woofagill-head where Potter beck coes into it. Thence East up Potter beck till you come at the foote of the hill called Moulds by the said water. Thence southeast to the top of the said hill, and so on by the Coale-way to Westland Pit house commonly called Hither Pit house where Brough and Bowes and Grinton parish meet (all this while dividing it from Brough). Thence upward in a direct line to Brownber Edge (Here Swadal claims to Browenber Edge's head [?] and Grinton clames to Wettsundale head which is a half mile one into anothers) and so lineally to the Nine Standers on Caudber Edge. Thence south on Caudber Edge till you come at an hurrock voc. [= *vocatur* = called] Caudber Standerd. Thence and W down Lady dike till you com at Lady Bog and so on in a straight lne to an Hurrock of stones called Hollow-mill cross. Thence again W to a Gray Stone at a place called Fells End. Thence S to Uldale gill head. Thence again W to an Hurrock of Stones on top of Fells End. Thence S on Mallerstang Edge as heavens water divide to the top of High Seat. This Swalidale claime. Then S lineally from Uldale Gill Bar to High Seat Top. Thence as Heaven Water divides To Hugh Morvil's Seat. Thence S to a standard half a mile of [= off]; where Grinton, Aiskar and Kirkby parish meet, all this while dividing it from the Grinton in the Co. of Yorkshire. Thence from the said Standard linell descending near to Lile Helgill Head (where Eden springs). Thence W in a straight line to a Stander of Stones at the south end of Swarth Fell (Little Baugh) where Aisker and Gaphill [?] meet Russendale (on Swarth Fell edge) to a place called Galloway Gate where Gaphill [and] Russendale meet. (marginal note: Question in William Wallers of Stanemore at Swine Stedy [?] wath has found an image of stone lately there?) [presumably at Galloway Gate?] Thence NW (by a straight line) to ye S end of Wilbright Fell: thence (by the NW edge of the said fell) to an upright stone called the Countess Mount on the Nab at the E end of Wilbert Fell. ~~Thence N (down the edge of the said fell to Whitewalls. Thence again N (by a straight line) to Dowfin Stye. Thence again N (lineally descending) to Lowgill [Cowgill?] head. Thence N down the old cartway till you come at Tarnmire hole near Tarn House. Thence W (down the Tarnmire sike) to the till [?] runs. Thence NW (in a direct line) to Scandal Beck head; thence again NW down Scandal Beck. From the~~ and from Sth Run Keld N in a right line to the Build (shield for sheep) on Askfell Edge. Thence NW as heaven water divides to a Little Hillock or hurrock of stones called Hound Tuft; thence NW (on the edge of Ash fell) to Russendale High park gate; Thence W to Gerrards Cross in the park wall. Thence W (by the parke wall) to Smardale bridge where Ravenstonedale parish and Crossby Gerrard meet. Thence down the river to Crosby miln: ~~thence NE to Soulby mill by the way down the said river~~ and Thence W to Waterhouses by the Outring of Soulby low pasture til you come at Gallansy Yeat – and so up the lonen still Westwards till you come at Waterhouses where Asbby parish comes in; thence NW to Oglebrow all along down Waterhouse beck till you conme at Uglybrow. Where Musgrave P[arish] comes in. Thence N to High Hobkins house by Graskil house (beloning to Will Robinson) Then N. by a straight line to Great How Sike at the place where Appleby way crosses. Thence N. down the said sike to Low Hobkins house. Thence N. by the outside Ring of Low hobkins grounds to a plce called Dubber Dike where a sike runneth out of this parish. Thence N to the W. corner of Musgrave Intack. Then by the brig dike of Musgrave Intack till you come at Sandrig sike. Then NE by the same dike till you come at the Low end of Long Selme [?] where that dike ends: thence by an Hedge to the N. corner of Hard dales dike. Thence NE by another dike to a mossy pasture called Ladds; thence E. by Nobledale Hedge to Blanes Yate. Thence E. by the out Hedge of Blands pasture to Eden. Thence N. down Eden to the foot of Below where wee began."

Deletions as in the original have been retained as the reason for them is unclear; the places deleted appear to be on the correct line of the boundary, and are essential to the clear understanding of the boundary waypoints.

Post-1661; there is a reference in Machell MSS Volume 1, page 438, to William Ryley's *Placita Parliamentaria* 1661 in the British Library as a source for the "bounds of Burgh" [i.e. Brough]. This source was checked at the British Library but the boundary of Brough is not given; the text only states that the boundary needs to be definitively surveyed (see also the 1338 Commission below). While it is disappointing that no "bounds of Burgh" are given in Ryley, this source had to be checked out.

1651: "South Stainmoore Bounder ridd 1651 By My Lady Pembrooks officers and tenants. Winton-South Stainmoore and so on the east of South Stainmoore. The Marks and Bounders ridd the 23rd Aprill 1651." (CROK/WD/HOTH/Boundary Rolls)
1 Ffirst up the beck to the Ffletchers Close nooke
2 Thence up Wingill Beck
3 And so up Whingill wall by the South west corner of that wall
4 And so along Winton ring dike or Scarr edge up to Coat garth house
5 And so on Winton side of Langrigg Scarr to a stone within Hartley gate
6 Thence up by his raven scarr
7, 8 And so up Harnegill Beck to Harnegill Syde
9 Thence to a great Stone on Lowgrayrigg
10 Thence to a great Stone on Highgrayrigg
11 And so up the North end of Greenside by the Maior [= meer] pott
12 Thence to the Standers on Blacke Hill
13 Thence to a white harrock on Blacke Stone fell
14 Thence to a hurrock of Stones on Baystone fell
15 Thence to a Maior Stone on the South side of the 9 Standers.
16 Thence to a horrock on the midle of Benty Back.
17 Thence to another on the South end of Benty Back
18 And so directly East to the two becks meeting in Witsondale.
19 Thence to the little Tarne
20 And so directly to Hugh Seat Nabb
21, 22 Thence to Coth lake rigg
23 Thence to Tack and Tann...   [Waypoints 24-37 omitted]
38 And so to the foot of Bradstone greene
39, 40 Thence we came to Brough, in all about 30 Miles.

The names of those that ridd the bounders mentioned of the other side. Of Your Hono[rable] Servants Richard Clapham, William Edge, Gabriel Vinsent, Thomas Johnson, Christopher Swindon, John Breamer, John Allen, Thomas Lamb & John Darby. Thomas Gartle Steward od her hon[orable] Court and Bayliffe. Of ye hono[rable] Tennants Capt. Robert Scaife, George Rood, William Le Schoolmaster, Thomas Wharton.”

1651: “South Stainmoor Bounder ridd anno 1652.1 EAH & SRL. No. 1. Wynton South Staynemore and so on the west [*sic* – should read “east”!] of South Staynemore. The markes and bounders rid the 23th of Aprill 1651.” (CROK WD/HOTH/Boundary Rolls).
  “Winton South Staynemore and soe on the east of South Staynemore The Markes and Bounders Rid the 23rd of Aprill 1651
1   Ffirst up the beck to the Fletchers Close nooke
2   Thence up Whingill Beck... [Waypoints 3 to 13 omitted]
14 Thence to an hurrock of stones one Bayre Stone fell,
15 Thence to a Maior Stone on the south side of the 9 Standers.
16 Thence to a hurrock on the midle of Benty Back
17 Thence to another of the South end of Benty Back
18 And so directly East to the two becks meeting in Witsendale
19 Thence to the little Tarne
20 And so directly to Hugh Seat Nabb...”

This is actually a duplicate of the previous perambulation, in a non-professional scribe’s hand but with exotic and highly individual spelling. The full text is not given in Appendix C. Also this second version has no doubt interesting but largely illegible annotations at the foot, including notes dated 14 November 1705 and 13 December 1841.

1651: Boundary of Kirkby Stephen township. (CROK WD/HOTH/Boundary Rolls).
  “The Bounders of Kirkbystephen rid the 5th of September 1651 for the Right Honourable the Countess of Pembrooke as following:
1   First beginning att the corner of Kirkbystephen steeple.
2   Thence to Gelber Yate.
3   Thence along through Waiteby Intack
4   Thence along by Carnack Castle,

5   Thence to Waiteby Rigg
6   Thence to Waiteby Intack Head,
7   Thence to the Northwest Syde of Thorneypott hole
8   Thence to Whyte Rigg End
9   Thence to High Whyte rigg
10 Thence to the out Edge of Assfell
11 Thence through Tarnewett myre
12 Thence to Tarnewett hole
13 Thence to Kirby high way
14 Thence to Sandwath beck bridge
15 Thence along up the farr syde of Sandwath Beck
16 Thence along to Sandwath Beck Head
17 Thence to the Stand on Wilbor fell,
18 Thence to Wilbor Fell Pike
19 Thence to Dolphin Stye
20 Thence... [over?] graystone rigg
21 Thence to Wharniegill Head
22 Thence to Kirby waye
23 Soe along by a stone Bounder Mark and the Place a stone
    had formerly stood with the Clifford's name on it, it being in
    Asse fell end
24 Thence to Kirby intack Roade
25 Soe along by the Parke wall to Wharton Parke Yate that goes
    to Kirby stephen
26 From the Parke Yate downe by an ould hedge that Stands some
    4 or 5 yards without the Parke Wall to Eden water
27 Soe down Eden water to Kirbystephen steeple corner."

The underlines are as in the original. This does not contain any
references to the Nine Standards but it is included here because it is
the oldest perambulation of Kirkby Stephen in this collection, though
it only defines the township not the whole parish. Also it contains references to the Countess of Pembroke, Lady Anne Clifford; to Torphin
(in the place name Dolphin Sty); and to one of Lady Anne's Clifford
predecessors, a good example of the strong persistence of local memory of the prominent people associated with important places
described earlier.

1636; as noted above, A H Smith's reference was checked, and no

Musgrave boundary roll at this date has yet been located. But no other boundary roll at this date has been located so Smith may well have seen one, and it may turn up.

1617: "Boundary of East Stainmore." (CROK WD/HOTH/Boundary Rolls)

"At a Court holden at Brough the last day of June 1617 for the Right Honourable Francis Earl of Cumberland the Bounders were presented by the Jury whose names are here underwritten as followeth.

"Viz: To begin at Ffletcher Close adjoining to Sir Richard Musgrave's ground, from thence to Coat Garth, then to under Lannrigg Skarth, then to the standing stone within Hartley Yeat, Then to Raven Skarth, and up Harny-gill beck to Harny-side, then to a hurrock on Low Grayrigg, Then to a great stone on High Grayrigg, Then to the Meare Potts at north end of Greene Side unto the standers on Blackhill, then to the nine standers, then to the Benty bat, then to the meeting of the becks in Whitsondell, Then to the hew seat, Then to the Cocklake rigg in Stonsdell, Then to dry gill, then to the white stone in Easegill, then to the Swhart [?? Swart?] gill, then to the Reare Cross, then to the Beld how, Then to Mickle dod, Then to the ragged stone at the meeting of bounder beck and black, then to the east pind hill, Then to a hill between potter reads, Then to the foot of Braide Stone greene, Then to the east end of Dow cragg, Then to the white mynes, Then to the bout of Dow cragg, then down Rawton Sike, Then to a hurrock at the east end of Leasett Then to the Mastow [?] Sike, Then on the Sike to a hurrock in the bout to Mickle fell, from thence downe the Birks Sike to Maysbeck, Then to Swarth beck, Then to West Swindale foot."

Annotations on the cover include "1507-1617 = 109 signature Matthew Smithe by John Shal [?] 1710". In the text, the numerals 1-25 [oddly omitting 22!] have very distinctive sevens. This may be a copy of an older boundary roll, perhaps dating from 1507? This is the earliest dated perambulation on the Westmorland side to mention the Nine Standards by name: see plate 8 opposite.

These last perambulations are quoted extensively because they are the oldest so far found for the Westmorland side, and hence of more

Plate 8, 1617 perambulation for Brough Court, courtesy of Lord Hothfield.

than passing interest. Certain words in them suggest that the boundaries are much older, and not something being defined by this perambulation, and may present older spellings and pronunciations.

1577: Saxton's Map of Westmorland dated 1577 is the earliest map consulted by the OAN desk study; it shows 'Neatbye' with 'Holomill Crosse' on the Westmorland/Yorkshire North Riding border, but not the Nine Standards.

1534x1599? DRO Catalogue entry: "Joshua Fryer's Book: recipes, cure for bite of mad dog, miscellaneous remedies, potions etc: papers concerning Swaledale tithes, manorial boundaries, lists of tenants etc., 1735" (DRO D/HH 6/2/204).

"The Boundary of ye North Side of Swaledale Hollow Mill Cross to ye Lordship of Marrick.

"From Hollow mill Cross as Heaven watter Deales to ye Gray yawd in Cawbrigh. From ye Gray yawd in Cawbrige as Heaven watter parts to ye Nine Standers from ye Nine Standers as heaven parts to ye Hart horne Gcragg From The Harthorne Cragg as Heaven Water Deales to Brownbergh Edge from Brownbergh down ye White Gill from ye White Gill as Heaven watter Deals to ye tanne From ye Tanne as Heaven watter Deals to Taggon Tanne From Taggon tanne as Heaven water Deals to Thomas gill head, From Thomas Gill head as heaven watter Deals to East Stonedell Grove head From East Stonsdill Grove Head as Heaven Water Deals to ye Hight of watter Cragg From ye Hight of watter Cragg as heaven water Deals to Mosedill head from Mosedill head as Heaven Watter Deals to mickle Punchard from mickle Punchard as Heaven Watter Deals to ye Hight of Penseit From ye Hight of Penseitt as Heaven watter Deals Waytshaw Head by Lineall Line to Forgill Yate From Forgill yate by Lineall Line Down forgill to Sindergaite & Soe Down to Arkell Beck to ye foot of Carngill Beck & So up farnedaill to ye Hight of Mosedayle Rigg as Heaven watter parts & So forth Aldmond Crag from Aldmond Cragg to ye Edg End From ye Edg End by Lineill Line to Methorn yeat from Methorn Gate by Lineall Line to Awme poole in Swale & So down Swalle to Stollerton Stile.

"The Bowndrey of ye South Side of Swaledale Betwixt Stollerton Stille to Hollo mill Cross.

"From Stollerton Stile to ye Head of Codgin & So forth towards ye Soutth to Brown Seat & forth as heaven water Parts Betwixt Swaledale & Wensledale unto ye Hight of Bolton Greets & So forth as Heaven watter parts to ye Hight of Windegates & So west as Heaven parts unto Stonegrave gill & So forth betwixt Swaledale and Wensledale as Heaven Watter parts to Rede Keld & So forth as Heaven Watter Parts to ye Hight of Shume Fell & So forth as Heaven Water parts unto the Head of Middle Sedeck and So forth betwixt Swaledale and Molerstang as Heaven Watter parts unto Hude Seate Morvill & So forth as Heaven Watter parts unto White Stone in fels End & So forth as Heaven Watter Deals to Hollow Mill Cross."

The above material is an undated perambulation, but the whole hand-written book is chronologically arranged, and this boundary roll occurs between two transcriptions dated 1534 and 1599 respectively, dating the boundary roll perhaps to 1534x1538. These J Fryer texts are thus much older than the book they are in.

The first six lines of the item dated 1534, which precedes the above perambulation, describes the division and sale of the tithes of Fremington, thus:

> "I sold my part to ye Viccar North by consent of ye Prior and ye Sellerer Wm. Brownne right Prior and Wm. Wood ye Sellerer. Written ye fourth day of ye month of October in ye year of ye King Henry ye Eight ye 25th [= 1534] with there witnesses Thomas Covill, Wm. Conyers of Mask – Esquire, Robert Cook 1534 by me Thos. Covill Sener, Ralph Metcalfe of Healay park, Concords with original."

The text implies that it was written while the monasteries were still actively managing (and profiting from) upper Swaledale, ie pre-1538, as the consent of the Prior and the Sellerer was deemed a necessary condition of the transaction: see plate 9 below.

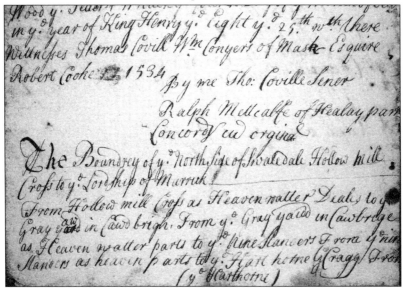

Plate 9, perambulation of Swaledale north side from Joshua Fryer's Book, courtesy of Hanby Holmes Estate archive, Durham County Council.

The item dated 1599 which follows the above perambulation is headed, "The Breist of ye Letters Pattens from her Gracious Majestie to Mr. Wiseman." It begins:

"Elisabeth by ye Grace of God Queen of England & co. By her Lettere Pattens dated ye Ten Day of November in ye one and fortieth year of her Highness Reigne in ye year of our Lord God 1599 for and in consideration of one thousand four hundred three score and three Pounds one Shillings and Two pence paid unto her highness Exchequer by Rich. Wisemand Citizen and Goldsmith of London Gentleman and to ye Heirs and Asings [= assigns] of ye said Richard Wiseman for Ever. All thatt our Manner or Lordship of Grinton and all those lands and tennements in Neither Whitay Overwhitay Harcayside Low Speng... Haverside & Somerluge, Late Percill of ye Lands and Possessions of ye Monastery of Bridlington within ye County of York And all those lands and tennements in Neither Whitay Overwhitay Harcayside Low Speng... Haverdaile & Somerluge, Late Percill of ye Lands and Possessions of ye Monastery of Bridlington within ye County of York And all Singular Messuages Milnes Houses Edifices Barns Stables Dovecotes Gardings Orchards Lands Tenements Meadows Feedings (Pasturs)..."

Joshua Fryer's book in turn is bound into the first part of a later book belonging to James Iveson of Angram, and dated March 1910. Contemporary textual evidence elsewhere in another document transcribed in full below under the title "An Extract of Particular Proves Concerning ye Manor of Grinton" (D/HH 6/2/204) also supports a possible date between 1534 and the Dissolution in 1538 as this other document speaks of the land as though at the time of writing it was owned by the monasteries. There is no mention in the quoted text that the metes and bounds which they record were given by Gilbert de Gant.

Pre 1400

1338: the Boundary Commission cited by A H Smith in the English Place Name Society 1968 volume for Westmorland as having been commissioned in this year was never undertaken in spite of repeated renewals of the commission, and revisions of the commissioned personnel, in ever more plaintive tones and in a variety of languages, over the succeeding decades. Smith cites this commission but clearly he never checked that it had in fact been carried out; it had not. So no mention of Nine Standards, obviously. This commission and subsequent events are discussed in more detail below.

1320-1340? The so-called Gough Map (named after the 18th century antiquarian Richard Gough, in whose *British Topography* it was first reproduced; see plate 6, page 76, 1780 edition). The original is at the Bodleian Library in Oxford. There is a current project to study this map and determine more accurately its likely date, and the Belfast University project website has an interactive version of the map. It is probably the oldest depiction of the main island of Britain (i.e. England, Scotland and Wales); it does not show Nine Standards (or the town of Kirkby Stephen for that matter, although it certainly existed at that time), but in addition to the main rivers such as Eden and Swale, it does show Appleby, Brough, the pass of "Steynmore" and Pendragon Castle!

It is worth a visit to the website; here the map is mentioned in passing, as an interesting curiosity and available on-line, but also as a very early cartographic source that had to be examined for any depiction of the Nine Standards. The Gough Map, like the others cited here, illustrates how the contents of maps and charters are extremely selective in what they do and do not depict. Their themes and contents reflect the instructions of whoever is paying for them, the preoccupations of their superiors, and the brief given to the cartographers or scribes. The contents of such early documents simply cannot be taken as an indication of whether or not something or somewhere existed at the time of their creation.

1325: In *Secrets and Legends of Old Westmorland*, 1992, on page 95 in the section on the Nine Standards, Dawn Robertson says, "The massive cairns have never been dated but are thought to have stood for centuries... They were marked on the earliest maps of the region in the eighteenth century and the first known reference to them was in 1325." No source was quoted for this date: it is being systematically sought in the 35 or so listed documents in her bibliography but has not yet been located.

1281: PRO Calendar of Patent Rolls for 9 Edward I, 1281, Membrane 17d, dated June 5 at Westminster.

"Commission to Geoffrey de Neville, Guichard de Charroun and Alexander de Kirkenny, to make a perambulation of the bounds between the counties of York and Westmoreland on the moor of Steynmor, between the land of John de Brittannia, earl of Richmond in Richmond, in the county of York and the land of Roger de Clifford and Is[abella] his wife, Roger de Leiburn and Idonia his wife in Brough, co. Westmoreland, the metes and bounds of which are the metes and bounds of the said counties."

This item precedes the perambulation given in Lady Anne Clifford's file of Charters and Evidences dated 1199-1377 (CROK WD/HOTH/A988/11), the text of which is given below. In a later section, there is a brief account of the records held in The National Archives at Kew that cover a number of years following, which conclude with Lord Clifford's statement, threat or boast "which perambulation may never be made." The transcription held at CROK is possibly by Roger Dodsworth in 1640x1650 or thereabouts (see the note below on some holdings of the Earl of Rutland at Belvoir Castle) from which it is evident that a perambulation <u>was</u> made at <u>some</u> date between 1338 and 1640. The source document has not yet been found, but the following partial boundary roll therefore appears to date from the period between 1338 and 1377.

1199x1377: Lady Anne Clifford's file of "Charters and Evidences relating to Westmorland and Yorkshire properties from John (1199-1261) to Edward III (1327-1377)" (CROK WD/HOTH/A988/11): see plate 10 opposite.

"These are the bounder of Stanesmoore - First Beginning att the Haight or Topp of a place or hill called Hearne hil, and thence unto Backston Fell, and from Backston fell to the heighte of Morvill, and from thence to the Frierwith Sike and from thence to a Whitestone in Easegill, and from thence to a place called Aesgill [?Aygill on OS map] poole And from thence to a place called Reerecross; And from thence to the Heade of a yellisike howe [heved? hewd?] and soe along a Travers unto Soutergill head and from thence to a place called Caldselehaw And so ascending by ye Shillipsike unto the westend of Nerigillfell [?] and from hence unto the Northern end of Little Fell and from thence directly to the haight of the westend of Swyndale and from thence descending unto the Bounders of Helton."

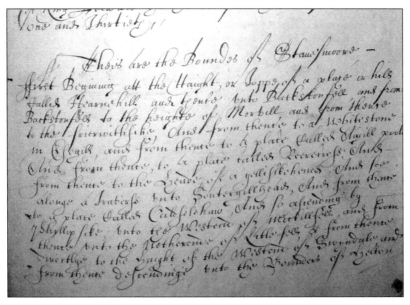

Plate 10, Lady Anne Clifford's Bounder of Stainmore, image courtesy of Lord Hothfield.

In this very early source it is interesting to note that the spelling of "Stanesmoore" recalls Harrison's later naming of this very distinctive stretch of upland as "Athelstane Moore", as noted elsewhere in this book. It is surprising that Smith (1967) quotes freely from Canon William Harrison's 1577 *Description of Britain*, but fails to include and comment on this particular name for Stainmore.

How close to the Nine Standards does this boundary roll approach, and why are they not mentioned? To trace the boundary in issue here, we must start at the first waypoint and ask, where was 'Hearne hil'? It is not shown on the First Edition of the OS maps, or indeed on any others so far examined, and the tithe and enclosure maps do not cover this high upland area. However, further research uncovered a relevant extract from Curwen's "Later Records from North Westmorland, East Ward." On page 147, the entry for 1746-7, 12 January reads:

"Presentment that John Birkbeck and others of Hartley did by hushing for lead ore in a place called Harnagill in the parish of K.

Stephen in such manner poison and pollute the stream of water in Hartley Town Beck and Eden that the said stream became unwholesome and corrupt so that those who had lands adjoining to the streams and cattle were hurt and greatly damaged thereby. On 7 April 1755, John Longstaff was indicted for the same offence and fined one shilling."

Hearne Hill, Harne Gill, or Harnygill (and variants) is also mentioned in several of the boundary rolls already cited above notably 1617, 1651, 1684 and 1709, from which it is clear that the gill is now named on the OS maps as Birkett Beck, and the hill must be Middle Grayrigg (the ridge on which the Lord's Stone is found), or Collin Hill. Hearne Hill and/or Harne Gill are consistently recorded as marking the boundary between the townships of Hartley and Winton within the parish of Kirkby Stephen, but this point is not on the extreme outer boundary of the parish of Kirkby Stephen where the Nine Standards are located.

When the above partial perambulation reaches the outer boundary of Kirkby Stephen parish, the waypoint is called Backston Fell; this is not named on OS maps, but it is probably the very long watershed ridge (running north-east from the 662m triangulation station) that lies between the Backstone Beck catchment (which flows east into Yorkshire) and the Baxton Gill Head place name (oddly located by the OS on the opposite side of the watershed, where drainage flows west into Westmorland). If this assumption is correct, the Nine Standards are located on this ridge, and it is surprising that they are not named.

On the other hand, if the waypoint named Backston Fell does not refer to the long watershed ridge on the north-west side of the Backstone Beck catchment, it may more correctly be identified with Bastifell (620m), which is shown on the OS maps. This is less than a kilometre north of the Nine Standards, and in a direct line between Hearne Hill and Hugh Seat Nab. In this case, the Nine Standards are not mentioned because they do not lie on the boundary being defined.

The problem is that we simply do not know, and perhaps cannot know with certainty, what names were used to identify each ridge, peak or fellside even within such a limited area before the era of the OS maps. In many cases, the names are very similar, pronunciations may have differed; rustic accents perhaps hard for scribes to grasp; and all that may have caused confusion. However, the perambulations

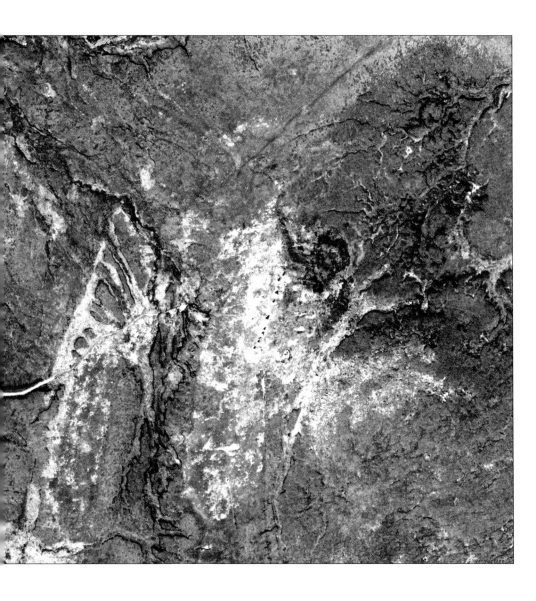

Plate 1, high altitude digital aerial photograph of Nine Standards Rigg, courtesy of GetMapping Ltd.

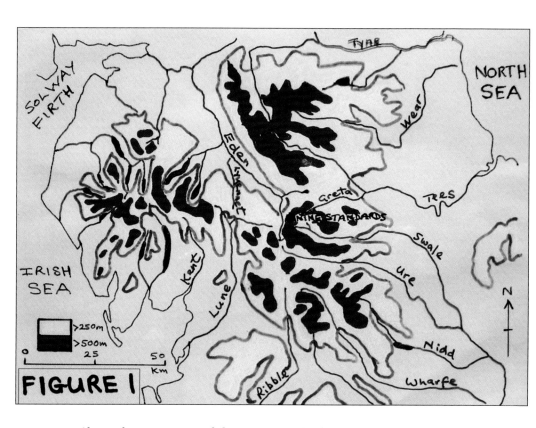

Above, location map of the Nine Standards in northern England, by the author.

Plates 2 and 3, opposite, top, low altitude oblique aerial photograph of Nine Standards, on 12 May 2005 before re-build, looking south-east, and, below, low altitude oblique aerial photograph of Nine Standards, on 6 September 2005 after re-build, looking south-east, both images courtesy of Simon Ledingham.

Plate 4, above, during the re-building, master waller Steve Allen and assistants, courtesy of Barry Stacey, Plate 5, below, Steve Allen and colleagues with Dick Capel and Alfie, photograph by the author.

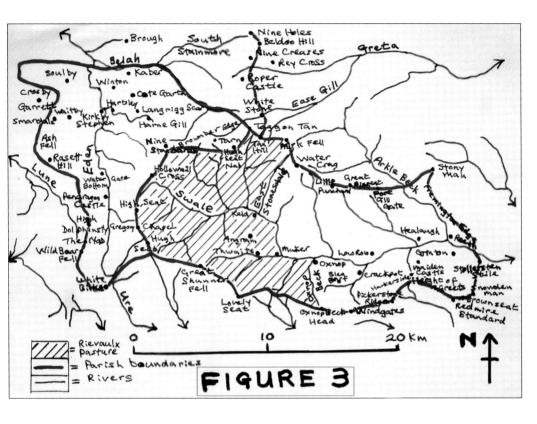

*Boundaries of Kirkby Stephen parish and Upper Swaledale, drawn by
the author.*

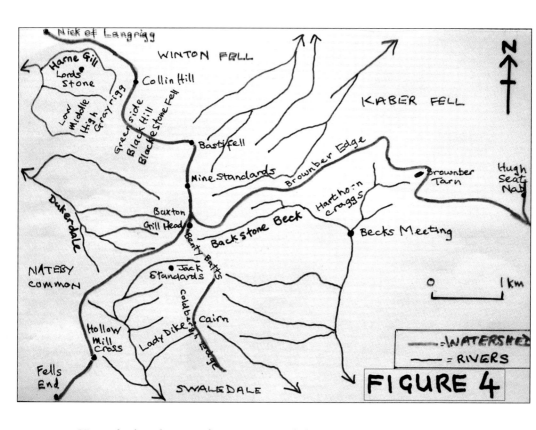

Watershed and major features around the Nine Standards, drawn by the author.

Above, plate 6, inscription on flat rock slab behind Tan Hill pub LW 1676. Below, plate 7, inscription on flat rock slab behind Tan Hill pub WPE B 1759, photographs by the author.

Plate 15, above, Nine Standards on the skyline seen from the easr.
Plate 16, below, Nine Standards on the skyline seen from the west.
Photographs courtesy of Barry Stacey and Simon Ledingham.

transcribed in this book, along with the various others that have been found, provide the raw material for a very interesting and useful piece of detailed research to establish exactly which name belongs to which place. The original OS surveyors' field notebooks for Westmorland are accessible to the public and can be consulted in the archives; the 1863 Books of Reference (i.e. Area Books) are in the British Library under shelfmark 'Maps O.S.'

1199x1377: A further jewel in Lady Anne Clifford's file of "Charters and Evidences relating to Westmorland and Yorkshire properties from John (1199-1261) to Edward III (1327-1377)" (CROK WD/HOTH/A988/11) is the following perambulation of Mallerstang. It is bound in as the last page of this book, and it follows straight after the above, as though it were part of the same perambulation. In fact, it is completely unrelated to it geographically, as anybody familiar with the upper Eden Valley would know. An explanatory note to this effect ought to be included in the *Charters and Evidences* book. If they have survived, it would also be rewarding to identify, locate and transcribe the original sources of these documents in the Clifford family archives, and see if other such papers may also have survived. This very early boundary roll is quoted in full in a later section; also see plate 11 (see page 74). It is included here simply to draw attention to it as a fascinating survivor, which may lead others to pursue the original source used by Lady Anne's researcher and indeed the identity of that researcher.

12th/13th Century? Lawrence Barker personal papers. At face value, this appears to be the oldest perambulation so far found that mentions by name the Nine Standards, and for that reason the full original text is quoted. See Plates 12 and 13 (see pages 77 and 78).
    "Metts and Bounder of the South Side of Swaledale 1743 taken from a Copp of Corns. [= Cornelius] Fryer.
    "Metts and Bounders given by Gilbert Gant Lord of Swaledale beginning at Stallerstone so riseing towards the South to White Stone in Sharra Ascending towards the South by Brounsitt And then between ye fforrests by the Height as ye Watter of Heaven Divids Towards ye West to the Limitt on ye Greets And then towards ye West as Heavens water [divides] to High Couvill and then towards ye West as the Heaven Watter Divids to Piecessea

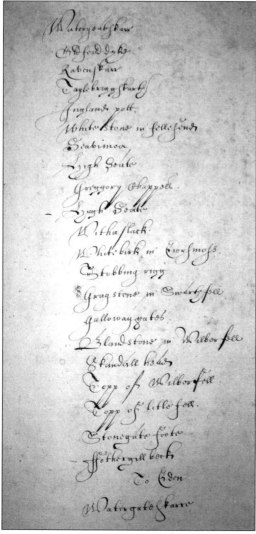

Plate 11, Lady Anne Clifford's Boundary of Mallerstang, image courtesy of Lord Hothfield.

Rigd So then towards the West as ye Water of heaven Divids to Winngates So then as the Watter Heven Divids to Tarn Seate So then towards ye west as Heven Watter Divids to Oxnopp head So then towards ye west as the Watter Heven Divids to Ellerad Pott So then as Hevin Water Divids to Watter Pott so then towards ye west to the height of Backstone Edge So then towards the West as the Watter Heaven Divids to Stoney Gill head So then towards the west as the Watter of Heaven Divids to Topes Cragg So then towards the west as ye Heaven Watter Divids to Digsomerseat so then towards the West as the Watter of Heaven Divids to Lovelseate So then towards ye west as the Watter of Heaven Divids to troope head So then towards the West as the Water of Heaven Divids to little Shunner fell So then Towards the West as the Watter of Heaven Divids Unto Mikle Shunner fell. So then towards the West as the Watter of Heaven divids to He Seat So towards ye West as the Water of Heaven Divids to How Seate So then towards the West as the Water of Heaven Divids unto White Stone in ffells End between Richmond Shire and Westmoorland."

"The Boundery of the North Side Swale from Hollowell Cross to the Lordship of Marrick...

"From Hollowell Cros as Heaven Water Deals to the Gray Yoad in Coad burneth as Heaven Water Deals to the 9 Stande as Heaven Water Deals to Harthorn Cragg from the Hart Horne Cragg as Heaven Water Deals to Brownber Edge Down the [White] gill from the White Gill as Heaven Water Deals to the Tann from the Tann [as Heaven Water Deals] to Tak and Tann from Tack and Tann as Heaven Water [Deals to Thomas Gill] head from Thomas Gill head as Heaven Water Deals to East ... [?] ... Head to the Hight of the Water Cragg from the Hight of the Water Cragg as Heaven Water Deals to Mosedale head from Mosedale head as Heaven Water Deals to Little Punshard Standert as Heaven Water Deals to the Hight Pinseat from Pinseat as Heaven Water Deals to the Wet shaw head from the Wetshaw head by Linyell line to forgill Gate from forgill Gate Down forgill to Arkle Beck so Down that Beck till you come at farndell So up that beck to Sinder Gate from Sinder Gate to Ackman Cragg from Ackman Cragg as Heaven Water Deals to Beals head Pasture So down to Batt Yeatt so down Goat to Swale Down Midrever Swale to Stollerstone."

The page is torn in several places, but in this fortunately repetitious style, the missing text is clear enough and has been inserted above in square brackets.

As Lawrence and Sheila Barker have pointed out, the second part appears to be in a different hand, and transcribed with more modern and consistent spelling. It is also worth noting that much of this text is the same as Joshua Fryer's text above; but crucial minor waypoints located in the heart of lower Swaledale are not, and the reference to the Nine Standards waypoint is not repeated.

This is the last and apparently the earliest perambulation so far located. It contains several points of great interest that may help in deciding on a likely date for the original material, the nature of that material, and the reliability of what is presented. This will form the starting point for the next major section of the book. Meanwhile, it is worth reviewing briefly the various place-names in the above peram-bulations that have been used over the centuries for drystone cairns such as the Nine Standards.

Names given to drystone cairns near Nine Standards

Digressing for a moment to explain why this analysis has been includ-ed, the science of onomastics (or 'the study of the principles of nomenclature,' in old money) studies place names first and foremost to yield the meaning of the name. But it can also identify the people who invented those names for prominent landscape features from the particular language they spoke. This is very useful, because the his-torians think they know roughly when the various groups of people arrived in Westmorland, and what their languages were. So while place names cannot be used to determine the actual age of the cairns, they do prove the cairns existed when those languages were spoken, and were named by people trying to find their way around. How else could they have acquired the names we now know them by?

In the original texts faithfully transcribed above, the surprising thing is how many different words have been used over the centuries to describe the same type of landmark, namely the simple drystone cairns that are such a common feature of the watersheds and other ridges on the upper fells in this area. Eight clearly different words are listed below, in some fifteen variants. They derive from civil and ecclesiastical perambulations of the townships, parishes and manors of both the upper Eden valley and upper Swaledale, in the small area between Stainmore and Mallerstang Edge, many of which are quoted in this book.

The various similar forms of what appear to be the same basic word may reflect change over time, differences in dialect or pronun-ciation, or simply the literacy level of the various people reporting and recording these boundary place names. Spelling was only standard-ised very recently, and we find variations in name even within the

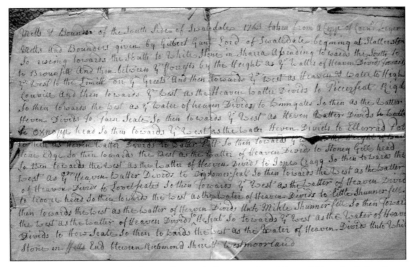

Plate 12, Metts and Bounder of the south side of Swaledale from Cornelius Fryer, image courtesy of Lawrence Barker.

same document; it must have been a challenging task to accurately record words spoken in different languages and dialects, by people from widely different backgrounds.

BEACON
>Lovely Seate Standard or Beacon (1710)
>Rowlandson Beacon (before 1811)
>Water Cragg Beacon (1812)
>Lovely Seat Standard or Beacon (1812)

CARN
>Sod Carn (1812), Arkendale Carn (1812)

CURRACK
>Carter Currack (1812)
>Reynoldson's Currack on Mick Fell (1812)
>New Currack, Old Currack (1842)

CURRICK
>Stony Shaw Rigg Currick (1724)

CURROCK(S)
>Windygates Currocks (undated, c.1700)
>Cuddy Currock (1812)

HURRISY
>Rollison Hurrisy (1812, twice)

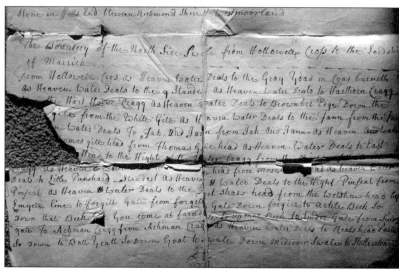

Plate 13, Metts and Bounder of the north side of Swaledale from Cornelius Fryer, image courtesy of Lawrence Barker.

HARROCK
    White Harrock on Black Stone Fell (1651)
HURROCK
    Hurrock on Low Grayrigg (1617)
    Hurrock at east end of Leasett (1617)
    Hurrock in the bout to Mickle Fell (1617)
    Hurrock of Stones, Hurrock (1651)
    Hurrock of Stones on Baystone ffell (1651)
    Hurrock of Stones on Bayre Stone Fell (1652)
    Hurrock on the middle of Benty Back (1651 and 1652)
    Hurrock of Stones called Hollow Mill Cross (1664x1698)
    Hurrock of Stones on top of Fells End (1664x1698, twice)
    Hurrock of Stones called Hound Tuft (1664x1698)
    Hurrock of Stones on Baxton Fell Side (1684)
    Hurrock of Stones on middle of Benty Batts (1684)
    Hurrock of Stones at south end of Benty Batts (1684)
    Hurrock of Stones in bought of Middle Fell (1684)
    Hurrock of Stones at Arneside Rake (1684)
    Hurrock of Stones at North end of Little Fell (1684)
    Hurrock of Stones on Basson Fell Side (1709)
    Hurrock of Stones in middle of Benty Batts (1708)

Hurrock of Stones at South end of Benty Batts (1708)
Hurrock of Stones in middle of Benty Batts (1709)
Rawlinson's Hurrock, Hurrock of Stones (1710)
Hurrock on Blackstone Edge (1710)
Mickle Shunner Fell Hurrock (1710)
Great Hurrock at Heugh Seate (1710)
Hurrock of Stones (1724, four times)
Hurrock of Stones in Grayston Rigg Edge (1749)
Hurrock of Stones in Stoney Band (early 19th C)
Great Hurrock or High Seat (early 19th C)
Hurrock of Stones, Rawlinson Hurrock (1812)
Hurrock of Stones on Stoney Band (1812)
Great Hurrock or Hugh's Seat (1812)
Hurrock on Knowlberry (1812)
Great Shunner Fell Hurrock (1812)
Hurrock on Height of Blackstone Edge (1812)
Hurrock of Stones side of Swaledale-Askrigg Road (1812)
Hurrock of Stones in Grayston Rigg Edge (1842)
Tarn Hurrock (1882)

MAN

Snowden Man (undated, c. 1700)

PILLAR·

Lady's Pillar (1812)

STANDARD(S)

Solomon Standards (undated, c. 1700)
Nine Standards (1708)
Nine Standards (1709, three times)
Mirk Fell Standard (1710)
Nine Standards (1710, four times)
Ogrome Gate Standard, Lovely Seate Standard (1710)
Standard att West End of Hood Rigg (1710)
Nine Standards (1735, twice)
Nine Standards (early 19th century)
Nine Standards (before 1811)
Nine Standards (1812, six times)
Lovely Seat Standard (1812)
Standard at West End of Hoodrigge (1812)
Nine Standards Rigg (1836)
Principal pillar of Stones called the Nine Standards (1843)

Standards Tarn (1843)
Nine Standards (1896)
STANDARTS
Nine Standarts (1811)
STANDE
Nine Stande (12th/13th century?)
STANDERD
Caudber Standerd (1664x1698)
STANDERS
Nine Standers (1534x1538, twice)
Nine Standers (1617)
Standers on Black Hill (1617)
Standers on Blacke Hill (1651)
Nine Standers (1651)
Nine Standers on Caudber Edge (1664x1698)
Stander of Stones at South end of Swarth Fell (1664x1698)
Nine Standers (1684)

The spellings in the various perambulations over the centuries differ, and they often vary also even within the same record. However, it is clear that *carrick*, *currack* and *currock* may be taken to be the same, and derive from *currick*, a Modern English dialect noun meaning 'cairn, heap of stones' (Smith, part ii, page 245), or from *carrec*, Old Welsh, meaning 'rock' (Smith, ii, 240). Similarly, *harrock* and *hurroc* derive from *hurrock*, a Modern English dialect noun meaning simply 'cairn' (Smith, ii, 265). The earlier forms *stande* and *standers*, and the later forms *standards, standerd* and *standarts*, derive from *stander* an early Modern English noun meaning 'upright pillar,' as also found in Jack Standards, (Smith, ii, 289). This drystone cairn is a major landmark not mentioned by that name in any of the perambulations cited here, but it is only about one kilometre or half a mile to the south of the Nine Standards, and thought by Fleming (1998) to be of "probably Bronze Age" though he cites no evidence for his assertion. 'Man' is a Modern English noun meaning 'cairn, pile of stones' (Smith, ii, 273). The words beacon, carn (Irish and Gaelic for 'cairn'), and pillar are self-explanatory.

'Hurrisy' is more interesting: it derives from *hreysi*, an Old Norse noun meaning 'cairn, heap of stones,' and my text here corrects an error in Walker (2007). Quoting from the section on 'Elements in

Westmorland place-names and field-names' in part ii of Smith, 1967, pages 229 and 264, we find:

> "*hreyrr* Old Norse = cairn, boundary cairn e.g. Rey Cross; and *hreysi* Old Norse = cairn, heap of stones. These can occur as the final element of a compound name in which the first element is a significant word eg Stan(e)rays(e), 1220-1247; Stanirase, 1200; Staynraises, 1294."

Elsewhere in Lakeland, the term 'raise' is found, from Icelandic *hreysi*, "applied originally to mounds or cairns raised over the dead, as in Dunmail Raise, grave of Dunmail a Cumbrian king; also the village of Stone Raise in Cumbria" (Ellwood, 1895). A further example is the hill Raise Howe, a few kilometres south-east of Crosby Ravensworth, on which the OS 1:25,000 map shows a tumulus or burial mound. As the blurb on the dust cover of the EPNS volumes on Westmorland states, "The most striking feature of the nomenclature [in Westmorland] is the extensive Scandinavian element, and the evidence of the names proves this to be of Norwegian and Irish-Norwegian rather than Danish origin. The best parallels... are to be found in Iceland and the Faroes."

These variants all mean literally 'stone cairns', and hence Nine Stande or Standers (the earliest forms of the name recorded in the documents above) simply mean 'nine stone cairns.'

Some of these words for drystone cairns have been used at different times to describe the same landmark; e.g. Rollison Hurrisy (1812), Rawlinson Hurrock (1812), Rowlandson Beacon (before 1811), Rawlinson's Hurrock (1710). Occasionally two 'cairn' words are used together as in the phrase, "Lovely Seate Standard or Beacon" (repeated in both 1710 and 1812). Equally, there are cases where the same landmark is known by a different name to people in manors or parishes on opposite sides of the watershed.

It also appears that the name by which a landmark is known may change over the centuries; for example the geography suggests that Rollison/Rawlinson Hurrisy, Beacon or Hurrock, and Jack Standards are one and the same place. Similarly one should verify whether the Standers (1617 and 1651) on Black Hill, and the hurrock of stones on Baystone ffell (1651), Bayre Stone Fell (1652), Baxton Fell Side (1684) and Basson Fell Side (1709) also all refer to the same place. This identification might be substantially aided by an expert study of the place names themselves in the field as well as in the library. There is, in short, a need for detailed topographical research on the fells to iron out the queries and inconsistencies apparent in the many peram- bulations quoted in this book, and to identify by hand-held GPS (Global Positioning System) and corresponding Ordnance Survey map grid references the exact locations of all the places listed to avoid any ambiguity or confusion in the future.

In conclusion, the present name of the Nine Standards therefore appears to derive from the word *stander*, a choice originally influ- enced by French usage, and later used by others in a transferred min- eral sense, and hence it dates from no earlier than the middle of the 15th century (Margaret Gelling, personal communication) or mid- 14th century following Smith (1967). When earlier original texts which mention the Nine Standards are unearthed, it will be interesting to see what names they are given, and what language is used to name them.

At least one other cairn in the vicinity, Rollison Hurrisy, may derive its name ultimately from Old Norse, so it must have been in existence when the people who spoke that language named it on arrival in the upper Eden Valley, at least by the 9th and 10th centuries, and possibly earlier. In the case of the 'currock' names and close vari- ants, these may derive from speakers of Old Welsh, dating possibly from very much earlier times. Going further, and at the risk of enrag- ing the place-name scientists, it does not seem fanciful to a rank ama- teur to discern a connection between 'carn' as used here and its Gaelic or Irish equivalent meaning 'cairn.' Equally, it would be interesting to get an expert view on possible precedent forms of the very fre- quently used dialect word 'hurrock' and its variants. Any volunteers?

So we do not know, and may never know, what the Nine Standards were called by the several groups of inhabitants who preceded the early Modern English speakers, those groups who variously spoke and/or wrote in Norman-French, Anglian, Saxon, Norse, Irish, Gaelic, Latin, and even British (Brythonic) or Early Old Welsh, though in the latter case an intriguing possibility is given in a later section where speculation and downright heresy are briefly entertained.

THREE

The Search for Gilbert's Charter

We return now to the last of the perambulations quoted above, from the personal collection of Lawrence Barker of Healaugh in Swaledale, who kindly made it available to the author, so that we can pursue in detail several points of great interest. In brief, it is said to be a copy, perhaps made in 1743, of a document belonging to one Cornelius Fryer. The document is contained in an envelope on which there are two annotations. The first, in black ink and a script very similar to the script of the document itself, reads, "The Boundary's of Swaledale." The second, in blue biro and a much more modern script, reads, "HEALAUGH MANOR 1747 GILBERT DE GANT." The first would seem to be contemporary with the document itself; the second is probably in the writing of Roger Fieldhouse who catalogued the Barker papers in 1973, possibly as part of his work with an adult education group in the area. The envelope and enclosure were described in Roger Fieldhouse's partial catalogue of the Barker papers under section 4 "Manors of Healaugh and Muker" as item 10, "Healaugh Manor boundaries, 1747, (fragile)."

The document is in two parts, listing respectively the "metes and bounds," in other words the boundary markers or waypoints, along the south and north sides of the upper Swaledale watershed, and it states that these were given by "Gilbert Gant Lord of Swaledale." These are presented here as plates 12 and 13, (see pages 77 and 78) as noted above.

The actual script of the two parts seems very similar to the non-expert, but as Lawrence and Sheila Barker pointed out, the spelling and grammar are different, and the south side ("as ye watter of Heaven Divids") is noticeably more archaic than the north side ("as Heaven Water deals"). Much of the text is formulaic, perhaps reflecting its original transmission to succeeding generations by word of mouth, repeating an apparently well-established pattern of words. The formulaic text is reminiscent of chant-like sequences of verses to aid memory in a pre-literate society. Interestingly, this formulation persisted in Swaledale through the centuries, as seen in the perambulations quoted above, but it is uncommon, if not completely absent, on the Westmorland side of the border.

Eventually the words were written down, and the text we now have states that it is "taken from a Copp of Cornelius Fryer." Since this is a copy, the Cornelius Fryer document was in English. It was probably transcribed from the original more ancient preceding documents, some of which – as noted in D/HH 6/2/259, page 41 – are thought to have been in Latin. But we do not know if Cornelius Fryer himself translated the Latin document into English, or whether he simply transcribed an existing English language translation. The copy we have does not appear to be in his handwriting. The Barker text may not be the script of Cornelius Fryer himself, since we can see an example of his signature on the lease of Smarber Hall from the owner Thomas Lord Wharton to the two brothers James and Cornelius Fryer, both of whom sign their names with the double Ff commonly used at that time. But if we assume, not unreasonably, that it is an accurate copy, the information it contains is coming to us second-hand. There was a Latin original; it was translated into English, and we have an accurate copy of that translation. But we need to know a lot more about the owner of this document as well as about the document itself before making a judgment on its reliability and the credibility of the information it contains.

Lord Wharton's Bailiff

First, the owner of the copied document: who was Cornelius Fryer, where and when did he live, why would he have possessed, maybe transcribed and possibly even translated, an old document defining the boundaries of upper Swaledale? Cornelius Fryer would appear to have been a figure of local importance, and so information about him – as with the perambulations quoted above – is best sought at local level, in parish papers, in manorial estate documents now kept appropriately at the relevant county record offices, or still in the possession of local residents, often as descendants of agents or bailiffs of the various manors, or of others with vested interests in the resources of the area.

Searching the Grinton Parish Registers in the decades before 1743, we find the following entry: "1667: February 2. Baptised - Cornelius, son of James Frear of Low Row."

Similarly, 74 years later we find the entry: "1741: November 13. Buriall - Cornelius Fryer of Law Raw."

And he had a family: "1692: June 19. Baptised James son of Cornelius Fryer of Fetholme." After his daughter "An" was born on 25 April 1697, there follow seven more children including a second Cornelius: "1699: November 26. Baptised Cornelus son of Cornelus Frear of Law Raw."

He was followed by Ely, 14 December 1701; Hanna, 3 April 1704; Ralph, 7 October 1706, Matthew, 5 January 1708 (but he died in October 1710); Jane, 5 February 1711 (but she died in September 1716), and ending with Abraham, November 4, 1713.

The move of house from Fetholme to Low Row, possibly into the ancestral home, may be related to the death of his parents, or at least of his father James. Or it may simply have been to accommodate his large and growing family. Sadly we also find the following entry: "1739: November 3. Buriall – Jane wife of Cornelius Fryer of Lawraw." There is no record of their marriage in the Grinton Register, so Jane must have been from another parish.

And there is yet a third Cornelius Fryer: "1728 July 31. Baptised Cornelius son of John Fryer of Lawraw." John being presumably a brother or cousin of the original Cornelius Fryer. There is also a James Fryer in the same generation. But there is no mention of a Joshua so the author or compiler of *The Book of Recipes* was probably from an earlier period, before 1650, the date of the earliest surviving Parish Registers of Grinton.

Cornelius Fryer (1667-1741) was one of more than 90 witnesses at the court proceedings over mineral rights in the dale between the then Lord Wharton and Reginald Marriott in year six of Queen Anne's reign, namely 1707/8. In the National Archives (TNA) at Kew under reference E 134/6 Anne/Mich 38 the original manuscript parchments of the Exchequer Depositions by witnesses contain the following:

"Cornelius Fryer, Yeoman, of Low Row, 39 years, who rid the boundary [of Swaledale] two years ago at Lord Wharton's order, after first giving notice at Reeth Market. His dead brother James Fryer was bayliff to the late Lord Wharton [Philip Lord Wharton died 1695], and Cornelius Fryer is Bayliff to the present Lord Wharton for the Manor of Helawe."

The depositions were evidently taken in 1706 (1667 plus 39 years), so the Swaledale boundary must have been ridden by Cornelius Fryer in 1704 or thereabouts. He was therefore intimately familiar with the various waypoints.

Similarly, in one of the Hanby-Holmes papers (DRO D/HH 6/2/263) we read:

"In 1742 there was a Law Suit between Gibson & Co. who sold the Swaledale Estate and Smith who purchased. The latter having laid claim to the Lead Mines in the Common Pastures at Spout Gill Keldscale [?] ...Cornelius Fryer aged 72 deposed that he was born in Swaledale & he lived there all his life. Was Bailiffe of the two Manors of Healaugh above 30 years & of the Manors of Mukair above 16 years, which mannors were ye Estate of ye late Duke of Wharton, and lately purchased by ye defendant Smith. That he is owner of a Copyhold on Customary Tenement in Low row within ye manor of Healaugh and in that capacity intitled to a right of depasturing his Cattle upon the Common Pasture called Lowrow Common Pasture & upon the out Common or Moor thereto adjoining. That by & under ye said several circumstances he became and is very well acquainted with the several Commons and Common Pastures in Swaledale within ye said Manors & with ye nature & usage thereof. And saith that ye said Commons and Common Pastures do most of them contain large quantities of land, & are for ye most part hilly and mountainous & containeth great variety of Soil some part good but for ye most part Ling & full of Bent Sieves & Peat – And that ye said Common Pastures are most of them inclosed with walls or fences from ye out Moors which are usually maintained by ye persons having a right to depasture."

Since he died in 1741 at the age of 74, Cornelius Fryer would have been 72 in 1739.

From these extracts it is clear that Cornelius Fryer was a pillar of the local community, and a man totally familiar with upper Swaledale. As bailiff or agent for the Wharton manors in Swaledale he had professional responsibilities that required him to know in great detail the boundaries of those manors, and to be able to defend the interests of his Lord against incursions and encroachments by people from neighbouring manors: to do so, he held the estate record books including all ancient documents defining their "metes and bounds." He is therefore entirely credible, both as an authority on the detail of the manorial boundaries and on exactly who had defined them in the first place.

The Norman Lord of Swaledale

Secondly, who was 'Gilbert Gant Lord of Swaledale,' mentioned in the Cornelius Fryer document, and why and when might he have defined the boundaries of upper Swaledale? Gant was a figure of more than purely local importance, so the information on him that follows was gathered at regional and national levels.

Bear with me: if it was confusing to find at least three men bearing the name Cornelius Fryer, we now have to identify which of the five men all bearing the name Gilbert Gant might have been the one named in the Cornelius Fryer document, so that we can determine the origin and nature of his interest in upper Swaledale. To minimise the confusion, I have numbered the five candidates I to V, as one might with monarchs, although they were not of course referred to or known by those numbers in their lifetimes. The account of the Gant family given below is based on several sources, notably the Roger Dodsworth manuscripts (in particular his Manuscript 95, in the Bodleian Library at Oxford; Short Catalogue reference 5036), but also the Farrer/Clay 'Early Yorkshire Charters', Page's *Victoria County History* volume for North Yorkshire, material in the British Library at St. Pancras (which since 1974 has housed what was formerly the British Museum manuscripts collection), and material in the Society of Antiquaries of London library at Picadilly. The several sources do not all agree on the dates, nor on the details of wives and children. The following is the best I could do!

The first Gilbert de Gant was born around 1042 and invaded England in 1066 with his uncle William, Duke of Normandy, better known to us now as William the Conqueror. Gilbert's father was Baldwin, Earl of Flanders, and his mother was Matilda. She was the sister of William, Duke of Normandy. Baldwin was the brother of William's wife, another Matilda. So Gilbert de Gant was very well connected, and for his military services in the conquest of England, King William gave him the large estate of Folkingham in Lincolnshire, where the Domesday Book lists him as tenant in chief; this became the seat of Gilbert's Barony. Around 1065, Gilbert de

Gant the first, or Gilbert I, married Alicia, the daughter of Hugh de Montfort, on whose death Alicia inherited the de Montfort estate. Gilbert I and Alicia had three sons, Robert, Walter and Geoffrey, and they owned lands and estates in both France and England. Gilbert de Gant I died around 1095.

Robert de Gant I (1085-1158?), said to be the eldest son, inherited his mother Alicia's estates in France, and stayed there. The second son, Walter de Gant (born 1090?), inherited the English lands, and the Lordship of Folkingham. Around 1108 he married Matilda, some-times called Maud, who was the daughter of Stephen, Count of Brittany and Earl of Richmond, with whom he received, as her dowry, the whole of Swaledale. This was originally part of the Saxon Count Edwin's lands of Richmondshire. After the Conquest, Edwin was dis-inherited, and his lands were given by William the Conqueror to Allan Count of Britanny, and they were then inherited in turn by his son, Stephen. Geoffrey de Gant, the third son, had lands in Lincolnshire from his father, but (according to Plantagenet Harrison, 1779) he later became Chief Forester of Swaledale to his brother Walter. Walter de Gant and Maud had three sons and two daughters, Gilbert II, Robert II, Hugh, Agnes and Matilda. Camden names the second daughter as Alice. Other sources state that one of the sons of this marriage was called Baldwin. Walter de Gant died in 1138 or 1139.

Gilbert de Gant II (born 1118 or 1120) inherited Folkingham from his father, and also became Earl of Lincoln in the right of his wife Hawysia. By her or Rohese de Clare he had two daughters, Alice who married Simon de St Luz, and Gunnora. Both Alice and Gunnora died without offspring so when Gilbert II died without a male heir in 1156, ownership of the Gant estates then passed to Gilbert's brother Robert II de Gant, by now Lord Chancellor of England.

Robert de Gant II (born 1125?) is thought to have actually man-aged Swaledale from 1185-1191, so between 1156 and 1185, and after his death, possibly in 1191, it may have been held and managed by Hugh de Gant, or possibly Matilda and her husband. Robert de Gant II married Gunora, niece of Hugh de Gurney, a great Northampton Baron and with her had four sons, William, Gilbert III, Maurice and Stephen. Robert was also married to Alicia, heir of William Paynel, possibly in 1167 before Gunora, and later still to Hawisia who sur-vived at least until 1216. William was the eldest son, but died with-out issue. The second son, Gilbert III, was born around 1185.

On Robert's death, Gilbert de Gant III was still under age, and therefore initially in ward to William de Stuteville. On maturity, perhaps in 1206, he became Earl of Lincoln, and at some time married Alicia, sister and co-heir of Ralph, Lord of Naburne. Gilbert III was known in Lincolnshire as Gilbert the Good. He and Alicia had four sons, Gilbert IV, Henry, William and Adam. In 1216/7 Gilbert III joined the barons in rebellion against King John, and after the defeat at Lincoln he was imprisoned in 1217 and (according to Page, 1923) "he [Gilbert III] remained a captive until his death in 1241/2." Certainly the Gant lands were in the hands of the King in 1219, though this may have been temporary. Burke's Peerage (1831) states that he purchased a pardon from the King. The Patent Rolls for Henry III (1216-1225) record he was in jail as a hostage in 1217 (membrane 2) but by 1224 (membrane 5) while Gilbert III – evidently a free man – was serving in the wars in Wales, the King sent him letters of protection for a military campaign in 'Pictland' (Scotland today) with other named knights. So he was too useful to be left long in captivity, in spite of his temporary lapse of judgement.

In Dodsworth's account, the son of Gilbert III, Gilbert IV who was named Lord of Folkingham and of all Swaledale, was born around 1220. Clearly Gilbert III was either released before that time, or he enjoyed liberal family visiting conditions. More likely, he had been accepted back into the King's favour as Burke says, in exchange for an appropriately large consideration. Gilbert IV had one son, Gilbert V, and four daughters Helewise, Nichola, Margaret and Juliana de Gant (Burke does not list Helewise). Gilbert IV died in 1274; his Inquisition Post Mortem was held in the same year (see the Calendar of Inquisitions Post Mortem, 1-19 Edward I, entry 55).

Gilbert de Gant V was born around 1248, married Lora, sister of John Balliol, King of Scotland, but they had no children. He died on 17 March 1298, the last to bear the name Gilbert de Gant; his Inquisition Post Mortem in 1298 has also survived. His sisters Helewise, Nichola, Margaret and Juliana all died without children of their own, but Nichola's husband Peter de Malolacu III, Baron of Mulgrave, had a son Peter de Malolacu IV; Margaret's husband William de Kerdeston, Lord of Kerdeston, had a son also called William de Kerdeston, and these two, along with Juliana de Gant, Gilbert V's only surviving sister, jointly inherited the Gant lands. An alternative version has Gilbert V alienating the Gant lands to his uncle

Adam de Gant without the King's permission, though that indiscretion seems to have been overcome, no doubt by a suitable gift to the King, and the lands duly restored to the Gant family line.

The purpose here is not to produce a definitive genealogy of the Gant family, perhaps an impossible task given the widely different versions available, but to use the several genealogical accounts to outline the acquisition and subsequent descent of the upper Swaledale lands through the various generations, and to establish a sequence of approximate dates for important events. This should enable us to see which "Gilbert Gant Lord of Swaledale" may have defined the detailed boundaries of his territories, and in so doing recorded the existence of the Nine Standards at the earliest time (so far).

The above sequence eliminates Gilbert I from consideration; Swaledale was not acquired by the Gants until about 1108 when Walter married Maud, and received Swaledale as her dowry. Gilbert II the son of Walter is therefore the first who could have defined the boundaries, and he inherited Swaledale in 1138 or 1139. The last Gilbert, Gilbert V, died in 1298, 150 years later. We are therefore looking at the various Gilberts who lived in the period between 1138 and 1298, and we are seeking a manorial perambulation or just possibly a charter of some kind that one of them is known to have made.

The search for Gilbert's document began at the local level and gradually extended to regional and national levels. Starting at the Cumbria County Records Offices at Kendal and Carlisle, with occasional visits to the National Archives at Kew, and the British Library at St. Pancras in London, progress was at first slow. But enquiries at the North Yorkshire County Record Office at Northallerton were very helpfully and fruitfully redirected to Durham.

Durham County Record Office (DRO) holds a very large collection of papers accumulated by the Teesdale Record Society which was founded in 1934. E R Hanby Holmes, a local solicitor, and his clients R H Edleston and Miss S A C Edleston were the leading figures. The society was in abeyance from the end of the Second World War, punctuated by occasional short-lived revivals of interest and activity. The Hanby Holmes Collection of papers is referenced under D/HH, and the Edleston collection under D/Ed in the Durham Catalogue. The D/HH papers have been extremely useful, and I believe the present research has not exhausted them as a major source of valuable information on Swaledale.

The Russendale Book

One item, D/HH 6/2/257, from the Steward's Papers section in the Hanby Holmes collection is of particular interest in the present context; and the second page is accurately reproduced below:

"Swaledale Boundaries

"It is believed that Walter de Gaunt, Nephew to Wm. the 1st who had a part of Swaledale had at first no Boundaries described in his Grant but there is a Record 9 Edward 1st [= 1281] with a Verdict & Judgement obtained by Gilbert de Gaunt upon Quo Warranto showing that He had not enlarged his Liberties And it is believed that there is a Book called the Russendale Book (Westmorland) temp. Jcs. 1. in which the same Boundaries, i.e. The Heaven water deal are described as those of Gilbert de Gaunt.

"The General Boundary of the Maners of Yorkshire which have extensive Moors & Wastes is that of Heaven water deal upon the Mountains."

This document, (DRO D/HH 6/2/257), is undated, but in my view probably late 18th or early 19th century, and from a comparison of the script with other papers in the collection, it was possibly written by Ottiwell Tomlin of Low Row, and later of Richmond. The phrase "as Heaven water deals" indicates that between the two points mentioned, the boundary runs along the highest ground between two river catchments, that is, along the watershed. It is frequently repeated in almost all the perambulations cited above, to the extent that the phrase has usually been omitted to save space.

The original text contains several minor deletions and amendments, removed for clarity from the above transcription. The original is presented as plate 14 (page 92). The year '9 Edward I' is 1281 but other sources quote 7 Edward I, i.e. 1279, for this; it must therefore have been Gilbert V who obtained the court judgment. The important points here are that the Gant family still held the whole of Swaledale, that its boundaries had been defined and were well known, and that the Gant family had not enlarged the boundaries of their manors (one may assume, though it is not stated, that the Gants had not reduced their boundaries either!) The full Latin text of the relevant *Quo Warranto* [= 'By What Right'] roll is given in DRO D/HH 6/2/253, and an English extract is quoted below.

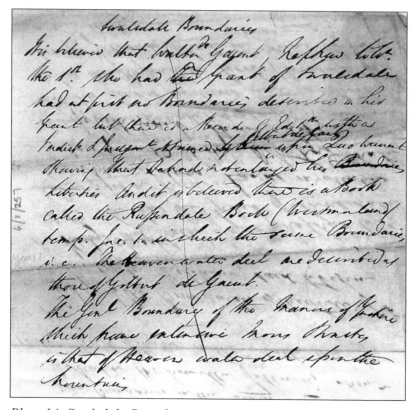

Plate 14, Swaledale Boundaries; manuscript note by an anonymous author. Image courtesy of the Hanby Holmes Estate archive, Durham County Record Office.

In the 'Swaledale Boundaries' document, the date of the 'Russendale Book' as I see it is given as 'temp. Jns. 1'; and according to the Durham Archivist this should be read as 'in the time of King James the First' (i.e. 1603-1625). The relevant abbreviation is therefore reproduced here as 'Jcs.' though it might also be read as 'Jns.1' and thus referring to the first year of Johannes or John (i.e. 1199/1200), an improbably early date. Have a look and see what you think; if the correct reading might be 'temp. Jms. 1', then the abbreviation used here is a personal shorthand. If the Russendale (= Ravenstonedale) Book could be found, the question could probably be resolved.

My best guess is that the Russendale Book was compiled by Wharton agents or bailiffs when Ravenstonedale was the principal seat of the Lords Wharton, probably when the deer park at Ravenstonedale was being created and walled in, with entries dating between 1544 when Lord Wharton acquired Muker, and 1738 when the Wharton manors in Swaledale were sold off. It is possible that the Cornelius Fryer document in the Lawrence Barker papers already cited above was copied from something in the Russendale Book, but it is more likely that both of them derive from a common source of earlier date, perhaps the original Latin language Charter of Gilbert de Gant defining the boundaries of upper Swaledale.

When asked, none of the archivists at the relevant regional county record offices had ever heard of such a book by that name, though they suggested several documents in their respective collections that might be the one referred to.

The Carlisle County Record Office (CROC) suggested their D/LONS/5/2/24/1 "Wharton manors 1560-1580" might be a Russendale Book candidate. This is a survey and valuation of the Wharton manors, including Ravenstonedale, and has 328 pages. It is in Latin, in a leather-bound volume whose title can be roughly translated as: "Extent and annual value of all lands, tenements and other hereditaments of the hon. Thomas Wharton, knight, Lord Wharton, in the counties of Westmorland, Richmond, bishopric of Durham and Cleveland in the County of York, examined and approved by the supervisors Ambrose Lancaster, Michael Wharton, Charles Wharton and Philip Machell, clerk, gentleman commissioners... by commission... directed to them dated at Helaugh, 15 January 1560/61." The survey records manors in Westmorland, County Durham and Yorkshire as well as Cumberland. In Yorkshire, the relevant ones are:

"Manerium de Helaughe infra Swawdale. Liber tenentes maneri.
[Manor of Healaugh below Swaledale. Free Tenants of the Manor]
Manerium de Mewacre infra Swawdail. [Manor of Muker below Swaledale]"

Most entries are confined to a statement for each manor of the free tenants' names, the size and nature of their holdings, and the amount paid by them each year. For full details see Arthur Raistrick, *Documents relating to the Swaledale Estates of Lord Wharton in the 16th and 17th Centuries*, edited by M. Y. Ashcroft, NYCRO Publication No. 36, April 1984.

Is this, then, the Russendale Book? There are no manorial

perambulations in CROC D/LONS/5/2/24/1, but a search for any reference to Gilbert de Gant and his definition of the boundaries of Swaledale was commissioned from the CROC Research Service in March 2008. Mrs Helen Cunningham reported that page 168 records that on 6th September 1682 this tome was produced in the case:

"in Chancery between Phillip Lord Wharton plaintiff and Edmund Millner and others defendants. This Booke was shown to Mr John Gunter and Mr William Mortimer as Wittnesses, produced on behalfe of the Plaintiffe att the time of their Examination before us Edw. Place, Antony Brathwaite, Matt. Smales and He. Robinson."

She concludes, "I can see no evidence of any reference to Gilbert de Gant or any boundary descriptions."   So probably not the Russendale Book.

The Kendal County Record Office (CROK) suggested their WDY/32 "Four and Twenty Ravenstonedale 1583-1903," and their WDY/32/3 photocopy of "The End (second) Book containing ends and verdicts of the 24, 1583-1730," as candidates for the Russendale Book. Dawn Roberston was kind enough to undertake an initial scan of the text, and commented by email as follows:

"The book is a monster, more than a foot high and almost six inches thick, though quite a few pages are blank. It was compiled by Anthony Fothergill of Brownber, public notary, [and as it happens one of Dawn's ancestors!] and concerns parish and manorial matters mostly. There are numerous accounts of the elections of the four and twenty men (often called the 'grand jury' of Ravenstonedale) who organised Ravenstonedale parish and church matters. There are accounts of tythes and poor rates plus quite a bit of information relating to the various vicars. The years it seems to cover are 1680 to 1790 but the entries are not in date order and, obviously, Anthony Fothergill was not alive throughout the whole of that period and occasionally the writing is not as neat as his, suggesting that someone else was involved in keeping the records. There are lots of financial accounts.

"There's an interesting piece about Robert Lowther, Lord Lonsdale, who owned part of the parish and who refused to pay his land tax! It also emerges that there were always two Russendale books – one kept by the public notary on behalf of the four and twenty men and the other kept by a person employed by Philip

Lord Wharton. The books were exact copies of each other and this fact was checked from time to time. One of the books was called the End Book and the other was called the Parish Book. Quoting from the article: 'The End Book of Ravenstonedale is kept by Anthony Fothergill, public notary, that all the ends and verdicts within the said lordship may be registered therein according to the order of the jury.'

"Another excerpt refers to a previous, older, Russendale Book. Anthony Fothergill copies from this: 'On the 28 day of January in the 27th year of the Reign of our sovereign Lady Elizabeth, 1583, renewed and rewritten by Anthony Fothergill in 1729-30.' He offers no clue as to what happened to the older book or what information it included. So, the mystery deepens... and I wonder if the older book and the copy book stayed with Lord Wharton's papers and have ended up somewhere other than Kendal?"

Enquiries at the Kendal Record Office revealed that the correct title and reference for the above are 'Ravenstonedale Parish End Book' (WD/MG A1717), and it is part of the Metcalfe-Gibson deposit. I have now read this from cover to cover and cannot improve on the above summary, except to add that it does not contain any boundary rolls, nor any statement about Gilbert de Gant having given the boundaries of Swaledale. WDY/32 "Four and Twenty Ravenstonedale 1583-1903," and WDY/32/3 in the CROK catalogue are photocopies. The archivists are aware of the references to an older Russendale Book, but despite their extensive enquiries, it still has to be located.

The search for the "Russendale Book" continues, on both sides of the Pennines as well as down south. Online searches of the catalogue databases of the National Archives, the British Library and the Society of Antiquaries of London Library have so far failed to find it either. But for the time being, another lead has temporarily run into the ground.

The National Archives at Kew

The search for Gilbert's document was simultaneously extended to the many official records kept by the government over the centuries.

A brief overview of the sorts of general source materials that have so far been consulted available in the archives might be of interest here.

Most county record offices hold reference copies of the many volumes of the Calendar of Charter Rolls, published by the Public Record Office (PRO) in various editions. The earliest Charter Roll Calendars date from about 1200. The National Archives and larger regional or cathedral offices also contain PRO calendars of the Close Rolls, Patent Rolls, Fine Rolls, *Placita de Quo Warranto* Rolls, Chancery Inquisitions Post Mortem, Parliamentary Rolls, Original and Confirmation Rolls and so on.

These were an excellent starting point in the search for the Gilbert de Gant document. But like all summaries they are selective and abbreviated, and in the case of the first calendar of the Charter Rolls for 1199 to 1483, and the Inquisitions Post Mortem for 1307 to 1461, the earliest years, and, as it happens the ones of interest to me, were known to be incomplete. The Deputy Keeper of Records, Sir H C Maxwell-Lyte, produced new versions over the period 1903-1927, and had this to say about the earlier edition, "The Calendar of Charter Rolls printed in 1803 was based on a manuscript of the time of James I [1603-1625] which was both incomplete and inaccurate, and no attempt was made to supply these defects by comparison to the original rolls."

While the later editions are a great improvement, they do not in every case contain all the entries on the original parchments, nor the full text even for those entries which they do include. Therefore, if and when found in recently published Calendars, important material has to be verified by inspecting the original parchments held at Kew. Some may be examined in the open reading rooms, under general supervision; older, more precious or more fragile ones can only be seen in safe rooms under close supervision, where researchers are locked in and have to apply to be released! But the printed Calendars are one of the best sources of information available, and provide an excellent starting point.

The earliest Charter Roll Calendars date from 1199, the Close Rolls from 1200, the Patent Rolls start in 1201, and the others follow soon thereafter. The printed volumes of the earliest material are 19th century summaries of the various official records indicated, in the original language of the respective documents, mostly Latin, but also Norman-French and latterly in English. Detailed information is available on-line as well as helpful Research Guides at http://www.nationalarchives.gov.uk/catalogue which is already an excellent resource but rapidly expanding and improving in detail.

A limited amount of material from before 1200 has been calendared and printed, mostly in the two *Cartae Antiquae* or Ancient Charters volumes of the Pipe Roll Society, but there are over 1000 charters from this series that have not yet been published. At the National Archives at Kew, manuscript indexes are available for some of the 'Ancient Charters' series, and the Public Record Office has produced *A Descriptive Catalogue of Ancient Deeds* in six volumes, edited by Maxwell Lyte, covering the 11th to the 16th centuries. Fortunately this excellent compilation is now searchable on-line at the http://www.british-history.ac.uk website, which also has the original OS Six Inch First Edition maps and a plethora of other useful information.

I say fortunately because these six volumes alone, which only cover Series A, B, C and D, contain over 52,000 parchment membranes, and over 27,000 deeds. Series A contains charters from the Treasury of the Receipt of the Exchequer; Series B from the Court of Augmentations; C the Court of Chancery; and D the Queen's Remembrancer's Department. There are eight other series of Ancient Deeds, five of which are further subdivided. Other collections of ancient charters are indexed in manuscript in the series 'Miscellaneous Ancient Charters,' and have been consulted at Kew. In brief, a great many charters and deeds, and so far no complete on-line index, but the website is evolving so rapidly that it is worth checking frequently.

All of the above printed Calendars, on-line websites and manuscript indexes have been scoured for Gilbert's Swaledale document, from the earliest available date until the end of the Gant line in 1298. Effectively this means from about 1200 onwards. It emerges that the Gants, in common with many of their Norman-French contemporaries, were devout Christians, and generous in their donations of lands, wealth and privileges to the Church, both by building and endowing parish churches in their manors and lordships, and also by founding abbeys, monasteries and churches, and granting lands to support the religious communities and individuals within them.

The generosity of these landowners was not entirely philanthropic, more a happy coincidence of interests, perhaps. The parish churches were a source of income; and in addition to income, the monastic foundations provided a way of extending influence and control in remote, sparsely populated and often politically volatile areas, at least in much of the north; and in old age, many of the rich and powerful who had survived to old age retired to live out their days in the peace and tranquillity of their monasteries. These donations by the great feudal magnates were mostly placed on record by writing charters, duly witnessed by the landowners, their families and the religious beneficiaries; and since these great lords held their lands from the King, all such grants had to be agreed and confirmed by the monarch, and duly recorded. In some cases the original donor's charters have survived; in other cases only the King's confirmation charters have survived.

The Gant Donations

The Gant family made generous donations to various abbeys and other religious houses. Bardney Abbey was refounded in 1087 as a Priory by Gilbert de Gaunt I and was raised to free abbey status in 1115 by his son Walter. Walter de Gant founded and endowed Ruford Abbey in 1148, and Bridlington Priory early in the reign of Henry I (1100-1135). The Gants probably gave the Manor of Grinton to Bridlington Priory along with the Church in 1200 (Page, 1923).

Gilbert de Gant III favoured Rievaulx Abbey, a Cistercian house in the valley of the River Rye near Helmsley, founded in 1131 by Walter Espec. One of Gilbert's many donations to it was of pasture rights over lands in Swaledale; this donation was confirmed by the King in 1251 in the Charter Roll for 35 Henry III, Membrane 6, which is the most complete surviving version of the Chartulary of Rievaulx Cistercian Abbey. In it the King confirms the many gifts to the Abbey, including, *"A dono Gilberti de Gaunt totam pasturam de Swaledale infra divisas et metas in carta ejusdem Gilberti..."* A translation of the full text of the Swaledale entry on Membrane 6 is as follows:

> "The King to the Archbishop etc etc greetings. Be it known that we, in the sight of God and for the greater good... confirm... to Blessed Mary and the Abbot of Ryvalle... the following grants and concessions, they having been reasonably made, in alms: namely:-
> By the gift of Gilbert de Gant all pasture in Swaledale between the

metes and bounds named in the charter of the said Gilbert, which the same monks from that time forth have had, with folds and out-houses for their animals, and with houses of the brothers and ser-vants and their animals, gardens, enclosures, and all necessities for buildings, fences, hearths, shelters, workshops, and their other easements in the forest of Swaledale."

It is clearly stated that the metes and bounds of the area gifted were defined in the charter, and that the monks have enjoyed them, "from that time forth" but no date is given. Since in 1251 the King was happy to confirm this gift, the original charter must have been pro-duced and examined, and the extent of the gifted lands understood and approved. It is not clear from the phrase "between the metes and bounds in the charter of the said Gilbert" whether this gift included all the pasture in Swaledale, or just the pasture within a more restricted area. Equally it is not evident from this document which Gilbert is making the donation. We only know that the King confirmed the gift in 1251.

The gift was again confirmed in 1332/3 by the King in the Patent Rolls for 6 Edward III, Membrane 23, which reads in part: "*Donationem... quas Gilberti de Gaunt, filius Roberti de Gaunt, ... fecit Deo... de tota pastura de Sualedale, cum pertinenciis, infra cer-tas divisas in eadem carta contentas, tam in bosco quam in plano... etc.*" The full translation is as follows:

"The donation... which Gilbert de Gant, son of Robert de Gant, ... made to God... of all pasture in Swaledale, with appurtenances, between certain boundaries contained in the said Charter, as much in the forest as in the open country, holding [it] forever, and the right to have in that place their herds [of cattle or sheep] however many and of whatever sort they wish, and whenever and wherev-er they wish, and folds and outhouses for their herds, and dogs and hunting horns, and of making hayfields and enclosed meadowland, outside the same boundaries, wherever and however many they wish, and of having there the dwellings and outhouses of the monks and their servants and their herds, and enough gardens and enclosures, and of taking unlimited amounts [of wood] from everywhere in Gilbert's woodlands, within the aforesaid bound-aries, sufficient for all the needs of the buildings and enclosures and pinfolds and outhouses, and other easements in the said forests, and of lopped branches of trees to feed their herds, and of using all the aforesaid pasture however they wish, and of taking wolves by whatever means they can, and of freely leading out and returning their herds to the aforesaid pasture throughout all the lands of the said Gilbert and his heirs except cornfields and mead-owlands – so that nobody else may have any herds in that pasture except only the aforesaid monks...”

Later in the same document Gilbert de Gant, son of Gilbert de Gant, concedes the gift of his father, thus, “*Concessionem... de tota donatione patris sui quam fecit eis per cartam suam de tota pastura de Sualedale, cum pertinenciis, infra certas divisas in dicta carta patris sui contentas.*” In full:

“The concession which Gilbert de Gant, son of Gilbert de Gant, made to God... of the whole donation of his father which he made to them by his charter of all pasture in Swaledale with appurte-nances, between certain boundaries contained in the said charter of his father.”

And again, “*Remissionem etiam, relaxationem et quietam claman-ciam quas Willelmus de Kirckeston*, miles, filius Rogeri de Kirkeston, militis, fecit Abbati et monachis praedictis de toto jure et clamio... in Swaldale quae iidem Abbas et monachi habent ex dono et concessione Gilberti filii Gilberti de Gaunt, infra certas divisas in eodem scripto contentas...*”

My translation of this is:

“Furthermore the remission, relaxation and quit claim which William de Kirckeston*, knight, son of Roger de Kirkeston, knight, made to the Abbot and monks aforesaid of all right and claim which may have or can have in all lands and tenements, meadowlands, moors, wastes, woods and pastures, with appurte-nances, in Swaledale which the Abbot and monks have out of the gift and concession of Gilbert son of Gilbert de Gaunt, between certain boundaries contained in that written document...”

Thus in 1332/3 the King confirmed the donations to the abbey as listed above, and notes the relaxation of rights and the quit claims of the heirs and successors of the donors.

All three entries clearly state that the limits or boundaries of the gifted pastures were given in the original charter. The gift was for the

---

[* = husband of Margaret de Gant, sister of Gilbert de Gant V, 1248-1297]

benefit of the Abbot and Monks of Rievaulx, Rivalle or River Abbey, however spelt. We also learn that the original donor was "Gilbert de Gant, son of Robert de Gant," and therefore Gilbert III, who may have reached maturity about 1206 and died in 1241/2. We also learn that his son, Gilbert IV, agreed to his father's donation of the land between the boundaries laid out in the charter.

The Rievaulx Cartularies

The 1332/3 and 1251 documents are quoted from *Cartularium Rievallense* or *The Cartulary of Rievaulx*, written by J C Atkinson and published by the Surtees Society, as Volume 83 in 1889. That is the most complete statement of the lands and possessions of that abbey at the very peak of its power and prosperity. Atkinson described his work as a cartulary, but more accurately it is a comprehensive compilation of all the surviving documents relating to Rievaulx Abbey and its possessions that J C Atkinson could find, and it is a formidable achievement. The two Latin texts and translations cited above are from the original Charter Rolls and Patent Rolls in the Public Record Office at Kew (Series C53 and C66 respectively). But at best, the Rievaulx Cartulary compiled by Atkinson is simply a summary, a brief description of the donor, location, extent and possibly some detail about the appurtenances included in the various grants. It does not contain copies of the original charters, and only in exceptional cases do they include even approximate boundaries (the 'wastes' of Pickering in the North Riding is an interesting exception, but of no use here).

The earliest date that has so far been proposed for the Gant charter recording his donation of pasture rights in Swaledale to Rievaulx is taken from *Swaledale from Source to Richmond: A Visitors' Guide*, 1968, Dalesman Press by Ron and Lucie Hinson with J L Barker. And I quote:

> "All Swaledale above Cogden Hall [i.e. Stallerstone Style] was held by the Gants who in 1125 granted Grinton Manor to Bridlington Priory, and in about 1141 granted Muker Manor to Rievaulx Abbey. At the Dissolution they reverted to Henry VIII."

If factually correct, this would attribute the gift to Gilbert II, and date it after 1139 but well before 1156 when he died. But sadly no source for this remarkable statement is given so it cannot be checked against the original documents.

The original manuscript cartulary of Rievaulx Abbey is in the British Library, and is known as MSS Cotton Julius D.I. This is probably the 'book of Rivall' sent to Sir Robert Cotton (died 1631) by William L'Isle (died 1637), shortly before 23 July 1622, and bequeathed to the nation by Sir John Cotton (died 1702), entering the collections of the British Museum in 1753, incorporated as the British Library in 1973 – an impeccable provenance. The catalogue states that the cartulary has 193 pages, and lists some 235 charters mostly from its foundation in 1132 up to 1188, with few (and often much less legible!) additions thereafter; so it is not a complete record of all the abbey's possessions. The original compilation was made not earlier than 1179, and probably before 1189; there are very few entries after the 12th century, but the last dated item is from 1381. The charters are arranged by family and unfortunately almost all are undated within the texts though archivists have managed to date most of them. It is a beautiful quarto volume, the parchment as supple today as it must have been 800 years ago, the red and black ink still fresh, bright and clear.

I have checked it from cover to cover; but it does not mention Gilbert de Gant's Charter for Swaledale. Many sources state that gifting to Rievaulx was mostly completed between 1130 and 1160. Atkinson in Surtees 83, page 7, under "XXXVIII [17] Cartularium Index" gives a list of all the charters the cartulary contains; one item that needs to be rechecked is charter CCXIX, "Concerning the possessions and pastures of Rivalle" which may mention Swaledale, if not Gilbert de Gant. Again, this manuscript only lists the charters, usually by donor, location and sometimes a brief description of the nature of the gift; it does not quote the actual texts of the charters, and so does not include any boundaries that might have been specified in the original charters.

The Curator at the British Library, Claire Breay, pointed out that relatively few Rievaulx Charters for the period after the 12th century have survived. Some are in the British Library among the Additional, Cotton, Egerton and Harley collections, but again none of these is the Swaledale charter. Original Rievaulx charters are also held at Belvoir Castle, York Minster and North Yorkshire County Record Office at

Northallerton.   The archivist at Belvoir Castle was contacted in August 2006; he made a brief search but was unable to help. York Minster does not have the Gant charter, nor does NYCRO. At Claire Breay's suggestion, I also wrote to the Yorkshire Archaeological Society but with the same negative result.

Other cartularies or compilations of the possessions of Rievaulx Abbey are known to have existed at some time in the past. It is generally thought to be unlikely that any more will be found in the future, bricked up in long-forgotten priest-holes, hidden away in unfrequented wings of stately homes, or simply buried in the farthest reaches of old attics in the remote depths of the countryside. But, of course, it is still possible.

J R C Davis, in his *Medieval Cartularies of Great Britain: a short catalogue* (London, Longmans, 1958) mentions as item 812 an untraced register in the possession of William Lite of Wilbraham in Cambridgeshire in the 17th century. Also item 813 an untraced "Inventory of charters in book form, on vellum, in the possession, 1640, of the 7th Earl of Rutland, Belvoir Castle", but this is not recorded by J H Round, in the Historical Manuscripts Commission, Rutland iv (1905). And in any case, even if found, these both appear to be simply lists of the charters, not transcriptions.

Surtees 83 quotes material found in an old cupboard at Belvoir Castle in 1730, printing extracts from folios 1-7 in the Bodleian Library Dodsworth MSS 85 (Short Catalogue ref. 5026), folios 53-7, and 71v-2, which show it to have been arranged topographically, with the royal charters (down to Edward I, and with those of Edward III added) at the beginning. Under I, *Cartae Regum*, item 35 (B.ix) translates as "Confirmation of those [charters] for Neuton, Kayton, No[n]ington and Swaldale," and item 36 (B.x) as "Confirmation of those [charters] for Swaldal, Lebberston, Neuton and No[n]ington."

These probably refer to the two royal confirmations already quoted above; the first certainly does. If found, these registers and inventories would again simply be summaries; there is no indication that they included original charter material, or the boundaries of the gifted lands.

The Ecclesiastical Antiquarians

Adopting a different approach, the foremost antiquarians on the eccle-

siastical history of England and Wales were consulted in various
Libraries, notably Canterbury Cathedral Archives and Library, the
British Library and the Society of Antiquaries of London Library.
The results for the principal authorities are summarised below.

Burton (1710-1771) in his *Monasticon Eboracense* or *The
Ecclesiastical History of Yorkshire*, 1758, lists all the Rievaulx Abbey
possessions and all the donors (on 33 pages). It ought therefore to be
a very promising source of information, and indeed it was probably
the most useful of the group. But he does not give any dates so we
cannot establish from this source when the Gant donation was made,
and he does not quote the full text of the charters, so we cannot check
the "metes and bounds" Gilbert specified. Instead, on page 363 we
read, "Gilbert de Gant gave all his pasture in Swaledale; which the
king confirmed, p." Footnote 'p' reads, "Cart. 35 Henry III, m6;
Dodesworth, C.15; Johnston's MSS.v.K.1.p.78 in the tower of
London, no. 6 in my catal. p.11." Unpacking this complex three-part
riddle took quite some time.

The first section, "Cart. 35 Henry III, m6," is straightforward and
refers to membrane six in the Charter Rolls for the 35th year of the
reign of Henry III, namely 1251/2: this is quoted in full by Atkinson
in Surtees 83, and was already quoted in translation above.

The second section of Burton's footnote "Dodesworth, C.15"
refers to Roger Dodsworth (1585-1654) whose manuscripts, fortunately copied by Dodsworth from originals in St. Mary's Tower at
York before it was blown up in 1644, are now housed at the Bodleian
Museum in Oxford where I studied them. Joseph Hunter (1783-1861)
in his 'Three Catalogues' (1838) explains that Dodsworth's systematic labelling of his 160 manuscripts was in six series, marked by single, double and treble letters, then letters in circles, letters in squares
and lastly in triangles! When sent to Oxford, they were unbound and
unnumbered, but the Bodleian Librarians numbered them I to CLX
with no reference to the content or sequence as given by Dodsworth,
and the 'Finding Aids' (so-called) do not tell you this.

It therefore took some time to find out that "Dodesworth C.15" is
known to the Bodleian as "MS Dods 120" and is listed in the
Bodleian's Summary Catalogue (Clappinson and Rogers, 1991) under
reference SC5061; and it was no pleasure to discover the relevant
entry, which can be translated as follows:

"York: the King confirms to the Abbey of Rievaulx the gift of

Gilbert de Gant of all his pasture in Swaledale with sheepfolds and outhouses and all conveniences in his forest of Swaledale."

This is merely a repetition of Membrane 6 of the Charter Rolls for 1251, or 35 Henry III in old money, and not a copy of the charter itself. One cause of delay was the fact that the word 'Swaledale' which appears twice in this text is not included in the index. The one useful finding was that it also confirms the gift of Albert fitz Richard of Sproxton, West Newton; and of Gilbert de Maltby of Nonington, both cited in the Rievaulx Cartulary entry with the Swaledale dona-tion, as noted above.

The third section of Burton's footnote proved even more character-forming to disentangle. The 'Johnston' referred to is Dr Nathaniel Johnston (1627-1705) of Pontefract who made a large collection of Dodsworth's papers, but, "in such an awkward Arabic scrawl as to be scarce legible" according to one Drake Nicholson, quoted in Gough (1780); he goes on, "only death prevented the publication of what its readers would have been weary of"! Illegible or not, Johnston's man-uscripts eventually found their way to Richard Frank of Campsall, and later to the Bodleian Library at Oxford which now provides a 'Finding Aid' to the collections of Nathaniel Johnston and Richard Frank; details can be found in the *Summary Catalogue* (SC) by Clappinson and Rogers (1991) already cited above. Or at least so I thought.

The reference is to 'Johnston MSS v.K.1.p.79' and Volume K.1 is item SC 55297, known by its Bodleian Library shelf mark as Top. Yorks. c.24 but the catalogue states that this volume deals with the Wapentakes of Buckrose, Holderness and Dickering, not with the Wapentake of Hang West, where Muker, Healaugh Old and New Lands, and Fremington are to be found. According to the catalogue, Hang West Wapentake is in SC 55299, which is MS. Top. Yorks. d.10, but this is Volume K.3, not Volume K.1, and in any case there are no references to Muker and the others under Hang West. The catalogue has no further suggestions to offer.

There is also the 'Finding Aid', which says that Hang West Wapentake material is in MS. Top. Yorks. c.84. However, I found that MS. Top. Yorks. c.84 is not included in the *Shorter Catalogue*!! When examined, there was no material there for Muker and the oth-ers under Hang West, though it did include Grinton, Aysgarth, Wensley and Middleham, each perhaps classifiable as a 'near miss' if charitably disposed. Quite by chance, reading the Durham material over once again, it emerged that in the 17th century Muker etc., were not in the Wapentake of Hang West as they are today, but in Gilling West. Which explains the failure to find them. Or at least it gives a partial explanation; another was soon to follow. Yet another visit to Oxford; yet another examination of c.84 but under Gilling West this time; and yet another wasted day. By this time the wine cellar at home was shrinking fast! On the next trip up the M40, I decided to go back to basics, and on arrival I ordered up Johnston's Volume K.1 for the second time, resigned to learning about Buckrose, Holderness and Dickering, wherever they were, in spite of the index.

The index was interesting too; interpretation was easier when one realised that there were on each page three entirely separate numbering systems. The experience had a familiar feel, after the catalogues and finding aids. The catalogue does not say there is any Gilling West material in Top. Yorks. c.24, only in Top. Yorks. d.10; and it does not even mention the existence of Top. Yorks. c.84. The finding aid, on the other hand, does not list Top. Yorks. d.10 though it is certainly a Johnston and Frank manuscript. So – and I am trying hard not to overstate my case – care is needed throughout.

Anyway, in c.24 there were references to Rievaulx, Grenton, Helaugh-in-Swaledale and Fremington. The relevant manuscript seems to read as follows: *"Et Ab de Rival ten. quanda pasturam voc. Meuaker, et reddit p. ann. 0:66:8 Et Gilbert de Gant est propinquior haeres, plena oblatis"*

That is, "And the Abbey of Rievaulx holds a certain pasture called Meuaker, and it yields per year 66 shillings and 8 pence. And Gilbert de Gant is the next heir, fully paid."

This is dated 1274, or just possibly 1224; it is difficult to read the script. From the context, this seems likely to be a quote from the Inquisition Post Mortem of Gilbert IV in 1274, recording his holdings of the king, what they yielded, and their status at the time of his death, including Gilbert's payments due to the king. Was it worth the struggle? It only confirms what we already knew from other sources about the gift of pasture around Muker to Rievaulx; it adds nothing on boundaries, but as one of the very few references to the Gant donation in the recognised major sources of reference on medieval monastic holdings, it had to be found and checked. The final part of the reference, to "Number 6 in my catalogue," was pursued for a while but eventually dropped for fear the search might induce apoplexy and cardiac arrest.

This cautionary tale is included here at length deliberately. Enormous resources are now being made available to the general public on the internet by major archiving bodies, so that it is now possible to inspect in detail many of their catalogues, and even digital copies of the original works, to download or print them, and thereby to save yourself time and money for the visits that may in the end be essential to successful research. But be not deceived: the existing catalogues, finding aids and indexes are only a good start, they are not infallible; in fact some of them are frankly appalling, as librarians may admit. So be prepared to query the recognised authorities, the existing indexes, the experts; and always go back to the original material and see for yourself. And record your findings to benefit others.

A few guidelines: many catalogues and indexes are not complete, if not actually selective and partial; some have simply been copied uncritically from older materials that were never checked against the original parchments or manuscripts, but it is those very same originals that you want to identify and see. And finding the right ones is not at all a simple matter. To be really disheartening, sometimes the material you want but which is not indexed under any logical description, may be embedded within another, larger item which is indeed indexed, but has nothing to do with your target; Robert de Gant's gift of Fremington to Bridlington cited below is a case in point. You may in short come across what you are looking for purely by chance. Or maybe not at all; but that does not mean it does not exist, merely that you (like me) have not yet found it...

It is true that internet search engines are rapidly improving and can find information on even the most obscure topic or place, but sources on the internet are unchecked, certainly not subjected to peer review, and can be of dubious quality, accuracy and credibility, unless they have been created by recognised authorities such as the National Archives, the British Library, the Society of Antiquaries of London, the Bodleian Library at Oxford and so on. It is also true that online catalogues even from reliable sources can only be as good as those original catalogues were originally. So use the internet, but question everything you see, and verify it for yourself. As with the famous phrase, "It must be true. I saw it on telly."

Dugdale's 'Monasticon Anglicanum' was originally published in

Latin but it later went through several major revisions and modifications. The most complete and the most useful version dates from 1817-1830, has eight books bound into six volumes, and was edited by Roger Dodsworth (1585-1654), John Stevens (died 1726), John Caley (1763-1834), Henry Ellis (1777-1869), Bulkeley Bandinel (1781-1861) and Richard Taylor or Richard Cowling (1789-1851), heavy hitters all. So no surprise that this is unequivocally the authoritative text on English monasteries. According to Richard Gough (1768) it was authored jointly by Roger Dodsworth and Sir William Dugdale (1605-1686) but was actually collected and written totally by Dodsworth. Not all acccept this, and many give greater credit to Dugdale. Much of it is based on Burton, though Dugdale usefully included copies of the main deeds; but disappointingly the reference to the Gant donation to Rievaulx (found in Volume 5, page 361) is identical to the text in Burton, "Gilbert de Gant gave all his pasture in Swaledale which the King confirmed. z" Footnote 'z' reads, "Cart. 35 Henry III, m6: Dodsworth, c.15: Johnston's mss. v.K.1.p.79." Enough said; we've been here before. Dugdale also lists all the possessions of Rievaulx, but it is based on Burton's '*Monasticon Eboracense*' so it adds nothing to what we already know.

Burton says in his 'Proposals' for the next volume that he has four times the number of manuscripts accumulated by Dugdale; but in the British Library copy I used an anonymous manuscript note on page 8 of the only Appendix states:

> "Dr. Burton began printing the second volume of the Book but never printed more of it than these 8 pages [an Appendix of some 38 documents on Whitby Abbey in Latin never before printed]. The Originall manuscript was sold along with the rest of the Doctor's manuscripts to William Constable Esq. of Burton Constable Anno Dom. 1769."

John Tanner in his '*Notitia Monastica*' 1744 lists material on Rievaulx [a.k.a. River, Rievall, Rivisside, etc] in great detail, in some cases summarising the content, but frustratingly in others merely listing them. Material he specifies include the MS Cotton Julius D.I. sections 2 and 4, the lost Rievaulx registry of William Lite of Wilburgham, the Roger Dodsworth manuscripts and others mentioned elsewhere in this book, as well as membrane 6 in the Charter Rolls for 35 Henry III. The very large number of various unspecified references helpfully listed by Tanner remain to be checked, as there is no indication of which donation they refer to.

Continuing this rapid survey of antiquarian authorities, John Stevens, before he died in 1726, wrote what is usually referred to simply as his 'Continuation'. It must have been completed before 1686 because it was edited by Sir William Dugdale who died in that year. The full title is:

> "The history of the antient abbeys, monasteries, hospitals, cathedral and collegiate churches: Being two additional volumes to Sir William Dugdale's *Monasticon anglicanum*, containing the original and first establishment of all the religious orders that ever were in Great Britain ... not spoken of by Sir William Dugdale and Mr Dodsworth... Collected from above two hundred of the best historians extant and from antient manuscripts in the Bodleian and Cotton libraries, and many more in the hands of learned antiquaries. Adorned with a considerable number of copper plates."

An impressive title, hence the familiar abbreviation. After all that, he only has three extra Charters for Rievaulx, they are incorrectly referenced and are in any case not relevant to Swaledale! But it is a major source that had to be checked.

William Farrer compiled a huge number of early Yorkshire Charters, and these were published by the Yorkshire Archaeological Society, duly edited by C T Clay, in 1914. The Honour of Richmond material is in two parts, Part 1 in Volume 4, and Part 2 in Volume 5. Volume 5, page 341, reads as follows:

> "To Rievaulx Abbey, Gilbert son of Robert de Gant, who died around 1241 gave pasture in Swaledale within fixed boundaries, specifying several privileges, including the right to take wolves. FN." The footnote reads: "Rievaulx Cartulary p. 304. This gift was the origin of the Manor of Muker with its members (ibid. p. 328 + VCH-NR,i,242)."

This is a reference to the 1889 Surtees Society publication number 83, by J C Atkinson, of which Farrer had this to say in his introduction:

> "The texts in the printed edition are often robbed of important passages, regarded as of common form" adding – in a rather waspish footnote – "the text has been so effectively relieved of 'common form' that it is impossible to say whether the document in question is a grant, a confirmation, or a release."

The Rievaulx Cartulary referred to is the manuscript known as MS Cotton Julius D.I. (sections 2 and 4) in the British Library. VCH-NR,i refers to volume one (1914) of William Page's *History of the North Riding of Yorkshire* in the Victoria County Histories series.

In the Hanby Holmes collection at DRO, one paper sugggests securing a copy of the documents relating to Muker from John Caley at the Court of Augmentations. Caley's 1820 '*Cartae abbatiarum in Curia Augmentacionis*' or *Charters of the Abbeys in the Court of Augmentations*, in 20 volumes, ought to have been a major asset to the research, but in the event it turned out to be seriously disappointing, but it had to be checked.

So that in brief is what we can gain from the recognised antiquarian authorities on the monasteries of England. They confirm what we already knew from other sources, but they do not contain the crucial original texts that we are looking for. After exhausting all these national luminaries, and finding them wanting in various ways, it is fitting to ask, but what do the locals have to say in the matter?

Other views from Swaledale

Joshua Fryer's Book was already mentioned above, (DRO D/HH 6/2/204) and it is of considerable interest, reading as follows:.

"An extract of ye Perticulars Proves concerning ye Maner of Grinton. Itt appeareth in ye Book of Domesday of Ancient Record yt. Grinton was called Grinto ad Gele and Containing a Court or a Parte of a Court. Troptino had his manner there and (after him)... after him Bodin before ye Conquest. Itt & ye whole Daile of Swadale was maid waist in ye Conquest after ye Conquest being in ye King's Hand Grinton was measured to a league in Length and half a League in Breath & in ye Time of King Edwd. ye First itt was valued at 5s.

"After ye Conquest all Swaledale was given by ye King Jnh... [John?] to Gaunt, John Gaunt who was Son and Heir to ye Duke of Britayne & Earle of Richmd. & marryed Beatrix of King Hen. he gave certain Lands in Swaledale unto ye Monstrey of Rivisse now called Riviside wch. was from Oxnop beck on ye South to Dale Head & on ye north from east Stonedill beck to ye Dale Head. He also gave unto ye Monstrey of Briglinton Grinton in wch. Dale are Several Township Viz. Grinton where ye Parish Church staneth wch. was ... a Manner & in Record before ye Conquest as is above Sd. [= said] Standeth on ye one sd. [= side; here, the south side] of ye River of Swale wthin. ye Wapentake of Hang West and Deanery of Cathrick & ye Township of Reeth wherein is ye Manner of Healeah standeth on ye other side [= the north side] of Swale in ye Wapentack of Gilling of Gillinwest and Deanery of Ruen... [Richmond?] ye Township and Manner of Grinton was given by Gaunt & his heirs to ye Prior & Monstrey of Briglinton who was ever Lord thereof & had all maner of profitts whasoer Cometh Growing & Arising thereof without ye memory of man to ye Contrary as may appear by sundry Grants and Confirm-ation. *Finis.*"

So he gets an 'E' grade for history since it was not the famous 14th century Lancastrian John of Gaunt, granted the Honour of Richmond in 1342, but his less well-known ancestor Gilbert de Gant of Lincoln who donated the pasture rights in Swaledale to the Abbey of Rievaulx. But we can allocate him an 'A' grade for geography as he clearly knew both the manorial boundaries and ecclesiatical divisions of North Yorkshire. He speaks as though at the time of writing the monasteries in question were still enjoying "all maner of profits" from the granted lands, so it must have been written before the Dissolution of the Monasteries in 1538.

It also indicates that only the upper part of Swaledale, that part west of Oxnop beck and East Stonedale beck, was given by Gilbert de Gant to the Monastery of Rievaulx. This conclusion is supported by post-Dissolution accounts of income and expenditure for the Muker holding, which had formerly been the property of the Monastery of Rievalux, which are published in the "Ministers' Accounts for 30-31 Henry VIII [= 1539/40], No. 162. Rievaulx, until recently a Monastery, Yorkshire." Folio 7 lists the accounts for that period at "(Me)wacre in Swaldale with appurtenances."

The incomes listed for the several parts can be summarised as follows: Swaledale with Muker £16:0s:0d; Oxhoppe 106s:7d, Thwate £9:6s:8d, Angrame 56s:3d, Kelde £6:13s:4d; Birkedale £4:0s:0d and Keisden 40s:0d – total for Muker in Swaledale therefore £46:2s:10d. Each village has named tenants, and the income is from meadows and enclosures, except Keisdon where lead mines are mentioned, though curiously there is no income recorded from them. In the deductions and payments for fees and expenses to officers of the court, bailifs etc in the last paragraph, various officers and their duties are given: these include supervision of the woodlands and lead mines. See Surtees Society, Vol. 83, page 310. Item CCCLXXIV [= 374] for 1539/40.

This definition of the area donated by Gilbert de Gant is also supported by the 1569: "Escheators Inquisition (Esch.A.R.) [= Escheator Augmentations and Revenues?] Series II. File 257. Membrane 22. 11 Elizabeth (AD 1569) taken on the death of Thomas Lord Wharton" (extracts translated) (DRO D/HH 10/17/143) which reads:

> "Inquisition indented taken at the Castle of York on the 22nd day of March in the 11th year of the reign of Lady Elizabeth [= 1569] before Charles Jackson... by virtue of a writ... by the oaths of... who say upon their oath that the said Thomas Wharton, knight, Lord Wharton in his lifetime was seized in his demesne as of fee... of and in all that Lordship and Manor of Mewacre in Swaledale [bought by Lord Wharton in 1544] and of and in all messuages tofts gardens villages lands tenements feedings pastures and hereditaments whatsover with their appurtenances now or lately in the several tenures of William Braderigg, Geoffrey Metcalfe, James Miller, Edward Mylner, George Metcalfe, James Miller, Edward Mylner, George Metcalfe's wife, Alexander Metcalfe, Margaret Metcalfe, Edmund Mylner, Edward Mylner, Ralph Mylner, Reginald Alderson and William Metcalfe or their assigns situate lying and being in Swaledale in the said Co. of York lately belonging and appertaining to the late Monastery of Ryvalls... and of lands and tenements in the tenure or occupation of various persons named in Oxhoppe, Thwayte, Angram, Kelde, and Byrdsdale all described as being in Swaledale..."

Another local view dated 1738 has the title, "Notes on the history of the Swaledale Manors and extracts from conveyance Denton and Gibson to Smith (1738) endorsed: 10 October 1828." (DRO D/HH 6/2/254). It reads as follows:

> "The Manor of Muker in Swaledale formerly belonged to the Monastery of Rivellys or Rivalx near Helmsley in Yorkshire. Wholly consisted of Lands and Tenements of Gavelkind Tenure, holden of the Abbot of the Monastery by certain fined Rents, Fines, Suit, and Service at the Lord's Court. After this Monastery

was dissolved and given to the Crown, then the said Lands were holden of the King by the Tenants upon the same Conditions for about 5 years. Then King Henry VIIIth on or about the 2nd of December 1544, granted under certain Yearly Rents, his rights in the Manor of Muker to Philip Lord Wharton and Sir Thomas Wharton, Knight, which was then held by 53 Tenants upon the Conditions aforesaid till about the 12th day of November 1618 when the Decree was obtained at which Time the number of Tenants was 111.

"Gilbert de Gaunt Lord of the Seignority of Swaledale gave and granted to Rivaux all his Pasture in Swaledale which the King confirmed. 53 Henry III." [= 1269].

The date of "53 Henry III" or 1269 given at the end of this account may be a transcription error for 35 Henry III, which is the King's confirmation of the Gant donation in the Charter Rolls for 1251, quoted elswhere. I have checked; no other confirmation which dates from 1269 has yet been found in the Charter Rolls or Patent Rolls.

There is also an undated, untitled and unattributed document (DRO D/HH 6/2/257, 2 pages) again from the Hanby Holmes Collection of Stewards Papers. The text, which seems to be in the hand of Ottiwell Tomlin, an Agent living at Low Row [who was active at least from 1815 to 1842,] reads as follows:

[Page 1] "There are 4 manors in Swaledale – Grinton laying on the South Side of the River Swale which belonged to the Priory of Bridlington & was granted by Queen Elizabeth [1558-1603] to Rich[ard] Wiseman & Francis Fitch. Anno… [1599: see Joshua Fryer's Book of Cures]

"Healaugh which is divided into 2 Maners called the Old Land & the New Land, and

"Muker which belonged to the Abby of Rievaulx or River in Yorkshire.

"Of the Boundaries on the South & West Sides of Muker… following… V. [Insert?]

"1. And of those on the North the following

"2. And as to the Boundaries of the whole of Swaledale, the following said to be from Kirby Quest *

"3. The Maners & their Lands in Muker were granted 36 Hen. 8 [= 1544/5] to Lord Wharton of which Grant I [i.e. the writer of this note, whom I suspect to be Ottiwell Tomlin, Agent, of Low Row] have a Copy." [this grant may be D/HH 6/1/1 which is dated 2 December 1544, q.v.]

* [see D/HH 7/4/157, page 2 – where the text states that Kirby West or Quest is a reference book, also known locally as Doomsday Book; this actually refers, it is thought, to Kirkby's Inquest of Yorkshire, an inquiry dated 15 Edward I i.e. 1287 into the various knights' fees due to the King; it also includes lists of vill names by Wapentake or Honour. This was part of a survey of several of the counties of England, made in the reign of Edward I, by, amongst others, the King's Treasurer, John de Kirkby, Bishop of Ely, who died in 1290.

"Under the authority of a royal commission he enquired into the fees held by the immediate tenants of the crown and as such it was something akin to Domesday Book. It doesn't, though, give details of boundaries. The work was published by the Surtees Society in Volume 49 (1867). It has been digitised by the University of Michigan and is available to view at http://quod.lib.umich.edu/cgi/ t/text/text-idx?c=moa;idno=AHE1873.0001.001" [Personal communication with Ms M J Boustead, Senior Archivist (Collections), North Yorkshire County Record Office, Malpas Road, Northallerton, North Yorkshire DL7 8TB.]

So there exist many local documents stating that the area of land over which Gilbert de Gant gave pasture and grazing rights to Rievaulx Abbey consisted of the area around the village of Muker and west from there to the dale head. Although a vast area, this is still not the whole of Swaledale as defined by the boundaries named in the Cornelius Fryer paper. We therefore have to conclude that there are actually two documents out there, one of which spells out the manorial boundary of the whole of upper Swaledale included in the knight's fee of Gilbert de Gant, and the second of which is the charter by which he gifted pasturing rights to Rievaulx Abbey within the limits specified in his charter, believed to embrace only the extreme west of upper Swaledale.

The Gant Fee and the Rievaulx Charter

The one which we know most about is the charter by which Gilbert gifted all his pastures in Swaledale to Rievaulx, and from the foregoing we can safely conclude that this related to upper Swaledale, covering the head of the dale around and to the west of Muker.

The earliest date that has so far been proposed for the Gant charter recording his donation of pasture rights in Swaledale to Rievaulx is taken from *Swaledale from Source to Richmond: A Visitors' Guide*, 1968, Dalesman Press by Ron and Lucie Hinson with J L Barker. And I quote:

> "All Swaledale above Cogden Hall [i.e. Stallerstone Style] was held by the Gants who in 1125 granted Grinton Manor to Bridlington Priory, and in about 1141 granted Muker Manor to Rievaulx Abbey. At the Dissolution they reverted to Henry VIII."

If factually correct, this would attribute the gift to Gilbert II, and date it after 1139 but well before 1156 when he died. But sadly Hinson gives no source for this remarkable statement so it cannot be checked against the original documents. It is therefore hard to accept it at face value, as it is not supported by the Rievaulx Cartulary manuscript Cotton Julius D.I. It is possible that Hinson confused the Swaledale grant with the grant of Hundmanby to Rievaulx about that time, which grant has ample documentary support. An alternative suggested by NYCRO is that 1141 may be a typing error for 1241, the date of the death of Gilbert III.

My own view is that we can probably date the grant of Swaledale to around 1206x1217, on the grounds that Gilbert de Gant III reached maturity in about 1206 but was attained for treason and jailed in 1217, and his lands confiscated and taken back into the hands of the Crown. He may have spent the rest of his life in jail, though it seems more likely, given the birth of his son Gilbert IV in 1220, that he stuck to established precedent and purchased the King's pardon, and in that way redeemed his lands. In any event, we have to re-interpret the wording "all my pasture in Swaledale" in the grant to Rievaulx as meaning all the pasture that still remained at his disposal at that date, because we know that other grants of rights to pasture and grassland in Swaledale had been made before that date, particularly to Bridlington, by Robert son of Walter de Gant (see charter below for lands at Fremington), and to Bardney, which had pasture for twenty mares and their foals in Swaledale (see Dugdale, 1693, volume 1, page 143). Upper Swaledale may have been the only area left within which pasturage rights were still unallocated.

1200/01 Public Record Office publication *Rotuli Chartarum Anno 2° Johann* or Charter Rolls for the Second Year of the Reign of King John [John 1199-1216].   Page 88, column b. Membrane 10. Displaced second part of *Carta Henry fitz Hervey*.

"And [the King] further concedes and confirms Robert de Gant's gift to Bridlington Priory of Fremington and appurtenances, as in the bounds contained in the cyrography between them made in the court of King Richard our brother. At Carlisle, 21st Feb. in the second year of our reign."

Richard I reigned from 1189 to 1199, so this grant was made by 1199 at the latest, since it was confirmed by King Richard; this in turn suggests that the Gilbert de Gant charter to Rievaulx cannot be earlier than 1199. At this time, he was still a minor under the guardianship of William de Stuteville. This explains why in 1200 King John confirmed to William de Stuteville, "Healaugh in Swaledale with its appurtenances granted him by Robert de Rosel" (see Calendar of Charter Rolls, 1199-1216; Public Record Office). The King was simply giving de Stuteville custody of the rights in the Gant fee until the rightful heir Gilbert III came of age. If Gilbert's date of birth was indeed 1185, then he reached his maturity in about 1206.

The second document is the one we know least about; but it was almost certainly the earlier one. It is probable that its main purpose was to define the limits of the Gant fee in upper Swaledale as received from Stephen, Count of Brittany and Earl of Richmond and gifted to Walter de Gant with his wife Maud/Matilda, for which no bounds appear to have been defined at the time of the marriage (see the Stewards Papers document DRO D/HH 6/2/257 in the Hanby Holmes collection already quoted above). We know from the following translated excerpts that the limits were well known, and had therefore been placed on record at some time, because the Courts found in 1279/81 that Gilbert de Gant had not extended the limits of his fee:

1279-81: "*Placita de Quo Warranto* Temp. Edward I. Proceedings in which the claim of Gilbert de Gaunt to have free chase in Swaledale and Free Warren at Helaugh was established." (DRO D/HH 10/17/143)

"County of York. Pleas in Jury trials, actions and proceedings *de quo warranto* [by what warrant or authority] before John de Vallibus [= Vaux in National Archives] and his Bretheren Justices in Eyre in the County of York in the 7th, 8th and 9th years of King Edward [I].

"Gilbert de Gaunt was summoned to answer the Lord King on a plea of by what warrant he claims to have free chase in Swaledale, and free Warren at Healaugh, and wreck of the sea at Hundmanby. And Gilbert comes and says that he claims to have free chase in Swaledale by this Warrant namely that he and all his ancestors from time whereof memory is not to the contrary have had their free chase there and as to free Warren at Healaugh he says he claims to have it for this reason namely that his land of Healaugh is within Swaledale where he has his free chace as is aforesaid and beause he has free chase where he claims to have free warren. And he says that all his Ancestors from the time aforesaid have always enjoyed it. And as regards wreck of the sea he says that he does not claim any wreck other than whales only & co.

"The Jury say upon their oath that the said Gilbert and all his ancestors from time whereof there is no memory to the contrary have held and enjoyed the free chase in Swaledale and also that their free warren of Healaugh and they say that neither Gilbert nor his Ancestors have enlarged that chace and warren. And they say that the said Gilbert and his Ancestors from time whereof there is no memory to the contrary have been possessed of the right to have a whale whenever they shall have made it fast in the harbour of Hundmanby saving the head and tail of the whale to the Lord King Therefore let the said Gilbert go quit. (Roll 10 done)."

It may be that the bounds were defined as part of the proceedings brought against him in 1206 by Brian son of Alan, who challenged his right to the lordship of Swaledale, as recorded below:

"*ROTULUS Finium de anno regni Regis Johannis septimo (Pars secunda) (Exemplar Rotuli praecedentis). OBLATA Curie anno Regni Regis Johannis nono* [i.e. 1208] Membrane 13. Richmund."
This translates as follows:

"Fine Roll of the seventh year of John [i.e. 1206], second part.

Court Payments of the 9th year of John. Membrane 13. Richmond. Gillibertus de Gant gives one palfrey in the suit/action at the court of Richmond in the presence of the bailiffs of Richmond between himself the feudal land holder and Brian the son of Alan the challenger concerning the mesnalty [= the right of the mesne lord] of the forest of Swaledale and the profit-yielding land of the aforesaid forest which is in the gift of the Lord Richard [(= King Richard 1189-1199] and whence the said Gilbert holds it as a heritable warrant of the Honour of Richmond he lays it down in respite until his heir comes * which is uncertain and he can guarantee it to him."

[* his son Gilbert de Gant IV was born in 1220]

William Page (1923) summarises his understanding of the situation as follows:

"Despite the grant of all Swaledale by the Lord of Richmond to Walter de Gant, Brian son of Alan, probably tenant by inheritance from Bodin, sold half of the manor of Reeth to Gilbert de Gant in 1239 for £100. This sale and that of half the forest probably meant a quitclaim of the right of the lords of Bedale in Swaledale, and seems to point to Reeth having been the head of the lordship before Healaugh became so; moreover, a statement was made in 1303 that Healaugh was 'neither village, borough nor hamlet, but a certain site of the manor of Reeth.'"

So Gilbert bribed the King's court to find in his favour, made Healaugh the seat of his power, and then had to persuade the previous owners to drop their claim to their rights in Swaledale by purchasing half the manor of Reeth and half the forest of Swaledale, presumably the upper parts.

As an aside, the exact meaning of the Latin noun *medietas* varies between authorities. It is often taken to mean 'a half', but Trice Martin (1892) states unequivocally that it actually means 'the right of the mesne lord,' that is 'the mesnalty,' and in many contexts that makes much more sense. The sub-title of this work is *A collection of Abbreviations, Latin Words and Names Used in English Historical Manuscripts and Records*; it is extremely useful, and one of the standard reference works on the shelves of The National Archives at Kew, a recommendation in itself. Along with Latham's *Revised Medieval Latin Word-List* you will have a much easier time researching the last thousand years!

The other possibility is that the Gants were aware that the lack of any defined boundaries for their Swaledale lands was a grave disadvantage in managing disputes with the local largely Saxon landowners the Normans had displaced after the Conquest, and that they therefore sought at an early date to rectify the omission. Looking at the genealogy of the Gant family, the most likely Gilbert to have wanted and needed to define the limits of the lands acquired by his father in Swaledale was Robert's son Gilbert II (1118-1156).

These excerpts confirm that there are two Gant documents, and that we probably have to search for them at two periods in history, 1108-1156 and 1206-1241. In the meantime, until they are found, we have to consider the question of the level of detail likely to be found in such a document or charter. The purpose of both of these documents was to define the boundaries of upper Swaledale, and in so doing they should mention the Nine Standards as a waypoint along the catchment watershed that has always formed the border of the dale, but how detailed was the definition?

Examples of the earliest charters and perambulations

When the original charters are found, we will know if the Cornelius Fryer paper is what it appears to be, an accurate and unembellished transcription, providing us with the earliest written mention of the Nine Standards that has so far come to light. Or we shall find that the original was very short, mentioned only the main north-south and east-west limits, and was gradually elaborated over the succeeding generations until eventually the boundary markers were listed in considerable detail. The uncertainty arises because in fact we have some examples of early Swaledale and Westmorland charters that are very short and irritatingly vague, while others are commendably long and detailed!

For example, Robert de Gant's charter for his gift to the Monastery of Bridlington, dating from 1183x1191, and confirmed by King John in 1200/01, is quoted below. I have taken the Latin text given in Dodsworth's manuscript version in the Bodleian Museum at Oxford (Summary Catalogue Reference 4151, folio 144 verso) and checked it against the printed version quoted in Dugdale's *Monasticon Anglicanum* before translating it as follows:

"Robert de Gant, son of Walter de Gant, to all sons of holy church, greeetings. This should be a note to you that I concede and dedicate, and this present charter confirms my testimony, to the church of St. Maria of Bridlington, and to the canons of the same servants of God, in free and perpetual enjoyment all pasture and all herbage in Swaledale, in longitude towards the east from Hertay as far as the last waterfall which is called Hawardes dale beck, and which is closest to the hills called Blabergh; and in latitude from the river Swale, upwards towards the south, as far as my land extends; excepting my cattle sheds and my trees. I concede also, and this present testimonial charter confirms, in free and perpetual enjoyment, and permits them in this pasture to make hay as much as they wish, and [to take] from my woods excepting tree saplings enough material to make homes, and two cattle sheds, as much as the work requires, of which one vaccary is at Whallesheved and the other at Frithloc; and from my aforesaid woods they may have for firewood in those vaccaries, as much as necessary; the same canons may have also for the same vaccaries, four dogs with whole feet; the lords and dogs in their sympathy[?]. Which if the animals of the canons shall exceed the grazing capacity of the pastures they shall reasonably be taken and reasonably sent out. Witnessed by: Earl Henry de Gaunt my Bailiff, Master Robert de Escrop, Roberto the constable, William de Toup, Walter de Bovvington, William de Bucton, William de Siwardby, and Roberto his son, and the son of Gilbert de Speton, and Peter his son. Book V, Folio 136."

The limits here are clear and identifiable even today, but they only define the extremities, and leave out crucial details the absence of which may well give rise to disputes with neighbours. These disputes were not uncommon, even on the high fells where land values were relatively low, but the watersheds and prominent landmarks along them were very well known to all who worked there. This could lead to situations in which the correct boundaries were well known but ignored by the powerful, and the legal process of seeking redress could be – and was – deliberately dragged out over generations. The dispute between the Clifford lands in Westmorland on Stainmore and the Honour of Richmond in Yorkshire is a case in point; it was sufficiently serious for the King to instruct a commission to resolve the dispute, thus:

1281: PRO Calendar of Patent Rolls for 9 Edward I, 1281 Membrane 17d, June 5 Westminster.

"Commission to Geoffrey de Neville, Guichard de Charroun and Alexander de Kirkenny, to make a perambulation of the bounds between the counties of York and Westmoreland on the moor of Steynmor, between the land of John of Brittany, earl of Richmond in Richmond, in the county of York and the land of Roger de Clifford and Is[abella] his wife, Roger de Leiburn and Idonia his wife in Brough, co. Westmoreland, the metes and bounds of which are the metes and bounds of the said counties."

The dispute was still rumbling on over fifty years later in 1335 when Robert de Clifford was still grazing his animals on over 1000 acres of land on Stainmore which were in the upper catchment of a river flowing into Yorkshire. To Clifford, these lands were not legally in Yorkshire, but in Westmorland. He claimed that the case brought against him by Henry Fitz Hugh as tenant of the earl of Richmond in a Yorkshire court, where Clifford had no influence, should have been brought in a Westmorland court where his word was law! Clifford then brought the case to court in Westmorland, thus causing further delay and frustration. The case is documented in detail in the National Archives at Kew; see for example SC 8/53/2622 and 2623 for the year 1335 and SC 8/307/15314 for the year 1339. All decisons and actions are postponed repeatedly, for a wide and constantly changing set of reasons, "until the perambulation is made, which may never be done" A revealing comment!

The 1928 English Place Name Society volume for the North Riding of Yorkshire by A H Smith reports that in 1338 there was a commission, "to define by a perambulation the metes and bounds between the two counties" of Westmorland and Yorkshire. The parallel 1967 volume for Westmorland, also by A H Smith some 40 years later, states that, "the Pennine boundary with the North Riding was in fact the subject of a commission of enquiry in 1337." These statements are probably based on the Calendar of Patent Rolls for Edward III, 1334-1338, membrane 24d dated Westminster March 23rd 1337, in which a commission is issued to the Bishops of Durham and Carlisle about the boundaries between Durham, Yorkshire and "part of Westmorland by the commonalities of these counties that disputes frequently occur through uncertainty as to these metes and divides" and it lists the eight witnesses from each side, "who shall personally be present" – and that in itself became a major cause of delay.

In the Patent Rolls volume for 1338-1340, the document on membrane 35d dated 16 February 1338 at Westminster changes the personnel of the commission, in the light of complaints that key people are on duty elsewhere and not available, that the budget is not sufficient to ensure security of senior bureaucrats in such wild and inaccessible places, and so on. The document on membrane 7d dated 10 December 1338 at Kennington records, "there are still great disputes between those two counties touching the confines thereof" and reduces the witness list so that only "four out of eight have to be present in person to define by perambulation the metes and bounds of the two counties." In 1339 Membrane 30d dated March 1st at Kennington records that the commission had still not made the perambulation. The Volumes for 1340-1343 and for 1343-1345 do not even mention it. The issue kept reappearing in the Parliamentry Rolls, in a bizarre mixture of Latin and Norman-French, during the reign of Edward III, without any action. The perambulation by the royal commission seems never to have been carried out. It all sounds very modern; bury it in committee or set up a commission of enquiry.

However, a perambulation of at least part of the disputed territory was made at some date after 1345, but apparently before 1377. There was a long and bitter – but eventually successful – struggle by Lady Anne Clifford, Dowager Duchess of Pembroke, Dorset and Montgomery, to retain her rightful inheritance against the combined male chauvinists of the time, namely the monarchy and her closest male relatives. The problem was that her father George, Earl of Cumberland, had illegally left the Clifford lands to his brother Francis, and not to his daughter Anne, who therefore had to wait 38 years until both her uncle Francis and his son had died, to inherit, during which time she assembled all the evidence in her favour that she could dig out from the Clifford archives. Part of this can be consulted at the Kendal County Record Office. The paper relevant to the disputed lands on Stainmore quoted below is taken from a transcription now held at CROK as part of the Westmorland Deposit of the Hothfield family, probably made by Roger Dodsworth in 1640 or thereabouts, but the original source has not yet been found. The original may come from the Clifford papers at Skipton Castle or elsewhere. From the places mentioned, the perambulation began at a well known and undisputed hilltop landmark on the Winton/South Stainmore boundary between the parishes of Brough and Kirkby Stephen within Westmorland as far as the county boundary between Westmorland and Yorkshire, and then defined the course of the county boundary across Stainmore, the area of the dispute. It reads as follows:

1199x1377: Lady Ann Clifford's file of "Charters and Evidences relating to Westmorland and Yorkshire properties from John (1199-1261) to Edward III (1327-1377)" (CROK WD/HOTH/A988/11), see plate 10 (page 63):

> "These are the bounder of Stanesmoore – First Beginning att the Haight or Topp of a place or hill called Hearne hil, and thence unto Backston Fell, and from Backston fell to the heighte of Morvill, and from thence to the Frierwith Sike and from thence to a Whitestone in Easegill, and from thence to a place called Aesgill poole And from thence to a place called Reerecross; And from thence to the Heade of a yellisike howe and soe along a Travers unto Soutergill head and from thence to a place called Caldselehaw And so ascending by ye Shillipsike unto the westend of Nerigillfell [?] and from hence unto the Northern end of Little Fell and from thence directly to the haight of the westend of Swyndale and from thence descending unto the Bounders of Helton."

Note this early form of the word Stanesmoore, reminiscent of Canon Harrison's Athelstane's Moore for what is now known as Stainmore.

The first two places are very close to the Nine Standards, but the perambulation does not mention thém. 'Hearne hil' is not on the OS maps, but we can deduce where it was from later perambulations (quoted above under the years 1709, point 8; in 1651, points 7 and 8, and in 1617 for example). Harngill is also identifiable from Curwen *Later Records from North Westmorland, East Ward*, page 147, where the entry for 1746-7 dated 12 January reads:

> "Presentment that John Birkbeck and others of Hartley did by hushing for lead ore in a place called Harnagill in the parish of K. Stephen in such manner poison and pollute the stream of water in Hartley Town Beck and Eden that the said stream became unwholesome and corrupt so that those who had lands adjoining to the streams and cattle were hurt and greatly damaged thereby. On

7 April 1755, John Longstaff was indicted for the same offence and fined one shilling."

This gill is now shown on OS maps as Birkett Beck, although its correct name is consistently given in the documents cited here. The perambulation goes from Harngill to Harnegill side; this is the Hearne Hill at the start of the perambulation, at the Lord's Stone shown on OS maps at grid reference NY 3809E 5081N.

The second place mentioned after Hearne Hill is Backston Fell. It is not clear which fell top this refers to; it is discussed in the section on place names. This could be the fell named as Basti Fell on the modern OS maps, about a kilometre north of the Nine Standards. In the 1709 perambulation quoted above, this place is called Basson Fell Side; in 1651 it was called Baystone Fell, though it is more likely that Backston Fell is either the Black Stone Fell or Black Hill waypoints next to Basson or Baystone Fell. Finally, in the 1617 perambulation, the waypoint in this area is called Black Hill. These are all within a couple of kilometres of the Nine Standards, to the north of them, but they are not mentioned. This matter is discussed in the section on place names and the need for detailed research in the field to sort out these very similar names all in the same area. One can only assume that the Nine Standards did not lie on the boundary being defined, which appears to have passed to the north of their position.

The above perambulation is on the next-to-last page of Lady Anne's Evidences file. Curiously enough, on the last page, without any heading or explanation, is a simple list of places. It follows straight after the above, and a reader unfamiliar with the detailed geography of the upper Eden Valley might think that these places are part of the Stainmore boundary definition. But the area they define is far removed from Stainmore; the list is in fact a boundary roll of Mallerstang, starting from and returning to Water Gate Bottom on the Eden (see plate 11, page 74). It reads as follows:
"Wateryeatskarr
Hildserld dyke
Raven skarr
Taylebrigg Skarth
Anglands Pott
Whitestone in Fellesend
Seavimeer

High Seate
Greggory Chappell
Hugh Seate
Witherslack
Whitebirk in Gnar's [?] Moss
Stubbing Rigg
Graystone in Swarth Fell
Galloway gates
Blandstone in Wilbor Fell
Skandall Heade
Topp of Wilbore Fell
Topp of Little Fell
Stoneygate Foote
Fothergill beck
to Eden
Watergate Skarre."

Apart from its obvious interest to locals as probably the oldest per-ambulation of Mallerstang that has so far been unearthed, it is includ-ed here for two reasons. First, if it is true that all these Evidences date from the period 1199-1377 as the title says, it shows that detailed per-ambulations were being made and recorded at least as early as the 14th century, and possibly much earlier; it is therefore not unlikely that the Cornelius Fryer document defining Swaledale is an exact copy of an English translation of a very early original. And second, if such early records have indeed been located, although so far only as transcriptions or translations and not originals on the Swaledale side, then a more detailed and systematic search may well uncover peram-bulations of the Kirkby Stephen area or of the Hartley and Winton manors on the Westmorland side that do mention the Nine Standards.

It is worth noting from my experiences so far, that boundary rolls and perambulations are sometimes attributed to the wrong area, are often hidden away in an illogical place, and may be included in other quite different sets of papers! But the most important conclusion we can draw from this analysis is that if the Cornelius Fryer document is a translation of a Latin original that existed in the late 17th or early 18th century, then it is only second hand, that is only once removed from the original. If it is a copy of an earlier translation, even then it is only twice removed from the original.

So after this rather lengthy digression, one has to conclude that Charters were not all short, or all long; that over the centuries the names by which landmarks were known did change over time; and that the places people chose to select as defining landmarks also varied over time. Consequently on the balance of this evidence, it is just as likely that the Cornelius Fryer document is taken verbatim from a translation of a 12th or 13th century original as that he has copied a contemporary boundary roll that successive manorial bailiffs have elaborated and embellished over the centuries from an originally very short charter in the light of his own highly detailed knowledge of the manorial boundaries of his day. In the former case, we have a mention of the Nine Standards that can be dated to the 12th or 13th century; in the latter case, the earliest documented mention is probably from about 1534x1538. It may help finally to look at the context in which Gilbert de Gant may have been operating.

The Territorial Imperative

In *Yorkshire Boundaries* Le Patourel, Long and Pickles (Yorkshire Archaeological Society, 1993) provide an excellent introduction to the complexities of parish and township boundaries, and offer many insights of great value. Chapter Three on 'Perambulations and Boundary Descriptions' by Ann Alexander is particularly useful in the present context, and it is a very great pity that Chapter Four on 'Boundary Stones' could not be completed beyond a summary based on his field notes from 1975 to 1981 due to the death of the researcher J Howard Dobson. Though I have not yet seen them, his notes on the 1,281 boundary stone sites he visited, including the pre-1974 Westmorland border, are available at the Yorkshire Archaeological Society in Leeds as MS 1353. The level of detail throughout the book emphasises strongly how much better known and researched the Yorkshire side of the border is at present than the Westmorland side, reflecting perhaps the survival of more sources of useful material for such a study as well as the determination of a very large and biddable body of local enthusiasts, evidently supported by a wide range of institutions! It represents a major effort, sustained over many years by numerous people.

The parishes and townships covered in that book are mostly in lowland Yorkshire, the closest to Swaledale being Abbotside at the head of Wensleydale, but many of the conclusions reached by the researchers are no doubt applicable also to the Westmorland side of the border. For example, while the earliest boundary definitions are often vague, especially for the parishes in remote and sparsely populated areas, they found the detail and complexity of manorial and parish boundaries increased as time went by, development proceeded, and both agriculture and population intensified the pressure on resources especially land as a source of food, wealth and power, but also valuable minerals such as coal, iron and lead. This is a not unexpected conclusion, but while population pressure may well be a major factor in the rich lowlands of the Vale of York, in upper Swaledale the watershed of the main river has defined the limits of the civil and ecclesiastical units to the north and south since very early times. Equally on the Westmorland side of the border, boundaries in the rich lowlands have been progressively modified and elaborated, but the watershed between the Eden to the west and the Swale to the east along the crest of the Pennines has long been recognised as a significant natural and political boundary.

Another extremely useful book is Angus Winchester's *Discovering Parish Boundaries* because it deals with the national picture and provides considerable historical depth so that one can see what is unique in Westmorland and the North Riding, and what resembles the situation in other counties of England and in Wales and Scotland. While these two books have been very informative, their real contribution to the thinking behind this book has been to provide a very helpful national and regional perspective on what is in reality a very localised issue. And this section will conclude with a look at the social and political context within which Gilbert de Gant may or may not have defined in detail the boundaries of upper Swaledale.

This is not my field so I shall simply present brief extracts from two books on Swaledale which I have found very helpful in understanding a little of the complexity of land holdings and land users at that period.

The first book is R Fieldhouse and B Jennings' 1977 book *A history of Richmond and Swaledale,* essential reading for the North Yorkshire side.

"After the Conquest, King William gave extensive lands to his followers in reward for their support. Amongst these was the the vast feudal estate later known as the Honour of Richmond, which he granted to Alan Rufus, cousin of the Count of Brittany. Alan commanded the Breton contingent at the Battle of Hastings and later took part in the brutal suppression of the North in 1069/70... This extensive holding was created for military purposes, not so much as a defence against the Scots as has been assumed, but more as an offensive instrument for the conquest and colonisation of Yorkshire... to ensure the permanency of Norman rule in the north.

"Yorkshire was very much border country; the kingdom of the Scots extended to Rey Cross in Stainmoor... and the centre of Scottish power lay much closer to hand than that of the English and later the Norman kings. During the first few years after the Battle of Hastings Norman influence hardly reached into Northumbria and ideas of... an independent kingdom of Northern England under Scottish or Danish protection became a distinct possibility. William easily squashed such resistance in 1068, but in the autumn of 1069 the Normans were threatened by a more serious rebellion, encouraged by the arrival of a Danish army in the Humber. William was determined to suppress the rebellion and to ensure that it did not re-occur. He set out on a winter campaign of terror and destruction... of the whole region between York and Durham... whereby all crops, cattle and food... were burnt... Many thousands of people were killed or starved to death. The region was said to lie almost uninhabited and desolate for nine years, abandoned to bandits and wild animals.

"The Normans' military hold over Yorkshire was not really made secure until c.1080 when it was colonised. The old Anglo-Scandinavian aristocracy was replaced by Norman-French tenants-in-chief who, together with the king, held virtually all the land by the time the Domesday Book was compiled in 1086. The Domesday survey reveals the extent of the Norman devastation of the north... However by 1086 there were pockets of recovery... Some of the great landlords moved their surviving peasantry into the more fertile regions, to concentrate their scarce labour force in the most productive parts of their estates. Count Alan and his chief subtenants follow this practice. Whilst there is very little evidence of agricultural activity or even population in the Pennine dales in 1086... Richmond entered the medieval period as the growth centre of Norman fief, Swaledale did so as a depopulated and under-developed backwater."

The second is Andrew Fleming's 1998 book *Swaledale: valley of the wild river* where he writes of the de Gant/Gaunt family and the recovery of Swaledale:

"When Walter de Gant took control in the early 12th century, the manor which he established was named from Healaugh, and it occupied the whole of the upper dale... The tradition is that Alice, sister of Walter de Gant, married John de Swale and became mother of Alured de Swaledale (living 1157). Alured (Alfred) is an historical personage... It is tempting to suggest that when the Gaunts arrived... they found a large family of Swales, perhaps mostly in the Reeth area, some of whom claimed to be descendants of the old chiefly family. Perhaps Walter de Gaunt did find it politic to marry his sister to one of the leading male members of the older 'aristocracy' – especially if his arrival had deprived the Swales of some of their traditional rights, their title to land, for example... Walter de Gaunt established (or re-established?) the game reserve known as the forest of Swaledale, which took in all the old land of Swale... [i.e. upper Swaledale]

"Swaledale was a contested landscape. No doubt there were distinctions of power and status in pre-Conquest Swaledale, and they were probably intensified by the incursion of various groups of newcomers. Families trying to make a living here had to cope with the exactions and transactions of pre-Conquest lords, and then with their feudal successors. The de Gaunt family, who held the manor of Healaugh until 1298, imposed Forest Law on Swaledale; Arkengarthdale was also a Forest; and then there was the New Forest...

"The de Gaunts gave land in Swaledale to monastic institutions, notably Bridlington Priory and Rievaulx Abbey, far away to the east; it is interesting that they chose land on the well-wooded south bank of the Swale, and at the western end of the dale, rather than on the more populous north bank. These grants of land involved certain rights, privileges and restrictions, all of which had to be fitted into the existing scheme of things, individuals and families holding their land on the basis of various legal and financial rights and obligations. No doubt in practice certain things worked out rather differently."

Together these give a very clear picture of 12th century Swaledale, no longer a wilderness on the very edges of habitable land, where people could barely survive, but of an increasingly busy and lucrative pastoral system, with relatively large numbers of people making some sort of a living there, all of whom were subject to and rigidly controlled by the lords of each manor. No doubt too there was competition and conflicts of interest between the adjacent lords. The "harrying of the North" in the winter of 1069/70 was long over, and the region was recovering rapidly under its new Norman overlords. Mineral rights and exploitation are not mentioned above, and are not well documented for this period, though Fleming (1994) says that lead mining was, "evidently in being by the time of the Norman Conquest." Rievaulx Abbey was certainly involved in lead mining, as witnessed by the accounts at the Dissolution, and the Bardney Abbey horse pastures in Swaledale were probably a convenient source of pack animals for transport. The widespread coal measure outcrops and the millstone grit strata would also be lucrative resources even from an early date, and being located in the headwaters of the dale, detailed boundary definition would be essential.

Conclusions on the Fryer document

Viewing the Cornelius Fryer document in this light, the overwhelming balance of probability is that the boundaries of the 'contested landscape' of upper Swaledale were defined by Gilbert de Gant II (1118-1156) after he, as the oldest son, inherited the whole of Swaledale from Walter de Gant in 1138 or 1139.

We are told by the anonymous author of DRO D/HH 6/2/257 (on page 2) that, "Walter de Gant, nephew to William the First, who had a part of Swaledale had at first no bounds described for his Grant." In other words, it was customary to define the limits of land grants, but for the vast and remote area of upper Swaledale, perhaps not well known or not yet under the complete control of the Norman overlords, this had not yet been done. Thus Geoffrey de Gant, the third son who had earlier become the Chief Forester of Swaledale to his brother Walter according to Harrison (1779), could not impose Forest Law without knowing the boundary of Swaledale.

For his part, Gilbert II no doubt wanted and needed to find out exactly what lands he had just inherited, to establish control and to avoid encroachment by acquisitive neighbours. Knowing the generosity of his family, he had to define the limits of the Gant fee in Swaledale before Walter's second son Robert made the grant of middle Swaledale to Bridlington, and also before the gift of pasture south of the river Swale from Harkerside to Haverdale Beck was made to Bridlington. Equally, the imposition of Forest Law in the upper catchment required the detailed definition of boundaries, specifically to separate the Gant holdings in Swaledale from adjacent lordships in control of Arkengarthdale Forest and the New Forest on the north side, and the Forest of Wensleydale on the south side.

This makes it virtually certain that the original document, in whatever language, listed the same waypoints that are repeated in the transcription of Cornelius Fryer's translation. We can therefore accept with a high degree of probability that the Nine Standards were mentioned for the first time in 1138 or 1139.

Apart from the extracts in the preceding section, I have not followed tradition by including a detailed and critical review of the modern academic literature on boundaries, history or archaeology for this area and period. That might have been rewarding, but the information gleaned would necessarily have been general rather than specific, and the effort premature. The research had to be limited in the first instance to a search for and presentation of the documentary evidence for the modern creation or long existence of the Nine Standards.

The evidence for an ancient origin has proved to be compelling, and a strong case can be made that the earliest documented reference so far unearthed is from about 1138. So we have here ancient cairns rather than a modern folly, and they can now be examined from a very different perspective. Since they appear to have existed for over 850 years, it is not entirely idle to speculate on their likely origins by crossing the 1066 watershed of the Norman Conquest, so that we can visit briefly and in a rather lighter mood the previous thousand years, and perhaps beyond.

FOUR

Dark Age Speculations

In the pre-Conquest millennium, the evidence for the existence of the Nine Standards is more tentative, and that is only to be expected. The year 1066 might fairly be described as the crucial watershed between history and 'heresy'! Before 1066, there are very few relevant documents; and such as they are, they contain little concrete detail, and few clues. In this section, we are looking for possible links between known events in this geographical area and these very prominent features of the landscape of the upper Eden Valley.

At present, many of the pre-Conquest leads that follow are frankly speculative, an examination of the currently unsupportable but not unthinkable, perhaps to be followed up in detail in due course, and possibly dismissed. But no less interesting for that; the hope is that a fresh look at the various possible ties between these ancient monuments and proto-history, pre-history and even folklore and mythology may stimulate new lines of thought and enquiry as well as enquirers from different backgrounds and disciplines (without them jeopardising career, position, or peer esteem...) It is also highly likely that some reader more learned in the relevant disciplines and periods than the author might be able and willing to make a substantial advance on current knowledge about the Nine Standards... If so, do please get in touch!

King Eric's Memorial?

In 954AD Eric Bloodaxe, the last independent Irish Viking King of York (947-948, 952-954), was ambushed and killed with his companions on Stainmore, a pass three or four miles north-east of the Nine Standards. Local legend says Eric and his men were buried at the Rey Cross, but when it was excavated and moved during road widening in the late 1990s no burials were found. The cross was moved to Bowes

Museum for safe-keeping during the roadworks.

In the historian Machell's view, the geographical area named 'Steynmore' extended as far south as Hugh Seat Morvil, at the southern end of Mallerstang Edge, only five miles south of the Nine Standards.   The topographer Harrison also considered that "Athelstane's Moore" reached south to the head of Wensleydale. The massacre could in that case have been on any of the three major passes across the Pennines between York and the Solway Firth.   The Viking sagas tell us that when killed by Earl Maccus, son of Olaf, Eric had with him five kings from the Hebrides and two earls of Orkney. Stenton (1971) quoting Symeon of Durham and Roger of Wendover says that, "King Eric was treacherously killed in a certain lonely place called 'Steinmor' with his son Haeric and his brother Ragnold, betrayed by Earl Oswulf..." the Earl of Bernicia. Other sources simply state that his companions were 'high ranking', and that his opponents were King Eadward and the Northumbrian Angles.

There is no documentary mention of the Nine Standards in any of the sources quoted; but in the Norse tradition, it is conceivable that nine cairns were erected over their graves or maybe built simply as a memorial to the fallen by survivors or sympathisers, omitting some minor noble from the body count! If correct, this would provide an account of the origin of the cairns, an hypothesis which could be tested by excavation.

The name for the Nine Standards that has come down to us, as indicated above, appears to be of mid-14th century origin, though this may be a replacement of an earlier name. But there is at least one cairn in the vicinity with a name derived from Old Norse so this link is not completely out of the question. To state the blindingly obvious, it follows that there had to be Old Norsemen around in the upper Eden Valley to pass that name on to succeeding gernerations. More important, it also follows that the cairns had to be there at that time, staring down on them from the skyline, a readily recognisable landscape feature for use as a signpost for travellers, and therefore needing a name.

As it happens, if they were given a memorable name, it has not survived and has not come down to us. They are simply the nine stone cairns: a literal description and easy to remember, lying between the route over Tailbrigg to the south and over Athelstan's Moor to the north. But hardly a name to catch the headlines, and there is not the slightest indication in their present name of a connection between the

Nine Standards and Eric Bloodaxe, with or without his illustrious companions; more convincing would be a name such as 'Eric's Last Stand' or perhaps 'Resting Place of the Vikings.' If there were any link with the celebrated Eric, local memory would have preserved it, particularly since those who recall his last stand seem to have been sympathetic to his cause and ashamed of the betrayal that brought about his demise. As Stenton (1971) puts it, "nothing is certain beyond the fact that the manner of his death earned him the sympathy of those who recorded it." So they are not a memorial for Eric and his loyal companions.

Interestingly, it was rumoured locally that Eric was buried at the Rey Cross on Stainmore, but when the stone was moved from its original position during the widening of the A66 trunk-road, a search was made but nothing was found under it. That does not mean, of course, that he is not buried somewhere close by on Stainmore, just that he is not buried under the Rey Cross; and to my knowledge, no serious research effort has ever been mounted to locate possible sites, for example by stereoscopic analysis of aerial photographs followed by detailed ground investigation.

Urien's signpost?

There is a large and growing literature on Urien and the kingdom of Rheged, and the north of England in general, that needs to be researched as the last thousand years have been. But several points are worth making at this juncture in connection with the Nine Standards. Rephrasing the initial sentence from Charles Phythian-Adams *The Land of the Cumbrians* (1996), we read:

"The precise extent of the kingdom or even *imperium* of Rheged – whether confined to the Solway basin in general or to a wider territory extending beyond the Pennines to the east and the Lakeland massif to the south – remains at present a matter of uncertainty... The only precise geographical indications of the general location of Rheged are the facts that Urien of Rheged is described specifically as Prince of Catterick, and that he is associated with *Llwyfenydd* as a residence, what is now generally accepted as represented by the river name Lyvennet in north Westmorland. A territory that could have controlled the strategic Stainmore approach route from Deiran Yorkshire to the Cumbrian plain on the one hand, and on the other, the Swaledale line (via the Kirkby Stephen district), which was guarded to the east by Catterick itself, certainly seems appropriate. Urien himself is recorded as operating east of the Pennines."

In support he cites Williams (1952), Jackson (1955 and 1969), Higham and Jones (1985), Brooke (1983) and Miller (1975). He might also have mentioned Hogg (1946) who also argues in favour of a Lyvennet/Urien connection. *The Land of the Cumbrians* itself provides an in-depth analysis of the changing relationship of Rheged in the 6th and 7th centuries to Deira and York on the one hand, and to Bernicia and Bamburgh on the other, with Kirkby Stephen for example moving from the Diocese of Lindisfarne to the Diocese of York and finally of Carlisle. In this period, the British and Anglian entities coincide and conflict, affecting greatly the fortunes of the upper Eden and upper Swale valleys, but Phythian-Adams points out:

"It is evident that the British resistance to an increasingly vigorous Anglian presence was diminishing even before the close of the 6th century. That that in part was due to internecine rivalries is clear: whether at the battle of *Armteryd* (Arthuret) in 573, or when Urien himself was assassinated by an ally at the siege of Lindisfarne in perhaps the 580s. It is equally true, however, that the Britons were also savagely outfought at such battles as Caer Greu in 580 where Gwrgi and Peredur were killed, or Catraeth (c.600) where the cream of the British north were slaughtered."

This literature is full of British or Welsh names, and the search for references to the Nine Standards will be protracted, and require competence in the relevant languages. Many of the places mentioned have not yet been identified with certainty. Given the amount of traffic over Tailbrigg into Swaledale and over Stainmore into Durham and North Yorkshire, it would be surprising if there were no mention of the most obvious signpost between the two passes as viewed from the upper Eden Valley.

The place-name literature is already being used for historical purposes. For example, Fleming (1994) in *Swadal, Swar (and Erechwydd?): early medieval polities in Upper Swaledale* concludes that:

"According to Cox (1976), the name Swale comes from the Anglian dialect of Old English, the word *swalwe* meaning 'rushing water, whirlpool' and the name was mentioned by Bede (c.730). Ekwall (1960) followed by others (Jackson 1970, Cox 1976, Gelling 1978) suggested that the river previously had a Latin name *Cataractona*, referring to rapids or waterfalls; so the English name could virtually be regarded as a translation. With reference to the poems of Taliesin [a 6th century poet who served under King Urien of Rheged], Sir Ifor Williams (1975) argued that *yr Echwydd* is the Welsh counterpart of the Latin *Catarracta*. Thus *Udd yr Echwydd* or 'Lord of *yr Echwydd*' is parallel to *Llyw Catraeth* or *Princeps Catarractae*, [that is, Prince of Catterick]. Williams also suggested that, '*Erechwydd* (*Yrechwydd*) was Swaledale and that *Catraeth* [i.e. Catterick] was its chief fort'."

Later he concludes:
"Although the evidence of place-names and written records provides more satisfactory documentation for Anglian *Swar* than for its postulated British predecessor, the archaeological evidence tilts the balance of probabilites the other way. I suggest that the Grinton/Fremington dykes must be seen in the context of a horizon of east Pennine linear earthworks built by British polities against the Anglians, a horizon which includes Scots Dyke, Grims Ditch to the east of present-day Leeds, and the Roman Rigg in South Yorkshire (Faull 1974, Higham 1993). As a British polity the Upper Swale valley must at times at least have been part of the wider confederation of Rheged (Higham 1993). Rheged appears to have been centred around the Solway Plain and in Cumbria, but if the Taliesin poems are to be treated as an acceptable historical source, the description of Urien as Lord of *Catraeth*, usually interpreted as Catterick, brings the realm of Rheged further east, as Higham has suggested.

    "Sir Ifor Wiliams' comment about *Erechwydd* and *Catraeth* that 'all this... is speculation if not sheer guesswork' can at least now be juxtaposed against these new findings. Obviously a British polity in Upper Swaledale could have pre-dated the fullest extent of Rheged's power, and it could also have been a defensible territory in the wake of the (for the British) disastrous battle of *Catraeth* which, according to Higham (1986), took place before A.D. 600."

In relation to the perambulations quoted above, and the likely benefit to this research of a thorough examination of place-name evidence, Fleming notes:

"It is worth discussing the evidence of place-names, although the
replacement of British names by English names and of English
names by Norse names considerably reduces the potential of this
approach....Many Pennine rivers have retained their British names
(Thomson, 1964)."

In my view, this may be truer of the main settlements and valley floors
than of the words used to name the high fells and their main features
along the watersheds and down the becks. To my knowledge no place-
name research study has yet focussed on the material contained in
boundary rolls. A good selection of them are included in this book,
and more are available. I have scrupulously retained the original
spellings and grammar, exotic though some of them undeniably are;
they preserve many dialect words not in common use. My hope is that
they may be used to shed light on the meanings and origins of the
place-names in the area of the Nine Standards in the future, to help us
establish a more accurate context for them.

The Toothed Mountain?

The *Brut y Bryttaniat* or *The Chronicle of the Early Britons*, formerly called the *Brut Tysilio,* Tysilio's Chronicle and known as *The
Chronicle of the Kings of Britain*, after an early saint, is a 15th century manuscript copy of a 12th century original in *Kymraec* or Old
Welsh (now lost). First translated into English by Rev. Peter Roberts
in 1811, it was described by the celebrated archaeologist Flinders
Petrie in 1917 as "perhaps the best representative of an entire group
of chronicles in which are preserved certain important aspects of early
British history, aspects that were not finding their way into the published notices of those whose disciplines embraced this period."

The excerpt which follows is taken from Dr William Cooper's
2002 translation into English of the manuscript at shelfmark MS LXI
in the Jesus College Library at Oxford University, a translation duly
scrutinised for accuracy by Ellis Evans, the then Professor of Celtic
Studies at Jesus College. This was in fact the manuscript which

originated in Britanny, and was brought to Britain by Walter Calenius. According to Geoffrey of Monmouth (1100-1155), Walter the Archdeacon of Oxford who was unable to read Welsh or Breton himself, gave him "a certain very ancient book in the British language" and encouraged Geoffrey, who was of Welsh and Breton parentage, to translate it into Latin, which he did in 1136, and later translated it back from Latin into Old Welsh.

The time is 504AD, just after the burial of Ambrosius, Uther's older brother, at the Monastery of Ambri, within the Giant's Ring (ie Stonehenge).

"And when they knew that Ambrosius was dead, then did Octa, the son of Hengist, and Asaf [his uncle], rally the Saxons together. And they said to the Saxons that they were henceforth freed from their oath [of subservience] to Ambrosius. And so they sent to Germany and also to Paschent [who had sought refuge in Ireland] for help, and having gathered a mighty army they overran all Loegria [i.e. central England] as far as Eboracum [modern day York]. And upon their having invested the city, Uther came with his army and there was a great battle. And at the last the Saxons were routed and driven headlong to the mountain called Daned. And that was a great and high mountain, full of crags and stones. And there the Saxons rested that night. And Uther summoned his counsellors before him, and Gorlois, the earl of Cornwall, arose and said, "Our numbers are far fewer than theirs, my Lord. Therefore, let us attack them under cover of night, and we shall defeat them with little loss." And so did they, and rushed the mountain, slaying a great number. And they took Octa and Asaf captive, and scattered all the rest. And having won the day, Uther went up to Alclud [i.e. modern day Glasgow], and from there travelled all around the kindom, enforcing the rule of law so that no man dared harm another."

In his translation, Cooper has retained from the original manuscript the mountain's name *daned*; and in his footnote says: "the original Welsh text reads *mynydd daned*, literally 'toothed mountain' (*daned* later developing into modern Welsh *danheddog*)."

If Geoffrey of Monmouth had made a direct translation into Latin, we would have *mons dentulus*, toothed mountain; or just possibly *mons dentium* (genitive case, mountain of teeth) or perhaps even *mons denitibus* (ablative case, mountain with teeth). In fact his Latin version renders it as '*Mons Damen*'; he has departed from the original text, but what might his revised text mean?

The ten volume *Dictionary of medieval Latin from British sources* by R E Latham with D R Howlett, 1986, Fascicule III covers the letters D-E. There is no word that is directly comparable to *damen*, let alone one indicating teeth. The closest are *dama* or *damma* = a doe, especially of fallow deer, or the masculine equivalent *damus* or *dammus*, a (fallow deer) buck. Less likely are *danus*, a Dane; *damnum*, loss, damage or injury; or *donum* a gift.

A second authoritative source is R E Latham's *Revised Medieval Latin Word List from British and Irish sources*, 1965. There is again no entry for *damen*. The only close noun or adjective is *damer* from *damus*, a buck or fallow deer (and variants), as above. That would at least be appropriate: Leland (1506-1552) in his 'Itinerary' says of Upper Swaledale and neighbouring Yoredall [i.e. Wensleydale today] "Here is safe living for goats, deer and stags which for their great bulk and branchy heads are very remarkable and extraordinary."

If the word *damen* was used in medieval Latin, it would be in one or other of these dictionaries. And it isn't.

Plate 28, Mallerstang perambulation, 4 July 1906.
Photograph courtesy of John Hamilton.

So what are we to make of Geoffrey of Monmouth's *Mons Damen*, that is, Mount Damen? Bill Cooper pointed out to me (personal communicaton) that Geoffrey, "did not always translate his names. More often he transposed them into a form that his readers would be able to pronounce easily (*Sisilius* from *Saessylit*, for example). Whilst that did them a good service, it does not always serve us as well, alas." There is a further and more straightforward complication, as Cooper continues, "Geoffrey of Monmouth was no stranger to misreading his texts, as some of the Chronicle's footnotes testify" [i.e. in Cooper's translation]. Cooper then points out the possibility that what the scribe was copying actually said, '*mons dolmen,*' not '*mons damen*.' He continues, "I do know that the letters 'o' and 'l', if closely written on old and shrunken parchment, could easily be mistaken for the letter 'a' – which might explain how '*dolmen*' came to be written down as '*damen*'."

This might be clarified by checking as many of the surviving manuscripts as possible, Latin and Welsh, to see if this is a likely scenario. On the face of it, it seems a highly plausible explanation. Cairns are not dolmens, at least not by today's accepted definitions, but that distinction might not be evident even to a modern churchman, still less a 12th century cleric. We could expect him to know that dolmens were stone erections of some kind, and by enquiry he might have concluded that the name 'toothed mountain' was a poetic reference to some sort of stony or spiny crest on its summit; hence *mons dolmen* might seem to him to be a reasonable translation.

Can we identify this evidently striking topographic feature? If like Octa and Asaf you are driven into the mountains after a defeat at York, you are fleeing west or north-west, most likely back to Ireland, whence many of them had just come. Assuming they were fleeing towards Carlisle and the Solway Firth, rather than some port in Morecambe Bay, there are only three passes that cross the northern Pennines in this area: Stainmore, Wensleydale and Swaledale, all leading down the Eden Valley to Carlisle. Neither Stainmore nor Wensleydale could be described as a 'toothed mountain', but it is a graphic description of the Nine Standards at the western head of Swaledale, and may indicate that they were a well-known landmark to the Britons of the area in 504AD.

Whether the southern routes that pass such dramatic mountains as Penyghent, Great Whernside and Ingleborough have equally convincing candidates for the 'toothed mountain' is for others more familiar with their upper slopes than the present author to comment. But this does not imply an origin for the Nine Standards; the text simply mentions them to indicate the area where the battle took place; they are referred to as a prominent local landmark which already existed at the time of the actions described, namely in the first years of the 6th century.

Ninian's Stone Cairns?

A further possibility is suggested by the accepted derivation of the name Ninekirks, the ancient parish church of Brougham near Penrith, as meaning actually Ninian's Church. Its traditional title is the church of St. Wilfrid of Brougham, commonly called 'Ninekirks'. Wilfrid died in AD709. Clearly there are not, and never were, nine churches at that location, but a single church, founded by missionary monks from Whithorn or *Candida Casa* in Galloway, created by Ninian, who was born in southern Scotland about 360 and died in 432AD, and hence part of the sphere of influence of the Celtic Church in Scotland. By analogy, could the Nine Standards then actually be 'Ninian's Stone Cairns'? This is not as fanciful as at first sight it might appear.

Ninian is known to have preached mostly in southern Scotland but also around the Solway Estuary and in the Lake District. Ninian's missionary work in Westmorland has been dated to AD397 (see Simpson, 1940). Burton (1758) says:

"St. Ninian, Bishop of the Strath-cluyd Britons, whose espiscopal see was first at Glasgow till he erected a new church at Whithern or Candida Casa and made it the ordinary place of his residence."

Moreover, as late as the mid-13th century, John Cheyanne, who died in France in 1268, reports that the Bishop of Glasgow, "claimed as an ancient right to exercise his diocesan function as far as the Rere Cross on Stanmore" [from Cormo Innes *Sketches of Early Scottish History*, Edinburgh 1861, p.46]. John de Cheyanne was on his way to visit the Pope when he died, according to the Chronicle of Lanercost, page 65.

If the Bishop of Glasgow claimed the Rey Cross as the southern boundary of his ancient diocese, which thus preceded what Fordun in his *Scotichronicon* (see Walter Bower's version of 1722) described as

Henry II's unauthorised religious foundation at Carlisle, that boundary is likely to have been defined further south by the Nine Standards, Hollow Mill Cross on Tailbrigg, and the Brandreth Stone at Tebay, with its two St Andrew's crosses and local tradition as the southern limit of Scottish influence. Shap and Brough have long been mentioned as southern limits of the Kingdom of Scotland at this time; GWS Barrow's chapter on 'The Charters of David I' [1124-1153] speaks of the need to, "ensure the permananet absorption within the kingdom [of Scotland] of the country north of the Tees and the Howgill Fells" (Anderson, 1908).

This unity of the lands around the Solway is elaborated at very profitable length in Charles Phythian-Adams *Land of the Cumbrians* (1996) where he bemoans the unhelpful influence of the England/Scotland border and the consequent administrative separation of historical materials for studies of this crucial area. I have found that similar difficulties hamper research on communities in the Pennines, lying across the border between Westmorland and Yorkshire, that is, between upper Eden and upper Swaledale.

So the Ninian connection may not be so far fetched. If they are indeed in some way 'Ninian's Stone Cairns', then they must date from at least the fourth century AD. He did not build them, nor did his followers; but they may well have considered them as a diocesan boundary marker, inherited from even more ancient times.

The disgrace of Rome?

Another attractive idea – might the Nine Standards commemorate the defeat of the Roman Army's Ninth Legion, said to have been stationed at York, from which they are said to have marched north, only to vanish from the pages of history?

A tile stamped *LEG VIIII H* for Ninth Legion Hispana, so named because they were the conquerors of Spain, has been found at Scalesceugh south of Carlisle, probably dating from Agricola's time. Popular history would have it that they went north in 78AD under Cerialis against the Brigantes, and suffered a massive defeat further north in the Forth/Clyde area of what is now Scotland around 81-83AD under Agricola, who was allegedly deceived by the devious Picts into splitting his forces into three parts which were then wiped out in turn, which was possibly the reason why Hadrian later built the wall. It is thought that the Ninth was reformed, and sent by Hadrian to Spain as training to harden the men, and they were then posted to York. It is known they built a fort at York in 108/109AD, and legend has it they were ordered north again, marched out and were never heard of again. Was the Ninth Legion destroyed as it crossed the Pennine passes into Westmorland?

Some scholars believe it was annihilated by the Picts maybe in 117/118AD; but recent research suggests that Legio IX Hispana – or a sub-unit of it (or at least a small group of senior officers...) – was at Nijmegen and at Aachen around 121AD; others conclude it was destroyed in Judaea in the Simon ben Kosiba or Kochba rebellion of 132-136AD, in Cappadocia in 161AD, or just possibly on the Danube in 162AD. What is certain is that the Ninth Legion is not amongst the 28 legions of Rome's standing army listed by Marcus Aurelius in 161-180AD; so it must have been destroyed or disbanded before that date. The jury is still out, the evidence not yet conclusive. But there was certainly one, and probably two, major defeats in north Britain, so do the Nine Standards look out over the home territory of the Brigantes, conquerors of the Ninth Legion, as a perpetual reminder of their glorious victory? It might explain why there are nine.

But there may be other reasons why there are nine, and that discussion carries the inquiry conveniently out of a rather barren millennium, an era of pre-history or proto-history, with few documents but with an unresearched resource of place-names, to cross over another major watershed and into the pre-Christian era.

FIVE

The Pre-Christian Era

After the so-called Dark Ages, where we have neither the benefit of contemporary texts nor the certainties of known and well-researched history in eastern Cumbria, the millennia before the Christian era offer slightly more help.

Why nine?

Margaret Gelling, an eminent authority on place-names, states (personal communication):

> "Nine is quite rare in place-names. When it does occur it can usually be taken literally, unlike seven, which is frequent and does seem likely to have a folkloric significance."

This is certainly the case with the Nine Standards; there are indeed nine of them. Perhaps one should add 'usually' – ramblers, yompers and the local youth from time to time add extra ones, but these are of such dimensions that they are easy to distinguish from the originals, and of such construction that they only last for a season or two before disintegrating. Like the newcomer cairns on Wild Boar Fell, they are only chest-height, and look thin and under-nourished, as though the initial enthusiasm of the passers-by dissipated quickly. The Nine Standards are made of sterner stuff, dwarfing even the tallest person, and evidently constructed by a more determined and experienced breed of builders, as Wainwright noted.

And they are not alone; on the same natural watershed which extends away to the north-east from the Nine Standards are Nine Creases some eight kilometres away, now beside the main A66 trunk road over Stainmore (grid ref. 3883E 5126N), and Nine Holes, which is a hill (at grid ref. 3884E 5147N) a further two kilometres north of Nine Creases. Smith (1967) offers no meanings for either of them, and it is not at all clear why they are so called. Creases may be a reference to some agricultural land use type, or a geomorphological

Plate 17, pillow mounds at Water Gate Bottom, Mallerstang. Photograph courtesy of Simon Ledingham.

Plate 18, pillow mounds and tumuli beside the River Eden at Water Gate Bottom, Mallerstang.   Photograph courtesy of Simon Ledingham.

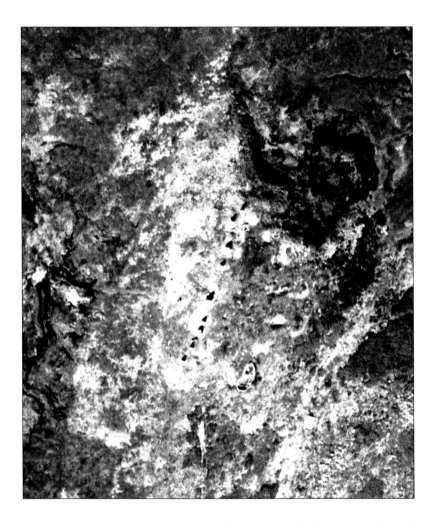

Plate 19, digital air photograph of Nine Standards Rigg, enlarged. Image courtesy of Getmapping Ltd.

Plate 20, above, low altitude oblique air photograph of Nine Standards looking south-east A circular ditch and mound features to the right of the closest two cairns, and there is a pit between the closest cairn and the bottom left corner. Plate 21, below, low altitude oblique air photograph of Nine Standards looking south-west with numerous pits in a line to left of cairns, ditch across front of central cairn and quarries in foreground. Photographs courtesy of Barry Stacey and Simon Ledingham.

Plate 22, above, low altitude oblique air photograph of Nine Standards looking west-north-west with large circular depression in front of second and third cairns from left, and quarries at bottom right. Photograph courtesy of Barry Stacey and Simon Ledingham. Plate 29, below, Mallerstang peramulation, 2006, photograph courtesy of John Hamilton.

Plate 23, above left, low altitude oblique air photograph of Nine Standards looking north-east, showing oval break of slope line around cairns, especially to left, and ditch at bottom right.

Plate 24, below left, low altitude oblique air photograph of Nine Standards looking east-north-east. Several mounds between oval break of slope line and five cairns to left, and ridge just beyond cairns.

Plate 25, above, low altitude oblique air photograph of Nine Standards looking east-south-east, showing barrow-shaped double mound with cairns on crest; also ditch and mound to left of central cairn. Photographs courtesy of Barry Stacey and Simon Ledingham.

Plates 26, above, Landscape and Arts Network visit to the Nine Standards, photograph by the author.
Plate 27, below, impromptu recital at Nine Standards, photograph courtesy of Irene Downing.

feature. No swallow holes (vertical solution holes in the limestone) are indicated on the OS map at Nine Holes. Whatever, somebody in the past believed there were nine of them. It is intriguing that these three places all featuring the number nine are located on the main watershed separating the Eden catchment from the Swale and Greta catchments.

Dick Capel of ECCP has also pondered long and hard over why there are nine cairns, and has suggested that they might represent the nine townships of Kirkby Stephen. These may date from very early times, as is often the case (Winchester, 2002) and would indicate that the cairns are a very early territorial limit, easily recognised and at an indisputable location. Exactly how early is hard to determine. The nine are named by Nicolson and Burn (1777) as Hartley, Winton, Kaber, Soulby, Smardale, Waitby, Nateby, Wharton and of course Kirkby Stephen itself. Whelan (1860) lists the townships as Kirkby Stephen, Hartley, Kaber, Smardale, Waitby, Wharton and Winton (eight) plus the two chapelries of Mallerstang and Soulby. At that time, Brough had four townships, Brough, Helbeck, Stainmore and Brough Sowerby. Kirkby Stephen and Brough parishes/manors separated in 1348.

There is a certain logic to this nine townships hypothesis, yet it has to be tested against the age of the settlements concerned and their likely dates of origin. Or origins; there is substantial evidence that settlements in the Eden Valley have had a chequered history, with numerous 'Romano-British' or Iron Age settlements on the dry limestone uplands, some within a few kilometres of the Nine Standards. These bridge the millennia, evidently abandoned, perhaps in favour of lowland sites, or maybe because of some disaster around the 6th or 7th centuries AD that depopulated the highlands. Candidates include such man-made disasters as the British defeats at Catterick and elsewhere, and any number of natural disasters, from plague, through famine and climate change to comet strikes, all of which have been postulated to explain the periodic devastation and abandonment, the re-peopling by newcomers from elsewhere, the choice of new sites or the re-occupation of old ones.

Previous thinking about 'waves of advance', Iron Age invasions, ethnic cleansing and population displacement are being revisited in the light of discoveries made using the techniques of DNA research, especially by Bryan Sykes (2001, 2003), Stephen Oppenheimer

(2006), and others, and gradually incorporated into main-stream archaeological thinking with appropriate caveats, notably by Francis Pryor (2003) and others. All worth reading, and a fascinating story that concerns us all. It is an enormously complex field, which extends as far as the revolutionary work of Colin Renfrew (1987) on the spread of Indo-European languages, but a much more realistic overall story is beginning to emerge, along with ecstatic shouts of, 'I told you so,' and 'I've been telling them that for years.' The agreeable din of academic mayhem, in short.

But the number nine, universally recognised as an auspicious number, also has other connotations. These can invoke a heady mixture of folklore, mythology and sheer New Age 'mysto-steam' that I find very hard to evaluate. On the basis that these fields are disciplines in their own right, and that they may be one of the few, if inherently uncertain and unprovable, ways such questions can be approached, they need to be mentioned and considered, however difficult it may be to arrive at defensible conclusions.

Waddell (1924) has this to say:

"The later title of "Brigid" (or "Bridget") for the female patron saint of the Irish and the Picts, which is usually supposed to have arisen with a more or less mythical Christian nun in Ireland... is now seen to be obviously the transformed and chastened aboriginal old matriarch wizardess who in the Gothic Eddas is called Frigg, or Frigg-Ida... Her alternative title also as "St. Bride" is confirmatory of this origin, as "Bride" was a usual title for Mother Frigg and her wizardess sisterhood priestesses in the Eddas. These sister wizardesses are often collectively called in the Eddas "The Nine Mothers" or "The Nine Maidens". This now acounts for the many prehistoric monoliths and series of nine standing stones, called "Maiden" stones or "The Nine Maidens", still standing in many parts of Ireland and Britain... as, for instance, "The Maiden Stone" standing at the foot of Mt. Bennachie to the west of the Newton Stone, and also "The Serpent Stone" monolith with the large sculpted Serpent, which stood not far from the site of the Newton Stone, and now placed alongside the latter.

In similar vein, Stuart McHardy's book *The Search for the Nine Maidens* (2003) presents the evidence for the existence in very early times of an almost universal tradition of the Nine Maidens, one of whom is the Mother Goddess. Amalgamating quotes from various pages for the sake of brevity, he has this to say:

"The religion they followed was based on Mother Goddess worship. This is generally thought to have been the earliest form of human religion, and the fact that we all have mothers is probably why humans developed the idea of a supreme Mother Goddess, giver of life and death... The material from Scotland... can be interpreted as showing the existence of an ancient dual Goddess figure portrayed in terms of light and dark, summer and winter, life and death. In Scottish tradition the goddess of Winter, the Hag, becomes the goddess of Summer, the Bride. In other traditions we see the Nine Maidens associated with the Norse goddesses Menglod and Fran, the Welsh Cerridwen, in Siberian shamanic traditions, in a foundation legend from Kenya and of course in the case of the [Nine] Muses we see them associated with the god Apollo... The earliest reference to the Nine Maidens is in a Magdelanian cave painting from [Cogul in] Catalonia, which is perhaps as much as 17,000 years old. This painting clearly shows some sort of fertility rite.

"A similar duality is expressed in the traditional Gaelic concept of the sun as having two seasons – the time of the Big Sun and the time of the Little Sun. These seasons were separated by the great feast days of Beltane and Samhain, which we know today as May Day and Halloween. Mackenzie (1935) mentions a Romanian tale in which a hag called Malvinia had eight female companions, situated on a mountain called Silash, actively involved in spreading winter. These nine witches were turned to stone on the mountain top, echoing the widespread British tales of standing stones and stone circles being witches, or sometimes called Sabbath revellers, who were turned to stone.

"A similar situation occurs in Early Welsh literature. The witches with whom Peredur is involved are based at *Caer Lyow*, and *Caer* generally refers to hill-top sites. Whether all hill top sites are forts is debatable. The standard military and aristocratic interpretation which promotes this idea ignores the fact that many hill-top sites in most parts of the British Isles were used for the great tribal fire festivals of Beltane and Samhain, and that hill and mountain tops are widely associated with Mother Goddess figures. Such sites were also likely to have been used in tribal society for a range of socio-political functions such as law-giving and land allocation.

He offers world-wide examples, and quotes a very great number of 'Nine Maidens' place-names in Scotland, the country he is principally writing about, associated with wells, mountain tops, and other sacred places. He also states that in Gaelic one word for maiden is *nighean* (pronounced nee-an) and argues that this is phonetically very close to the word 'nine'. He gives several instances where an initial reference to a nine maidens' well for example (literally nine *nighean* wells) has become contracted over the ages so that they are now known as Nine Wells, a single word now standing for what were initially two separate elements in the name.

One might then postulate that the original name of the Nine Standards meant 'the Maidens' Cairns.' They stand not more than seven kilometres from Maiden Castle on Stainmore. The Nine Standards are also only 24 kilometres from Maiden Castle in upper Swaledale. The double contraction might also apply to Nine Kirks, the Brougham church already mentioned above, which name would then become Maidens' Church, again not a totally unacceptable or unlikely etymology to the amateur (and with apologies to the professionals).

These are clearly modern names, and perhaps not susceptible to rigorous place-name analysis as conventionally understood. Other modern name examples from the area include King Arthur's Round Table, one of a group of earthworks just outside Penrith, and the stone circle now known as Long Meg and her Daughters. Although attempts to analyse such popular names have sometimes been made, the results are not really convincing.

Returning to Hardy's thesis about the Nine Maidens and stone circles, we can see on OS maps that this is not confined to Scotland. Dorset has its 'Nine Stones' stone circle; Devon also has 'Nine Stones', a stone circle on Dartmoor; Derbyshire the 'Nine Ladies' stone circle at Stanton Moor and the 'Nine Stones Close.' In Cornwall, there are at least six, taken from Payton (2004) and various OS maps; grid references for the sceptical are given in brackets:

'Nine Maidens' stone circle at Boscawen Un (SW 412 274).

'Nine Maidens' also known as 'Merry Maidens' and 'Dancing Stones' at Tregseal near St. Just in Penwith (SW 387 324).

'Nine Maidens' or 'Virgin Sisters' stone circle near Polgear, also known as Wendron north, south and west (SW 683 365).

'Nine Maidens' stone circle shown (SW 434 353) but not named on OS map.

'Nine Stones' stone circle Godaver Downs near Altarnum (SX 236 781).

'Nine Maidens' stone row at St Columb Major (SW 937 676).

Dates ranging between roughly 2500 and 1500BC mostly in the Bronze Age have been attributed to these, with what degree of accuracy I am not in a position to judge.

The last of these is particularly interesting; the Columb Major 'Nine Maidens' is a very rare, possibly unique, stone row. The nine stones are placed in a straight line which I recently measured as bearing some 22 degrees east of north. This orientation means that the stone row faces west-north-west, that is, in the direction of the Spring Quarter Day sunset, on the Feast of Beltane. This is, as noted elsewhere, exactly the same orientation as the Nine Standards, a row of drystone cairns on a hill-top in the north-west of England.

The closest archaeology

The closest archaeology has so far approached to the Nine Standards may be quickly and briefly summarised in quotations from either side of the Pennines:

Andrew Fleming (1994) when talking about the defensive earthworks known as the Grinton-Fremington Dykes near Reeth in upper Swaledale, offers a generalisation that may be applicable to the Nine Standards when he says for example:

"On the moorlands in this area there are walled enclosures, small cairns, and lengths of wall of varying character, some forming major land division systems of coaxial type (see Fleming 1987 *Antiquity* 61, pp 188-202), with long walls running across the contour; the latter almost certainly date from the middle Iron Age, c. 300BC... Also on the dalesides are grassed-over cairns of both 'clearance' and 'burial' types, and numerous house-platforms and settlement enclosures, as well as some sites set on prominent knolls and enclosed by banks and ditches. Our investigations suggest that during the Iron Age and Romano-British periods Swaledale was well settled, with a landscape relatively open and extensively subdivided."

Similarly, Fleming (1998) captions a photograph of a cairn on the Cumbrian side of the border as "a probable Bronze Age cairn at Jack Standards." This is a very close neighbour of the Nine Standards, only about a kilometre to the south. As noted elsewhere, Swaledale has received more archaeological attention than the neighbouring upper Eden Valley, though this is now changing.

A similar picture is beginning to emerge in the adjacent upper Eden Valley with the ground-breaking work, so far unpublished (as far as I know), of the local archaeologist Annie Hamilton-Gibney. She comes second closest to the Nine Standards in an email replying to a query of mine about boundaries (personal communicaton):

"What I can tell you is that ancient boundaries of 'White walls' on the lower ridge of Wildboar Fell and 'Lady Dike' at Tailbridge appear to be 'reaves' consistent with those set out denoting boundaries in the Bronze age (similar in style to those on Dartmoor). These are ancient linear ditch/mound features still recognised as marking the Mallerstang borders today."

Lady Dike is within three kilometres of the Nine Standards on the south side: it runs up from the Duker Beck near Hollow Mill Cross by the Tailbrigg road, onto Coldbergh Edge.

Neither of these are definitive Bronze Age identifications, but they are the closest so far, and suggest that a very early date for the Nine Standards may not be totally out of the question. They also indicate that many of today's landscape features, even the ubiquitous drystone walls, grassed-over mounds and ditches, are very much older than most pepole imagine, especially in upland areas round the Nine Standards.

Where similar drystone cairns in other areas have been studied by the archaeologists, a Bronze Age date has often been determined.

Recent research work on drystone cairns in Finland, Norway, Denmark and the Western Isles of Scotland have all come up with Bronze Age dates. At Crugiau and Crugiau Edryd in Dyfed, Wales, two lines of three and four drystone cairns respectively have been dated to the Bronze Age. The intriguing tri-radial cairns of Northumberland have also been so dated. There are doubtless many more examples, and if I were to hazard a view about the age of the Nine Standards, I would opt for Bronze Age, too.

And probably early Bronze Age, at that. Sir Cyril Fox in *The*

Personality of Britain (1938) was probably the first to note that early
Bronze Age cairns and burial mounds are characteristically located on
territorial boundaries, usually on high ground, and almost always on
the skyline, rather than the highest point. Plates 15 and 16 (page 72)
show that aspect of the Nine Standards to perfection. Other examples
of skyline mounds in the area include the Rasset Hill tumulus on Ash
Fell, and the tumulus right on The Nab of Wild Boar Fell (close to a
very large, and suspiciously rectangular, black slab set into the ground
near the highest point).

Machell (volume 3, page 307) reports on an excavation of what he
calls the Rassett Pike tumulus at Ravenstonedale where they found a
stone coffin in three pieces:

"like to a sheep trough wherein were ashes and some boanes of a
man like the links of a man's back and some round ends off not
reduced to Ashes which when they broake them they were
some[what] reddish... The coffin was all white rim [rime?] as if it
had bin don over with plaster, and the Ashes were white. Seen and
related by George Haton Wharton."

Two pages later, he also quotes another account, from the same
area but possibly not the same tumulus, in a different script and grammar:

"... Rassett where a great many deadmens bones have been digged
out of two round hills where severall Tomes [tombs] of... fashon
doth appear and bones (both mens skulls and other bones) found
of an extraordinary stregth, and greatness: it doth appear the bod-
dys have not beene buried East and West but round about each [?]
hill there heads all lying inwards towards the hill top and as far as
haises been discovered there hands have been taide upon their
breste. There remaines now [no?] tradition of truith what the
plaice haise beene. The hills are in forme of a piramid or something ressembling a sugarloaf, onley broken and... at the basses.
Anthony Prockter, Curatt and Geo. Fotthergill."

Machell offers no dates for these excavations, though they must
pre-date his death in 1698, and no doubt they have received more
recent expert inspection. His accounts are included here as curiosities
of which I was not previously aware, so others may also find them of
interest, (I have since found but not yet seen Tom Clare's 1979

TCWAAS article; see Bibliography.)

In the later Bronze Age, cairns and burial mounds are found on the lower ground, though still most commonly on the territorial boundaries. The Pillow Mounds at Smardale Gill are on low land close to territorial boundaries. Water Gate Bottom also provides a good example of this latter phenomenon: see plates 17 and 18 (pages 145 and 146). The Giants' Graves or Pillow Mounds at Water Gate Bottom were excavated in the 19th century, and inhumations were found; I have not yet tracked down the reference but I believe it was in the TCWAAS. The other examples I have given above may also have been written up in the relevant journals by qualified archaeologists; my apologies if so – I have not yet been able to search much of the literature before 1066 (work in progress!)

However, if the links to the ubiquitous Nine Maidens were somehow established, the age of the Nine Standards might well be pushed even further back than the early Bronze Age.

Cherry and Cherry (2002) speak of the east-west trade during the Bronze Age in Central Lakeland axes for East Yorkshire flints, a movement from west to east along the heads of the Lowther and Lyvennet rivers, Shap Fell, Gamelands stone circle and Rayseat long cairn, probably dating from the late mesolithic and enduring into the 4th century BC Iron Age.

These open limestone uplands provided a good all-season route through the middle Eden Valley, which passes along the watershed between the different tribal territories on either side and stays relatively dry under foot thoughout the year. But the wet Eden lowlands and the river itself had to be crossed at some point, and I think this was almost certainly at Water Gate Bottom. The upland route probably descended from Ash Fell Edge to what is now the Tommy Road or maybe Lammerside and down past the cairns, pillow mounds or 'Giants Graves' to meet the old track down Mallerstang at the Water Gate Bottom ford across the Eden: see plates 17 and 18 (pages 145 and 146).

The closest pass over the hills in that direction goes over Tailbrigg and down into what was then forested Swaledale, but the more open woodland vegetation may have made a route along the watershed more attractive to long-distance travellers on foot or on horseback. We forget how much the vegetation has changed, and how radically different are the ways and routes by which people now travel through the landscape. I have worked in heavily forested mountain catchments in the remote Cordillera of Central America, the Barisan Mountains of Sumatra and the volcanic ranges of Java and Bali, and in the foothills of the Himalayas; almost without exception the long distance footpaths and traders' tracks follow the ridges along the watersheds, avoiding the rivers in the valley bottoms. Similar conditions may well have prevailed in the northern Pennines until very recently: the Forest of Mallerstang, and in upper Swaledale, the Forest of Arkengarthdale and the New Forest, were heavily wooded and still harboured wolves and wild boar in the 13th and 14th centuries as noted earlier, as well as numerous 'vaccaries' or cow farms; only extensive lead mining finally cleared the trees in the 18th and 19th centuries. It is therefore probable that the preferred traders' routes followed the watersheds and stayed up on the high fells.

If true, the route would have past the Nine Standards and Tan Hill on the north side of Swaledale, or via Hugh Seat and Shunner Fell on the south side of Swaledale. Neither seems inherently improbable, but the northern side is the more likely as it appears to be the more ancient boundary.

The sharpest eyes would have guided the long-distance traders all the way along this ancient upland track from the Lake District axe factories by the view of the Nine Standards on the distant skyline. The Nine Standards are visible to the naked eye from Whygill Head near Little Asby, a distance of thirteen kilometres (eight miles). Younger eyes may have been able to see them from near the Lyvennet river. They would remain visible all along Ash Fell Edge at least as far as the present A683 (at the 336m spot height) road to Sedbergh from Kirkby Stephen. Beyond which point they rapidly become invisible on the descent to Water Gate Bottom.

Having forded the river, the travellers head up to Great Bell (at 375m) from which the Nine Standards are still invisible, so from that point they probably guided themselves by the deliberately placed series of cairns on successive skylines. The first is the cairn on what we always called Rowlandson Point at 547m on Tailbrigg (known to the OS as 'Tailbridge Hill,' a name I have never heard used locally). From the top of this cairn the five central cairns of the Nine Standards are in fact just visible. This is followed by the cairns now called Jack Standards (or Rollison Hurrisy, to quote the 1812 perambulation) at about 640m on the northern edge of Coldbergh; even from here the

Nine Standards are still invisible, but it is by now clear where the highest point is, and beyond that, at a lower level, the Nine Standards can at last be seen.

If the route along the southern watershed of Swaledale was favoured, one would expect to find a similarly prominent cairn on the northern end of Mallerstang Edge, clearly visible from Hollow Mill Cross. None has survived. There is a prominent disused quarry on the shoulder of Fells End, but it is not used as a marker. Instead the perambulations refer simply to a White Stone (or variants) in Fells End as the boundary marker, a much less prominent landmark further east and much harder to pick out from a distance. And the boundaries here on the south side of Tailbrigg are between townships or medieval manors, not between the major parishes, whereas on the northern side of Tailbrigg, the Bronze Age Lady Dike, leading as it does up Coldbergh Edge, seems on the face of it to be a much older and more significant boundary marker. It separates the Swale catchment from the Eden catchment. The boundary then continues north between the major parishes and lordships centred on the Eden and Belah catchments on the Westmorland side; on then to the watershed of the Greta River flowing down into County Durham and the boundary between the counties of Westmorland and Yorkshire; and finally to the boundary between Yorkshire and Durham.

All these are expressed in modern-day terms; but these are boundaries that in turn have evolved from very ancient land divisions. For long distance traders, sticking to a route that remained at the very edges of the major local territories would have a number of distinct advantages. They could pass by without attracting notice if they so wished, which might minimise conflict and even contact with the inhabitants, reduce the chances of being robbed of their precious cargo, avoid paying levies and taxes to local officials, stay away from wet lowlands, denser vegetation and hazardous river crossings, and generally make good speed on their journeys. Watershed routes also tend to be shorter and more direct routes than following the rivers.

A field visit to the Nine Standards

Throughout the ages, all visitors to the Nine Standards would notice much the same unique physical attributes of the site. Most noticeably, they are placed on the ridge which separates waters flowing west to the Atlantic Ocean down the River Eden from the waters flowing east to the North Sea down the River Swale. Not only that, but the several tributaries of these two major river systems radiate outwards from the Nine Standards Rigg.

At the Nine Standards, several other things strike you immediately. The cairns are virtually invisible to the east and south-east towards Swaledale and the Mallerstang valley: they face instead down the Eden Valley almost as if their builders could ignore the other directions. They are carefully placed not on the highest crest of the ridge, but on the skyline as viewed from the west; they survey a territory that appears to focus on Kirkby Stephen, but extends far beyond and to the west along the wide and open expanse of the limestone uplands on the south side of the Eden Valley, where a very large concentration of what are thought to be Iron Age/Romano-British settlements occurs, and then on towards the skyline of the Lake District, to the peaks of Scafell, Blencathra, Skiddaw, Saddleback and Helvellyn. This skyline location, as noted already, is itself a characteristic of Bronze Age monuments, marking territory and providing direction to travellers.

But as a signpost, they would only have been of use to travellers approaching them from the west; they are virtually invisible from the east until you are within a few hundred metres of them. Applying this general principle here, we may note that the west-east trade routes in stone axes from the Langdale factories of the Lake District to North Yorkshire, and in gold ornaments from Ireland, have now mutated into the Coast-to-Coast walk from St Bees Head to Robin Hood's Bay, preserving the west to east direction; and the ancient north-south Pennine Way, in use since the Neolithic and Bronze Ages, still draws hikers to the main watershed along the spine of England; these two major arteries cross each other at the Nine Standards.

And it is a reasonably good camp site. As well as providing an excellent look-out point from the cairns looking west, immediately to the north the land falls away to an extensive, flat-bottomed and enclosed area, sheltered from the prevailing south-west winds, and next to the Nine Standards well and at least two springs (though frankly water is not likely to be in short supply anywhere in these hills!) It is ideally suited to periodic or seasonal meetings of the local people, at whatever time in the past and for whatever purpose, and the site is still used by the hardier hikers and campers today.

Seeing at first hand the huge effort that went into creating this linear group of cairns, it is hard to believe that there was no serious intent behind all these features. But what was it? And are we to imagine them as being viewed from the Eden Valley, or were the observers standing at the Nine Standards and looking out from there? And if so, did they look west down the valley or east towards Rogan Seat, and possibly south to the hill fort and beacon on Ingleborough, just visible over the saddle of Gregory Chapel on Mallerstang Edge? Or were they observed from Kirkby Stephen as markers for sunrise or sunset, moonrise or moonset from some as yet unimagined observation point? More study is needed.

Other possibly significant points arise. My sketched ground-plan of the cairns in Figure 1 (page 66) shows the orientation, and also the diameter of each cairn as they stood in winter 2007. The diagram is a rather crude one, based on my own field measurements (in a blizzard, so no guarantees of extreme accuracy...), but the locations and dimensions have been carefully checked by reference to photographs taken on the ground and from low-flying aircraft, some of which are included in this book, and also using high altitude aerial photographs and satellite imagery, notably the excellent Google Earth and Memory-Map. So it is a reasonably accurate depiction.

The individual cairns are irregularly spaced, and they are of different shapes and sizes. Together they lie in a roughly straight line some 75m long, at about 22 degrees east of grid north; in other words, they point to the north-north-east. Though they are not now in a perfectly straight line, they do appear to be aligned purposefully to face west-north-west as a group: see plate 19 (page 147). They therefore face towards the setting sun on the Spring Quarter Day, around 1st May on the ancient feast of Beltane. This feast day falls between the equinoctial position on March 22nd and the summer maximum northward extent on June 22nd. It also faces the rising sun on the Autumn Quarter Day, around 31st October at the great feast day of Halloween. This day is between the equinoctial position on 22nd September and the winter maximum southward extent on December 21st. These are days of great significance to an agricultural or pastoral community, related as they are to key points in the apparent annual migration of the sun, marking the summer and winter seasons.

The above discussion of possible etymological links to the Nine Maidens would suggest that lunar orientations may also be significant, a specialist and complex subject into which, for once, I do not propose to venture!

Some of these physical aspects of the individual cairns and the Nine Standards group as a whole could have changed over the centuries, with collapse and rebuilding; but more likely they have not. During the recent reconstruction, great care was taken to rebuild the cairns on the same footprint, and in the same shape as in old photographs. But whether or not their precise positions and sizes may have altered over the centuries to some slight extent, their siting along the highest points of a relatively narrow ridge limits quite strictly any significant change of position over time. Also too much should not be made of the orientation – their site is determined in the last resort by the shape and orientation of the ridge on which they stand. And there is no recognised evidence that the shape or size of the ridge have been modified by man's activities. This cannot be ruled out, of course: in Britain there are many examples of man-made mountain tops (see Appendix D). In the present case, there are at least two compelling reasons why that possibility should be very carefully considered; their present name, and the general appearance of the Nine Standards Rigg.

The name Nine Standards appears to have been given to the monument by the very practical local population, who have been involved in both agriculture and mining for many generations, often as seasonal or part-time activities. Neither occupation is noted for producing (or tolerating) airy-fairy romantics and deluded fantasists, so when they give a name to a place, it rarely strays far from the factual and the literal, and therefore deserves our careful attention. The place-name discussion above concluded that the original meaning was a description of nine pillars of undisturbed bedrock that had been deliberately left in place by miners so as to support the roof of underground excavations. It was emphatically not a description of nine drystone cairns built along the top of a ridge using flat, loose stones, round and broad at the base and tapering upwards to a rounded point, structures moreover that were and are prone to periodic collapse, which is what we actually have here.

Early mining used the 'bell-pit' technique; a central shaft was excavated vertically downwards to the desired depth, and then the ore-bearing material, the coal or whatever, was removed to create a bell-shaped cavern underground. This method was also used in other areas for extracting flint. When the risk of collapse became too great, columns of undisturbed bedrock were left in place. The technique of shoring up the roof temporarily with pit-props or excavated slabs of rock, placed one on top of the another, evolved to cope with unstable strata, especially in the coal industry, reflecting a more sophisticated and profit-driven engineering approach, and was a much later development; the bell-pits were cruder, more direct and arguably a much less efficient technique.

If we are to take the name literally, therefore, and accept that the name derives from very early mining activities, we have to envisage a large cavern, or perhaps a series of caverns, in which according to the locals there were nine supporting pillars. Such activities will inevitably have left their trace on the general appearance of the Nine Standards Rigg. There ought to be substantial evidence that the natural surface has been disturbed, possibly in the form of spoil heaps, pits, scars of different kinds, maybe even workers' huts, and we would expect to see their visible impact on the slope, soil type and vegetation on the ridge itself.

Fortunately, I have had access to some excellent oblique aerial photographs, generously and freely supplied by Simon Ledingham working on behalf of www.visitcumbria.com and Barry Stacey of the Kirkby Stephen Tourist Information Office, whose invaluable help made this section possible. After many years interpreting black and white or infra-red false colour air photographs, I found them particularly interesting and informative. I only wish they came as conventional stereo pairs taken vertically, and that I still had access to mirror stereoscopes fitted with such trimmings as floating-point and stereo-plotter facilities! But I don't, so what follows can only be a first approximation.

A selection of these photographs is presented in plates 20 to 25 (pages 148-151), and the titles of the plates mention what to look for as well as the direction the camera is pointing. The features provisionally identified are summarised on figures 5 and 6 (pages 167 and 168), and they can be categorised as either natural or artificial. The natural features are mostly boundaries between vegetation, soil and lithology type, breaks of slope, and drainage lines. The artificial or man-made features include footpaths, the cairns themselves, excavations such as quarries or borrow pits, mounds, one or two possible shafts or mine entrances, circular markings in the vegetation, possible drainage lines and outlets.

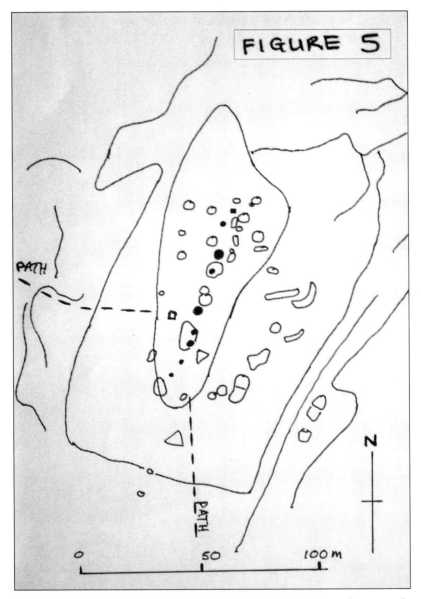

Figure 5, features visible on high altitude digital air photograph, image drawn by the author.

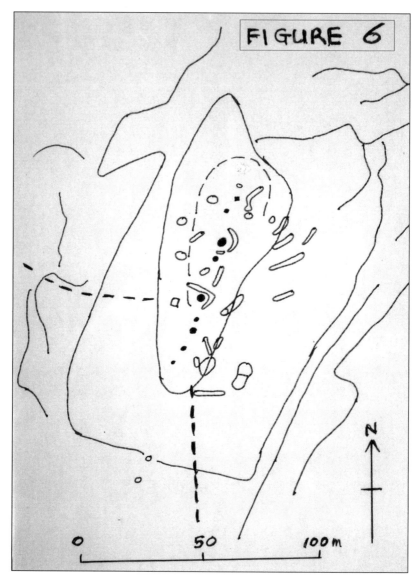

Figure 6, features visible on low altitude oblique aerial photograph, image drawn by the author.

The digital air photograph image, plate 19 (page 147), shows that there are clearly three different regions, each with its own type of soil/vegetation/lithology. Around the outside of the image, there is a wet region of poorly drained peat haggs, with coarse reeds, heather, sphagnum, etc. characterised by dark browns and dark greens with clear river and drainage lines. This encloses an inner zone, which is like an elongated rectangle, almost 300m north to south at its longest on the western side, and about 100m east to west; this zone is much better drained, with a drier surface and good long grass cover, appearing mostly yellow and green on the digital aerial photograph.

The central core of this zone is different, and quite distinctive. About 100m long at the western edge and varying in width from about 60m towards the northern end to perhaps 30m in the south, it includes the Nine Standards and is almost devoid of the green colour of vegetation. It is characterised instead by a high reflectivity, seen as white or grey on the image, which indicates little or no grass, a stony or bare soil, a very permeable or porous lithology, and a patchy, very disturbed surface. This is the area of main interest, and within it considerable variation can be seen. The section off the top north-east corner of this lighter zone is in shadow and therefore much darker; it is much lower than the main ridge, and the dark colouring unfortunately obscures any features that there may be in this area near the well and springs. Plate 20 (page 148) suggests one major item of interest north of the OS trig. station cairn.

The artificial and natural features provisionally identified on the sketch map combine material from both the high altitude digital air photographs and the oblique low altitude aerial photographs. The positions of features identified on the vertical digital air photograph and shown on Figure 5 (page 167) will be more accurate than the positions of features identified on the oblique aerial photographs used for Figure 6 (page 168). In addition, it has to be emphasised that the existence and nature of these features can only be verified by careful and detailed work in the field, ideally by experts. Most features will be positively identified; some will remain ambiguous or not evident on the ground. The First Edition OS Six Inch map (1867) shows 'quarries' in three places, mostly on the western side of the ridge, though the exact location of the cairns and the ridge are not clear (a confusion repeated on the Second and Third Editions where their location and orientation are actually wrong). More helpfully, the oblique aerial photographs show a wide variety of other features. It may well be that the underground features on Nine Standards Rigg turn out to be at least as interesting as the cairns that dominate the upper surface of the ridge.

An expert field archaeologist should look at all the features evident from the photographs and identify what they are, quarries, spoil heaps, mine shaft entrances and adits, old cairn sites, hut circles, bields, sheep folds, modern shelters built by and for ramblers, etc. (trying hard to ignore the recently constructed yompers' drystone sofa...), and separating all of them from the evident artificial and natural drainage lines. Only with this level of detail will it be possible to get a real grasp of what has happened on this very complex site over the millennia.

The real need as a next step is a detailed topographic map of the site, covering the whole ridge down to and below the two breaks of strata evident in the photographs, with a contour interval of at least 1m, preferably 0.5m, and a detailed geological analysis of the rocks making up the light-coloured summit area. The ridge is on the Millstone Grit formations, but the lithology varies over short distances, and the site is close to the boundary with the Carboniferous Limestone and Yoredale Series. Outcrops of coal have been exploited in the area, and other mineral resources, notably lead, but also copper and iron ore, have been mined, and there is evidence of considerable geological faulting locally.

Since it is a very small site, the initial analysis of air photograph pairs using a simple mirror stereoscope should be followed up using a parallel guidance mechanism equipped with appropriate binocular attachments to provide an adequately detailed and accurate base map.

The Nine Standards 'footprint'

Other lines of enquiry that may also lead to fruitful study of who built the cairns, why they built them and when, relate to the recently developing use of Geographical Information Systems or GIS in archaeology, employing digital elevation models (DEMs) or digital terrain models (DTMs) to study intervisibility. In other countries and regions where cairns have been exhaustively studied, such as those already mentioned above, Bronze Age dates have been confirmed in many cases by combining GIS approaches with archaeological excavations.

At its simplest, these tools can help us to answer the question: from what areas of the surrounding countryside can the Nine Standards be seen? Perhaps equally important, what areas can you see from the Nine Standards, over what areas do they cast their 'footprint' as it were? We know that beacons were used from very early times to achieve rapid communication between distant sites; fires were built there so that smoke during the day and flames at night could be seen from great distances and in several directions. It is worth noting that the great Iron Age hill fort on top of Ingleborough is just visible from the Nine Standards, perhaps explaining the stepped nature of the main central cairn, and a fire at either site would be visible from the other. This of course would be dependent on the weather, particularly cloud level, and may not have been a paticularly reliable means of communication without a back-up network at lower elevations.

Machel mentions six such beacons in this part of Cumbria, taking messages from Ingleborough in Yorkshire, and relaying them north. Messages were as frequently relayed south in the wars with the Scots. A familiar modern example is the speed with which news of the appearance of the Spanish Armada off the coast of south-west England in 1588 travelled the length and breadth of the country, via a network of beacons that had already been in use for centuries if not millennia, and indeed are still used as the sites of bonfires during Coronation and Jubilee celebrations.

In good, clear weather after rain, they are visible to the naked eye from some thirteen kilometres (eight miles) or more. A hawk-eyed youth on a clear day may even have been able to see them from the hills above the Lyvennet valley. It was hazy during my last visit to the Nine Standards, accompanying a group from the Landcape and Arts Network (Walker, 2007), so I could not test this (but such sunshine is rare on those hills at any time, and unheard of in April, so nobody was complaining!) But we were able to delight in the presence of the place, accompanied by dozens of other walkers arriving in a constant stream from the north, west, south and south-east, eating their sandwiches and having a well-deserved rest and drink before heading on.

How fitting in such an evocative and powerful place to hear the haunting music of the fiddle played by one of our party, Sara Melville, and thanks to Geoff Jones who carried the fiddle there, and back: see plates 26 and 27 (page 152). Aptly selected, we heard *Bennachie Sunrise* by Alasdair Fraser, after the Aberdeenshire hills which have nine distinctive granite torr tops, two with Pictish forts, and multiple associations with the Nine Maidens, including the 'Maiden Stone' at the foot, mentioned by Waddell as cited above. This music was followed by the *Solstice Reel* and *Fingal's Cave*. A very moving experience and surely a first for the Nine Standards?

Meanwhile, back in the Library

On my return to the world of books, I looked up 'cairn' in the twenty volume *Oxford English Dictionary* (Simpson and Weiner, 1989):

"Cairn page 768. *Carn* from Gaelic *carn* (masculine) a heap of stones. The word is found in all the Celtic languages.

"A pyramid of stones raised as a memorial or mark of some kind; as a memorial of some event or a sepulchral monument over the grave of some person of distinction (CF Genesis xxxi, 45, 2: Samuel xviii, 17). Hence "to add a stone to anyone's cairn" e.g. 1772 Pennant's *Voyage to the Hebrides* p.209 (JAM), "As long as the memory of the deceased endures, not a passenger went by without adding a stone to the heap..." To this moment there is a proverbial expression among the highlanders allusive to old practice; a suppliant will tell his patron, *"curri mi cloch er do charne"* "I will add a stone to your cairn," meaning "when you are no more, I will do all possible honour to your memory" e.g. 1805, Scott 'Last Ministr.' III, xxix. "On many a cairn's gray pyramid Where urns of mighty chiefs lie hid," e.g. 1878, H Stanley, *Dark Continent* I, vi, 137: "We raised a cairn of stones over his grave."

Possibly then an early observance, kept alive until the very recent past by the oral tradition obliging each visitor to add a stone to the cairns on every visit? Their recent near-collapse suggests that a reminder of this tradition might usefully be added to the orientation table on the highest point of what is now called Nine Standards Rigg, which was erected by the Kirkby Stephen Mountain Rescue Service to commemorate the wedding of HRH Prince Charles and Lady Diana Spencer. If each visitor added a stone to the cairns, as they used to, the survival of the Nine Standards would be guaranteed. I didn't see anybody else doing this when we were there, but they might have done.

I then looked up the word 'folly' which has also been used to describe the Nine Standards. After various other meanings of the word, we find under 5a: "A popular name for any costly structure considered to have shown folly in the builder"!

And finally, I looked once again at the OAN report; the summary ends thus:

> "It is recommended that a RCHME Level 3 survey is carried out on the cairns, which would seek to establish the visible phases of construction that have occurred prior to the proposed consolidation. It is also recommended that a topographic survey of the quarries and sheepfold be undertaken."

So far as I know, this survey has not yet been carried out. I think the terms of reference in the OAN report assumed that the RCHME survey would be carried out before the reconstruction; and in that case, it may not now be appropriate, nor reveal the answers that are sought. If a further study is to be made at this late stage, it should not have as its primary objective the undertanding of the phases of construction – it seems clear to me that the cairns have been continually rebuilt over the ages, with collapses at various times, and the continual addition of flagstones to the structures. But in my view, a re-think may be required, and funds should be sought to support a full and professional investigation by competent field archaeologists, supported by a range of appropriate specialists.

A comprehensive study is fully justified, and long overdue. It should seek to determine the age of the Nine Standards, by whatever means are the most likely to be successful and definitive. If it is a phased survey, it should begin by determining what, if anything, lies underneath them, dismantling at least the central, largest cairn, and preferably any others that ground-penetrating radar, resistivity surveys, or other portable geophysical methods, indicate to be of potential value. Samples should then be taken for C14 and other appropriate analyses, with sampling of the underlying soil and peat for pollen analysis. If positive results are obtained, this initial exploratory survey might then be expanded to examine the full range of features outlined above. A detailed topographic map of the whole site would be of enormous help in mapping the results of the separate investigations of the many and complex site features.

A survey of that kind would be worthwhile; to settle for anything less would simply be another missed opportunity. One golden opportunity was missed in 2005 when the cairns were made safe for public access, and the major central pillar was dismantled to below ground level, along with four others. It is extremely difficult to understand why there was no archaeologist on site, with a camera, a trowel and a few polythene bags, even if only for a single day – or even half a day – when the ground beneath the cairns was exposed for inspection.

SIX

The Story so Far

This book had the limited objective of finding and presenting whatever evidence could be gleaned from existing sources, of any or all kinds, that could be used to make some factual statement about the drystone cairns now known as the Nine Standards. The original intention was simply to decide whether they are ancient or modern, or perhaps - like the hymns - both ancient and modern. We need a definite statement, to justify further study. Or if we cannot decide on their age, if the evidence is too vague or questionable, we may have to accept purely on the balance of probability that one or other of these two alternatives is the more likely. Either way, we must try to establish who built them, when they were built, and why. This final section summarises the findings so far, and indicates directions that may be pursued in the future.

The search for information and material began in the most recent past, for a variety of reasons. First, we have a surfeit of information today, on virtually any topic, and it is easier to start in the present and work backwards; the availability of documents and the reliability of maps decrease rapidly as we move into the past. Tracing from a known position today into an unknown past is more likely to be successful than adopting a random starting date. When you do not really know what you are looking for, or where you ought to be looking, this is a great help, and may even be a more efficient search method.

Second, the closer we are to the present, the more likely we are to be able to read and understand whatever sources have to be researched, and the more probable it is that those sources will have survived in their entirety and in sufficiently legible condition to be researched. The English language in the last few hundred years is reasonably comprehensible to most readers, but going back more than five hundred years means that grammar, spelling and even language are not standardised, and the actual materials deteriorate into illegibility with age, neglect and abuse, the older they are and the longer they have survived. Working backwards gives you some practise and training before the real challenges emerge.

Third, and perhaps most important, if the Nine Standards have a recent origin, and we can locate answers to these three key questions in the historical past, there is no need to delve into the murky and very time-consuming waters of arcane disciplines specialising in the distant past: we can all relax, get on with our knitting, do the garden or paint a few more masterpieces, rather than sweat it out in libraries, secondhand bookshops and dusty archives located at opposite ends of the country. But if we can't find acceptable answers in the recent past, we have come too far now to turn back. And that is the problem: self-respect stops us admitting it has become an obsession, but honesty requires us to say it has all become absolutely fascinating.

I say 'we' not in the regal sense, but in recognition that a great many people have been involved in the story outlined in this book. They have given of their time, their knowledge and experience, their particular skill or background, as much as they were able, and my debt to them is considerable. In a sense I am just the story-teller, as well as the researcher. And it is a story, or rather history, merging through proto-history into pre-history, gradually getting clearer but with some way still to go.

The study of place-names tells you the meaning of the name, suggesting why a place was so named, and an indication of the people who gave that place its name. This is a useful start because place-names are facts, etymology and onomastics are sciences, disciplines with a long history of achievement and an extensive literature. The limitation of this approach is that names change over time, just as the people living in an area change over time, and different people may have different names for one and the same place; think of Byzantium, Constantinople and Istanbul. The name that survives today is only the most recent, and it is the name used by the people who created and preserved it. From the language, it can be traced back to a particular period and people.

What we cannot know is what a particular place was called before that period, by the people who lived there earlier. In the case of the Nine Standards, the early Modern English name appears to date from the 14th century, and may have been given by people new to the area who brought with them a mining background and vocabulary. So we know the Nine Standards existed at that time. We do not know if they were built at that time by the incoming lead-miners, or whether they simply used the cairns as landmarks to help locate mineral deposits and the shafts or adits to exploit them. To decide on that, we need to know what the Nine Standards – or the bare ridge on which they now stand – were called before the miners arrived.

Maps record the existence of the Nine Standards at least as far back as the early 18th or late 17th centuries, and possibly earlier. But the very early maps were selective in what they did and did not show; today they would likely be called 'thematic' maps. The earliest maps we have do not show the Nine Standards, as they have no military or strategic value, and so would be of little interest to early cartographers, more concerned with the coasts, rivers, passes, main settlements and fortifications of the country. In addition, the early maps are drawn at very small scales, making it hard to portray such small features.

The evidence of the historical record offers many examples in the form of agents' documents, perambulations, boundary rolls and charters of different kinds that provide a clear and fascinating paper-trail back into the past, dense in the 19th and 18th centuries, fading away into the 17th and 16th centuries but never quite vanishing. Finally in the 12th and 13th centuries, the Gant family provide what may be the earliest documents. In the 13th century, there existed a charter by which pasture rights around Muker and extending as far west as the dale head in upper Swaledale were granted to the Cistercian Abbey of Rievaulx around 1206x1217 by Gilbert, son of Robert de Gant, confirmed by King Henry III in 1251, and reconfirmed by Edward III in 1332/3. These are facts. In the 12th century, there existed a very early perambulation of the whole of upper Swaledale above Stollerton Stile, perhaps ridden and recorded by a previous Gilbert, son of Walter de Gant, probably around 1138 or 1139 when he inherited the lands from his father, who had received the grant without any boundaries being defined. The perambulation is a fact; the dates are my best estimate.

On the balance of probabilities, and comparing the level of detail with surviving examples of similar contemporary documents from Westmorland, in my opinion the copy of the Cornelius Fryer document that has survived does record the waypoints of the perambulation as they were listed in the original document, but that original document was in Latin and it has not yet been found. While I have argued for an early 12th century date, that cannot be confirmed without the original, and perhaps not even then.

Equally, the later donation to Rievaulx was also in Latin, and is stated in the King's confirmation charter to have spelled out the 'metes and bounds', in other words the waypoints, around the perimeter of the area over which pasture rights were granted; this again has not been found, but unlike the boundary roll, we do not know the actual waypoints, though we can date it with some accuracy. The search for these two documents continues because it is important to know exactly what words were used to describe the various landmarks around the boundaries of these two areas, because we can reasonably infer from other evidence that they both include the Nine Standards location, under whatever name was used in the Latin of that time to describe that place. But for now, on balance of probability, the perambulation of 1138 or 1139 is the earliest mention of the Nine Standards so far.

When one or other of these two documents, or a copy, is found, a further step can be taken. If the Nine Standards name remains the same, the date for the earliest use of the transferred mining term *stander* will have to be pushed back more than three hundred years, with appropriate revisions of etymology and dictionaries. If it emerges that the Nine Standards were called something else at that time, other revisions will be required. Even Edmund Cooper's vaguely remembered *neun standen* might alter the dates, if found. It may become clear whether the Normans, the Norse, the Danes, the Anglians or the British called them something else; perhaps 'toothed mountain' for example, was simply a poetic local version of 'Ninian's Cairns.' In any of these cases, a revised date for the earliest mention of the cairns would be possible; 'toothed mountain' would establish their existence in the very early 6th century AD, 'Ninian's Cairns' even earlier.

The Gant documents, a charter and a boundary roll, are quite likely to have survived in some form. Today nobody doubts the account given by Pytheas the Greek (380-310 BC) from Marseilles of his circumnavigation of the British Isles and his epic voyage to Iceland and Greenland where he saw and reported on the midnight sun and the aurora, the pancake ice and drift ice. Yet his original text has not survived, and is known – like so many other classical documents – only by quotations from it that are found in other, later documents. Much the same is true of the New Testament. So copies and translations are acceptable as proof that a particular document did once exist, and much can be gleaned from them. I have searched all the most likely repositories of very early charters for the north of England, as outlined above, so far without success.

The surviving Rievaulx Abbey charters have been well researched, but they have not all survived, and we know of the rest mostly through lists and registers, which are just summaries not transcriptions; and at national level these 'cartularies' as they are called are well known, if often poorly indexed. The National Archives at Kew, the manuscripts collections at the British Library at St. Pancras, the Dodsworth, Burton, Johnston and Frank manuscripts at the Bodleian Library at Oxford, and the recognised authorities on ecclesiastical history have all been searched.

Such is the chaotic and random sequence of many early compilations that it is not an easy task. I cannot say the documents are not there, only that I did not find them. In my view, they are more likely to be tucked away somewhere unexpected in the north of England, in one or other of the less well-known institutions or in private repositories such as Belvoir Castle, perhaps a treasure trove like the Hanby Holmes collection at Durham, some Yorkist or Lancastrian Gant/Gaunt collection, or in local manorial bailiff record books, than in the great national collections at Kew, St. Pancras or the Bodleian. But I am confident that they have survived, as translations, copies or even originals.

Beyond the Norman Conquest, the previous millennium has a very rich and wide-ranging literature which I have not yet begun to sift through, and of which I confess to being largely ignorant up to now. In addition to the huge amount of straight historical and archaeological research, some of which is referenced in the bibliography, one major source that has so far remained untapped is the place-name material in Brythonic or Old Welsh sources. Up to the 19th century, these early chronicles were accepted as the factual history of the British Isles before the Norman Conquest, but a Victorian combination of political correctness and Anglo-Saxon arrogance in the academic community smeared and air-brushed them out of existence and beyond serious consideration, dismissed as legend and mythology, pronounced anathema.

The attempts to eradicate the Welsh language and culture, the blue book scandal, and the imposition of a Hanoverian orthodoxy by the ecclesiastical establishment at the major universities are all well documented (recent examples include Gilbert, 1997; Berkley, 2007) so this is not a political rant. But the result has been for us all a mutilated history with only Roman, Anglo-Saxon and Norman components, an impoverishment and falsification that is only now being slowly and reluctantly redressed. Certainly, there is now no shortage of competent and well-placed Welsh academic linguists. Fortunately, no such control was exercised over Irish sources; Scotland has pursued an admirably independent line on its history and languages, and even Wales has produced its champions despite the best (or should I say worst) efforts of the Establishment. History, in short, is being rewritten - and corrected in the process. This revision is also supported by the latest DNA research, by Sykes, Oppenheimer and others, which is causing a major re-think in the corridors of academe. No doubt it will be resisted tooth and nail, so many hard-earned reputations at stake, peer-review exposed for what it is. Wonderful stuff.

More important, a renewed effort to identify all the many places mentioned in the available British, Brythonic or Old Welsh accounts, and to reconstruct with correct dates the historical events they record, may add to the evidence about the Nine Standards. This is in part to establish a credible context within which to place them. I have argued that there is little or no likelihood that they were built in the last millennium without that fact entering local folk-memory, in the way the visits to prominent landmarks on the high fells by Sir Hugh de Morville and Lady Anne Clifford have done. It may be that we need to add to those examples the association of Uther Pendragon with Pendragon Castle in Mallerstang, and Canon Harrison's unqualified naming of Athelstane's Moor for Stainmore, and perhaps others.

The context provided by a combination of early place-names and such limited archaeological insights as we have, is one of a very ancient landscape in the upper Eden Valley and upper Swaledale, much older than at first imagined, into which the Nine Standards fit very comfortably. They are surrounded by landmarks recognised as old. These include the Norse- and British-named boundary markers and rivers, the Bronze Age dating of the Lady Dike and the Jack Standards, their unique location on the watershed marking the territorial limits of very ancient land divisions in the company of Pillow Mounds, Giants Graves, a bewildering variety of tumuli, Bronze and Iron Age settlements around a horse-shoe of sites from Cote Garth through Hartley Castle; Croglam Castle at Kirkby Stephen; Carrock

Castle at Waitby; Waitby, Smardale and Crosby Garrett fells; Great Asby Scar, Burwens, Ewe Close and Ewe Locks at Crosby Ravensworth; and on towards the Lyvennet and the Lowther rivers.

All argue for antiquity: bronze artefacts and dateable pottery (Samian and Romano-British 2nd and 3rd centuries AD, RCHMW, 1936) have been found at very many locations, and some sites are known to pre-date the Roman roads that crossed the area. From the Mesolithic, the known traders routes from the Langdale axe factories in the west to the Yorkshire flint mines in the east passed along this anciently settled upland area, a landscape that evolved over millennia. In the late Bronze Age, "the route across the Pennines continued in use for trade in gold objects" (Fell, 1940: Webster, 1969). The Mesolithic, Neolithic and early Bronze Ages saw the creation of many other sites in the broader area such as the various stone circles of East Cumbria, the stone alignments at Shap, the earthworks at Tebay, Penrith, Warcop and Kirkby Thore, not forgetting Long Meg and Her Daughters near Little Salkeld.

The Romans seem not to have ventured very far from their major military routes through this area. Several possible minor Roman roads have been identified, from the forts at Brough under Stainmore to the Tebay fort at Low Borrowbridge via the A685 route, to Sedbergh past Street via the A683 route, and to Brough by Bainbridge in Wensleydale (Swailes, 1985), and Roman artefacts have been found at many local places, though these could well have been lost by locals, not Romans. The Roman roads crossed the country over the lowest passes and used the valley bottoms as their preferred routes. This suggests that considerable clearance of the forests had already taken place, and that many native settlements had earlier been established in the valleys, first perhaps at the major river crossings, later spreading out into the adjacent agricultural land. Where they do cross the uplands and approach the native settlements, the alignment of the roads makes it clear that the Romans avoided existing villages. This suggests that the upland settlements long pre-dated the Romans, and that 'Romano-British' may be an inappropriate label; indeed the HER database records Iron Age and Bronze Age for some.

The Roman trading accounts list corn, cattle, hides and slaves as well as lead, copper and other minerals; like all colonists they were here to make money, and if there had been nothing of value, they would not have bothered. The huge effort they made to build roads and forts, and to maintain them against fierce opposition, indicates that this was a prosperous and well populated region from which they were extracting wealth in large quantities. Trading posts grew up beside the main camps. This may have been one factor in the gradual abandonment of the upland sites, and the intensive civilisation of the valley floors. In this period, the land was only partly forested; the area of grassland slowly expanded from the start of the Neolithic; in Roman times, there is clearance and the re-introduction of cereals according to a core taken at Sunbiggin Tarn, but pollen analysis by others shows that in the mountain areas of Westmorland, the valley settlements were in dense woodland, and only the upper fells had been cleared (Webster, 1969). More recent analyses may have revised this.

As upland sites were progressively abandoned, or came once more to be used seasonally rather than occupied throughout the year, fewer people used the old routes, and gradually the broad green ways became the preserve of cattle traders, moving their herds from Scotland down to the major markets in lowland England. In this way, the ancient upland sites have been preserved, whereas the perhaps equally ancient lowland sites in the upper Eden valley and possibly in Swaledale have been repeatedly fought over by armies throughout the ages, periodically burnt and destroyed, continually rebuilt and expanded, so that little or no trace now remains of the original fabric of the oldest lowland settlements, nor of the tracks that led down to them.

This simplistic and perhaps contentious outline is included to support the proposition that there is enough evidence and inference and reasonable assumption to decide that the Nine Standards are not in fact a folly like Mr Carleton's Fox Tower above Brough, whose origin is known as noted above, but an ancient monument, arguably dating from the millennia before the Christian era, and part of an ancient landscape that some disciplines have long recognised. The very fact that their origin is unknown is itself a powerful argument for their antiquity. We may not know when they were built, why they were built, nor by whom. But we can be reasonably sure that they have been there for at least a thousand years; there are possible references to them over the preceding thousand years; and in the pre-Christian era, there is a well-authenticated and understood context into which they fit very comfortably. In particular there are many examples of similar cairns that have been excavated and dated to the Bronze Age.

The antiquarians and archaeologists have ignored them precisely because nothing was known about them, and these authorities therefore had nothing to say. Access to the Nine Standards is not easy; there are no convenient roads, or even bridleways until very recently, but they are not exactly remote either. You can walk up there from the Tailbrigg road in much less than an hour. Other similar sites were visited; these were not. If any excavations have been carried out up there, they have not been recorded. If anything had been found during the frequent partial reconstructions, it would have entered local folk memory, and it hasn't. They therefore remain a mystery, but evidently a very old one.

When were they built? A glib answer might be that they have been built and rebuilt many times, so they are indeed both ancient and modern. But my considered opinion now is that they were first built in the early Bronze Age, an integral part of an extensive ancient and possibly sacred landcape in the Eden Valley that extends throughout Cumbria, over much of the west and north of the British Isles, and perhaps beyond. This view has to be reconciled with the substantial evidence indicating that the site in general has been severely disturbed at some date or over long periods, and in ways that are consistent with mineral exploration and possibly exploitation.

So what are the cairns, and why were they built? The three most likely choices are boundary markers, signposts and burial sites. They may have been any or all of these at different times in the past, so they were probably built for a combination of these reasons. The first two are logical and easy to accept; the third can only be verified or rejected by exploration and excavation.

If they are burial sites, the results of detailed investigation may yield surprising results. Such research must ask in the first instance: are there any inhumations underneath any or all of the cairns? Superficially this only requires the cairns to be dismantled and the immediate subsurface probed for disturbances and burials. If nothing is found, and the results are negative, the obvious location for any interments has been examined, but the overall hypothesis cannot yet be rejected. The search simply extends into another phase, and the question becomes: is the site itself a burial site? Are the cairns simply a distraction, deliberate or fortuitous, if they are not themselves the sites of individual burials?

Members of the Magic Circle, an association of magicians,

illusionists and experts in the noble art of prestidigitation and sleight of hand, know very well that the best place to hide something is in full view of the audience. But you do need a clever distraction. If the uppermost part of Nine Standards Rigg is in fact a sort of long barrow opening to the north or north-north-east (suggested strongly by plates 23, 24 and 25, see pages 150-1), and thus a major burial site, or a sacred repository of cultural artefacts, what better way to distract the unwelcome attentions of future grave robbers or desecrators than to build a line of cairns as dummy burial sites for them to focus on? What better way also to mark and protect the location of the sacred remains and link them forever to the Nine Maidens, much as Christian communities erect crosses on hilltops, bury their leaders in churches, and erect gravestones in churchyards; much as Buddhists build stupas above their holy dead?

As already noted, one or two cairns would be enough to mark a boundary, or act as a signpost; but to build nine does seem rather over the top, so to speak. It seems very deliberate, and this in turn argues strongly in favour of some cultural significance, a view supported by the widespread Nine Maidens associations. These mythological or legendary aspects on their own are unlikely to be accepted as proof of age or origin by the academic community at large, but in this case, there may be physical remains that would sway the balance of probability in favour of acceptance.

As to the cairns themselves, almost certainly speculators have dug underneath them before; if they found anything of value, it is not remembered locally. So they appear to have found nothing; it therefore goes unreported by the diggers because there is nothing to report, and anyway they feel foolish; and the digging does not enter local folk memory – but people no longer dig there. So, the cairns remain, they occasionally fall down; people wonder about them, maybe they do occasionally dig around a bit before they rebuild them but they find nothing. What you see is what you get: to the superstitious and to the simple, they are just a line of cairns on the top of the hill, always guarding the valley and those who live there. Good picnic site, though.

This conjecture can probably be resolved in the immediate future as a by-product of a much-needed geophysical survey of the overall ridge site, supported by results from a detailed field study of tentatively identified features. It looks much better on a grant application to request funding for a geophysical survey and in-depth scientific analysis of samples on a potentially major industrial archaeology site, than for investigations of what might perhaps turn out to be a man-made mountain top. The latter approach has not always met with marked success (see Appendix D); perhaps it's time for the smoke and mirrors? Arable farming, hill farming and sheep farming are all very pragmatic – maybe grant farming should be too.

And who built them? The answer to this final question exists on several levels. A ruling elite decided that they should be built, and commanded or persuaded the tribe to carry out this massive task. The size of the cairns means that the builders decided that they had to be visible from far away, suggesting that they marked the territorial limits for the tribe and its close affiliates, or that they were signposts for long distance traders from Lakeland with stone axes and/or bronze artefacts, or from Ireland with gold artefacts, or perhaps as markers for the lead, copper, iron ore, silver and tin miners and traders from more distant lands. Or perhaps they result from the self-aggrandisement of a local leader who required his or her tomb to continue after death to dominate the kingdom they had enjoyed in life – but if so, why is their name or that function not remembered?

Signposts and limits are the more likely reasons for site selection for the additional reason that those attributes would remain important for centuries, supplying the strong and permanent incentive needed to maintain the cairns, after any memory of long-dead heroes was gone. In a very real sense, every generation could be named as the builders, building and rebuilding what the powerful natural forces at the site were continually destroying. This process continues up to the present day, the latest reconstruction taking place in 2005.

It is appropriate to close this contribution by placing on record my personal thanks to Dick Capel of the East Cumbria Countryside Project for appreciating the cultural value of the Nine Standards to the people of the upper Eden Valley, and deciding not to let them disintegrate and vanish for ever. By obtaining permission from the relevant authorities to make them safe for public access, and securing funding both for an initial assessment of them as historical monuments and for the actual reconstruction, he has nobly continued the work of generations. How many generations? There can as yet be no definitive reply to that, but an answer cannot be long in coming.

The report and the reconstruction stimulated me to spend a part of my retirement researching these enigmatic structures on the Westmerian skyline. Without much idea of where to start, I made very slow progress at first, asked the wrong questions and looked in the wrong places. But over the years, the detective story gained focus and direction as clues emerged and riddles were solved. Many people were helpful, contributing their time and knowledge, offering suggestions and guidance, all very much appreciated.

The results – both the relevant but occasionally inconclusive, and the irrelevant but fascinating – are now summarised and presented, not as the definitive statement I had hoped to make, but as a record of what has been found and where it was found, as well as what was not found and in which dead ends. It is not, then, the final word; and I acknowledge here the excellent beginning provided by the OAN report. So maybe this book is just a continuation, but I hope it will be both useful and interesting. I hope also that the historical material presented and the less outrageous speculations on pre-history may encourage others more appropriately qualified than I am to consider how a phased archaeological study of the Nine Standards might now be realised.

Appendix A

The 2005 Reconstruction

'Before' and 'after' aerial photographs are presented as plates 2 and 3 (page 67); plates 4 and 5 (page 68) show the work in progress and the drystone wallers. This Appendix is based on a phone conversation in May 2008 with Steve Allen about his 2005 reconstruction. Several important points emerged, and I summarise them here so that they are on record for future reference, should that be useful.

1. They removed all the stones for each of the five reconstructed cairns right down to, and including the lowest layer, which was just one round below grass level. The ground surface below that was gravel and stone, indistinguishable from the surrounding surface of the ridge.
2. The stones of the lowest round were the only 'footings' – there were no foundations as such.
3. Steve Allen did not notice any unusual signs on the ground surface below the cairns to indicate there might be something buried underneath them. No markings were noticed on any of the individual stones that were handled.
4. The work took three men eight days. The total project budget for the ECCP reconstruction and the OAN report was £10,000, of which the reconstruction itself cost £9,000.
5. The cost of dismantling the largest, stepped, main central cairn for an archaeological inspection and sampling of the ground surface and whatever lies below (if anything) and then re-building the cairn would be about £2000.
6. The last cairn at the northern end was obviously of much more recent construction (this is the one that the OS used as a trig. station and/or bench mark).
7. There were no large stones in the centres of the cairns, though some longer slabs were found in the lower levels of the cairns, as one might expect, especially on the eastern side of the larger cairns. The OAN report speculated that there may originally have been a number of large single stones on the ridge, of the rounded

or smoothed type known as 'glacial erratics', around which the cairns may have evolved over time, or which the cairns might have replaced, but the author did not offer any evidence of this. It seemed to be a speculation. There are no large rounded stones in the middle of the cairns, or indeed anywhere else on the ridge, certainly nothing resembling a menhir or standing stone, not even a small one.

Appendix B

The Ages of Man

Others may be as hazy as I was about the approximate periods of time referred to in the various Ages mentioned. While there is still debate about the exact dates that separate the major divisions, and the reasons why particular dates should be adopted, it is agreed that there were lengthy transitions between the major divisions, that one did not suddenly finish one night and a new one start the next day, and also that they began at different times in different regions of the world.

The following approximate dates refer to the British Isles, and no doubt even within that region, some areas were ahead of others in their response to the forces of change, and their adoption of new technologies.

Palaeolithic	450,000 – c. 10,000BC
Mesolithic	c. 10,000 – 4,500BC
Neolithic	4,500 – 2,300BC
Bronze Age	2,300 – 700BC
	(Early 2,300–1,200BC; Late 1,200–700 BC)
Iron Age	700BC – 43AD
Roman	43 – 410AD
Dark Ages and Anglo-Saxon 410 – 1066AD	

Palaeolithic, Mesolithic and Neolithic identify the Old, Middle and New Stone Ages respectively, and are defined on the basis of the technologies employed by man.

Bronze is a brown alloy of copper and tin, often 90% copper and 10% tin, or 8:1. Iron is not 'better' than bronze, but it is more widely available. For smelting, iron needs temperatures exceeding $1,100^{\circ}C$.

Appendix C

1. 1812: Copy boundary roll of the Manors of Healaugh and Muker, 29 June-2 July, 1812 (DRO D/HH 6/2/211).

"Be it remembered that on this 29th day of June 1812 the Boundaries of the Manors of Healaugh and Muker in Swaledale in the County of York were ridden and perambulated by the several persons whose names are hereunto subscribed and set with others in their Company. Notice in writing having been first given to all adjoining Lords several of whom met and attended at the said Riding as hereinafter mentioned where the said boundaries adjoined to their respective Manors or Lordships which Boundaries were ridden and perambulated in manner following that is to say on the said 29th day of June beginning at Arkle Beck and [proceeding?] up Foregill Beck to the Bridge at Arkle Town where formerly stood a Gate called Sinder Gate and so up Foregill Beck to the Head thereof and from thence by the Wall to a Stone or Stoup standing East of Arkengarthdale Low Mills where formerly a Gate called Foregill Gate and here We were joined by George Alderson Bailiff or Agent to the Lords of Arkengarthdale to which Manor or Lordship this Manor adjoined here together with ... Foxton their Gamekeeper and from the stone or Gate last mentioned We proceeded in a West or rather South West direction by the Corner of the Easternmost House at Low Mills crossing a Garden to the Beck called Bleabury Beck, and so up by the beck up Bleabury Gill to an Ancient Washfold and from thence up the Gill to the Head thereof and from thence as Heaven Water deals to Wetshaw Head and from thence in like manner to Great Pin seat and from thence by the Water Deal to Carter Currack over Sod Carn or Arkendale Carn and so from thence by the Water Deal to Little Punchett Head where there is a little pool of water or small tarn on the north side thereof and from thence in a northerly direction to two great Stones on a Hill which is commonly called Great Punchett Head as so from thence as Heaven Water deals to Water Cragg Beacon and then on the Height of Baxton Band to Moor Hens Nest in Water Cragg where we were joined by Mr William Walton a Fereeholder of the Lordship of Bowes, John Longstaff

Agent to Henry Percy Pulleine Esquire Owner of the Minerals in the said Lordship of Bowes and Thomas Holliday his Lessee And then We proceeded from Moor Hens Nest as Heaven Water deals to a flatt Stone and thence in the same direction to Reynoldson's Currack on Mick Fell where comes in the Lordship of Bowes And then We rid as Heaven Water deals and according to the Marks already put up by Order of the Referee to whom a former dispute as to the boundary was referred until We came to Tan Hill and then passing between the two houses we came to two flatt Stones commonly called the Goose Nest on the Westernmost of which Stones are placed the Letters and Figures L.W. 1676 and on the other W.P.E. B1756 and from thence to a Hillock by the road Side leading into Westmorland commonly called Tackan Tan and here We were joined by Mr Briggs Agent or Attorney to the Earl of Thanet for his Manor of Brough or Stainmore Dale And here We gave over for this Day.

"Present at this Day's Riding Ottiwell Tomlin, Edmund Alderson Knowles, Alexander Calvert, John Teesdale (flag man) Thomas Wiseman, Thomas Birkbeck, James Lonsdale, James Lonsdale Junr., George Arundale, Peter Batson, Anthony Clarkson, William Simpson and William Pratt (Boys), Mr John Grimes, Mr Michael Metcalfe, Mr John Clarkson of Satron, Edmund Metcalfe and others.

"On Tuesday the 30th day of June 1812 we whose names are hereunto subscribed with sundry other persons proceeded further in riding and perambulating the Boundaries of the said Manors of Healaugh and Muker the like Notice in writing having been first given to all the adjoining Lords who met and attended as hereinafter mentioned that is to say beginning at Tackan Tan aforesaid where we were joined by the said Mr Briggs and Mr Dickinson Mining Agent of the Earl of Thanet and others Tenants and Farmers of the said Earl for his Manor of Brough or Stainmore Dale and from thence as Heaven Water Deals to Hewseat Nab, from thence as Heaven Water deals to Tarn or pool of Water above the Head of Wyth Gill called Brownbery Tarn from thence as Heaven Water deals to the height of Brownbery Edge and from thence along the said Edge between the Head of Buxton Gill and Blobery Gill as Heaven Water deals to the nine Standards where comes in the Lordship or Manor of Hartley We were joined by Mr

Lancelot Dixon, Thomas Hamilton and others Agents Stewards or Tenants to Sir Philip Musgrave for the said Manor of Hartley and from there as Heaven Water deals to a large Hurrock of Stones called Rawlinson Hurock and from thence as Heaven Water deals to the Head of Duckerdale where begins the Lordship or Manor of Nateby and here we were joined by Mr Lamb Agent to the Earl of Lonsdale for the said Manor or Lordship and from thence as Heaven Water deals to the bounder stone West from Hollowmill Cross where we ended for this day.

"Present at this Day's Riding: Ottiwell Tomlin, Edmund Alderson Knowles, Alexander Calvert, Peter Butson, Anthony Clarkson, John Teesdale, Edmund Clarkson, John Raw, John Peacock, Christopher Peacock, William Turn, George Calvert, John Cottingham, John Calvert, Simon Peacock, Thomas Peacock, John Alderson, William Alderson, George Alderson, Edmund Alderson, John Scott, Charles Alderson, Anthony Cleasby and David Cleasby, George Knowles, Henry Harker, John Clarkson, Ralph Scott (Boys), John Lowis, Thomas Robson, Frans Stutzein [??], John Alderson, ... Hills ... C ... Alderson Senr., Birkdale, John Alderson Senr.

"On Wednesday the first day of July 1812 We whose names are hereunto subscribed with sundry persons more proceeded furtyherin the Riding and Perambulation aforesaid and Notice having been given to the Adjoining Lords who attended and met as hereinafter mentioned that is to say beginning at the Boundary Stone West of Hollowmill Cross where we left off yesterday and where this Manor adjoins to the said Manor of Nateby We were met by the said Mr Lumb and from thence proceeding to the grey stone in Fells End where we were met by the said Mr Briggs as Agent to the said Earl of Thanet for his Manor of Mallerstang which comes in here We proceeded to High Pike and from thence to High Seat and so to Gregory Chapel and so to a Hurrock of Stones on Stoney Band above the Head of Long Gill and all as Heaven Water Deals to the great Hurrock or Hugh Seat by some called Ladys Pillar where comes in the Manor of Abbotside and so from thence as Heaven Water deals by the Hurrock on Knowlberry to Great Shunnerfell Hurrock little Shunnerfell to the Standard at the West End of Hoodrigge and so from thence as Heaven Water deals to the Boundary Mark above Cliffe Gill or Trope Gill Head where we ended for this day.

"Present at this Day Riding: Ottiwell Tomlin, Edmund Alderson Knowles, Alexander Calvert, Peter Butson, Anthony Clarkson, Simon Peacock, Charles Alderson Jnr., John Alderson Jnr., Charles Alderson Jnr., George Alderson, John Raw, John Peacock, Edmund Clarkson, James Clarkson, George Alderson Senr., Henry Waistell, Christopher Kearton, Wm. Kearton, George Calvert and John Alderson.

"On Thursday the 2nd day of July 1812 We whose names are hereunto subscribed and set proceeded further in the perambulation and riding aforesaid having also in our Company divers other persons whose names are hereafter mentioned Notice in Writing having been first given to all the adjoining Lords who met and attended as follows Beginning at the Boundary Mark last mentioned and proceeding as Heaven Water deals to Lovely Seat Standard or Beacon where we were joined by John Taylor Gamekeeper to the honorable ... of Abbotside and so from thence by ... or Top Cragg to Organ Seat Standard and so to a Stone above Stoney Gill Head as Heaven Water deals to the Hurrock on the Height of Backstone Edge and so as Heaven Water deals above the Head of Oxnopp Gill to Black Hole where this Manor adjoins the Manor or Lordship of Askrigg where we were met by Robert Addison and afterwards by Mr George Winn and others as Agent and Bailiffs for Lord Grantham for the said Manor of Askrigg and so as Heaven Water deals to a Hurrock of Stones upon the East side of the road leading from Swaledale to Askrigg now called Cuddy Currock and then as Heaven Water deals to the Tarn called Summerlodge Tarn and from thence to Great Bull head and so to Bloody Vale by Bloody Wall down Blea Gill to Haverdale Beck and so down Haverdale Beck to the River Swale.

"In testimony whereof We have hereunto set our Hands this 2nd day of July 1812. Ottiwell Tomlin. Steward of the Manor. E.A. Knowles, Agent and Bailiff. Alexr. Calvert, Land Surveyor.

2. 1812: 3 February, 1812. Letter of Thomas Fothergill Slater at Nateby to Thomas Buston at Thwaite, Swaledale concerning manorial boundaries, quoting in full the Boundary Thomas Slater had from Thomas Robson of Wharton Hall from its meeting with Mallerstang to the Nine Standards, where a large area is in dispute between Lord

Smith and Lord Musgrave's Liberties. (DRO D/HH 6/2/210).

"Sir, There is a Coppy of the Boundery from Thos. Robson of Wharton Hall he informed me that Mr Alderson hase a beter boundry book of a Allder standing, which might be gott if your Sun hase not gotit sum time sine, I was over at Mr Aldersons that day before I Called for this at Wharton Hall, and we had a good deel of talk about the Boundreys in Swaledale, and I told him I had got a Discharge from Bridg of appelby for working In the Earle of Thenats wastes In Malerstang, when I got my discharge I was working upwards of a Hundred yds. to the South East side of Blew gill, Leeding Into Swaledale Comon, which Alderson told me that the Earle had No Maner of Right at blew gill, Neither had they aney Right to discharge me there, for working, Mr Alderson spoke to his oldest sun Richard, I lent Mr Knowles that, and he promised to bring It back the Next week and he hase ben at Kirkby Severall times and never brought It whiche semed very angry about It, which I thought It might have been The Boundrey book but he did not mention what It wass, If its Not It If you wish to see It I think I Can get It for you, If you Chouse to Have It, I looked the Coppey of Thos. Robson over From the Hugh Seat Is to The Hight of Fellsend There Is Eaven Water deall From there To the Whits Stone one Felsend Side adjoinint to the Blewgill To a gray Stone one the Rode side a bout a Hundred yards one the west side of the Hollow mill Cross Leding to Nateby There is Heaven Water deall, from the gray Stone To the Mear gill In Codber Side There is eaven water part It Runs both Into Swaledale and Westmorland I parts Lord Musgraves Libertes and Lord Smiths there was a Stone fixed betwixt other tow stones which was taken out caried a way sum distance from the plase and was Taken and Caryed and put In by one of your Lords Tenants. James Atkinson Keeps getting of Coles In the blew gill Leavel and taking them a way of the premises I went up to the blewgill to fetch sum work Toles from there and they were fetching of Coles away that day. The Next time they went that way they Looked for It and It was taken a way and could not be found.

"From the Meargill to The grey Yaud In Codber hight from There to the Nine Standards There I leave of [= off] for that is the most disputd ground, which will measure Near a Mile in Severall plases that Lord Musgrave Stewards Rode Into Lord Smiths Libertes.

"I know the boundry Markes betwixt the Huse Seat and The Nine Standards as well as the Garth be hind My own House which is a vallowabel part of The Comon which Is Eaten by the adjoinin Lords for want of Lord Smith Looking to his Right of former Tenants.

"I expect by this time that you have got an answer from the Lord that he will Look to have His right that I may be gin to work the Slate quareys one the blew gill Side of the fell. For I am Now Loosint of the best season of the year for working of that quarey If I have Not an Answer from you soon I shall be obleged to begin In sum other work and then the slate quareys will be of No use to Me after I have Ingaged My self other ways.

"From Your Humble Servant, Thos. Fothergill Slater at Nateby. Feb. 3 1812."

3. 1811: "Copy of a paper lent by Mr Edmund Alderson of Wharton in Westmorland to E. A. Knowles, Oct 28th, 1811" (DRO D/HH 6/2/209). Described in the DRO D/HH 6/2/210 letter above as "a beter boundry book of a allder standing." This is a perambulation of the boundary of Swaledale as a whole; the original book 'of older standing' has not yet been identified.

"The Boundary of Swaledale beginning at Stollerton Stile.

No. 1. From Stollerton Stile to the head of Cogden

2. Thence to the white Stone in Sharrow

3. Thence to Brownseat

4. Thence as heaven water divides between Swaledale & Wensleydale to the head of Bolton Greets

5 Thence as heaven water parts to the heights of Wind-gates

6 Thence as heaven water parts to Stone-grove-gill

7 Thence as heaven water parts to Red-keld

8 Thence as heaven water parts to the height of Shunnerfell

9 Thence as heaven water parts to the head of mickle Sleddale

10 Thence betwixt Sleddale and Mallerstang as heaven water parts unto Hew seat morvile, is Sir Hugh Morvill's Seat or Hugh's Seat

11 Thence as heaven water parts to the White Stone in Fells End

12 Thence as heaven water deals to the grey stone on Hollow Mill

13 Thence as heaven water deals to the Gray Yaud in Cawdbright or Coedber

14 Thence as heaven water parts to the Nine Standarts

15 Thence as heaven water parts to the hart-Horn Cragg
16 Thence as heaven water deals to the Brown bergh Edge
17 Thence down the White Gill
18 Thence as heaven water to the Tann * Tarn – viz. Brownber
tarn to Hugh's Seat Nab (Seat any thing to Sit on)
19 Thence as Heaven water deals to Taggon and Tann
20 Thence as Heaven water deals to (Question) Thomas Gill
Head, Raygill head
21 Thence as Heaven water deals to Eaststonsdale-Grove-Head
22 Thence as Heaven water deals to the Height of Water-cragg
23 Thence as Heaven water deals to Mosedale head
24 Thence as Heaven water deals to Mickle Punchard
25 Thence as Heaven water deals to Little Punchard
26 Thence as Heaven water deals to the Height of Pinseat
27 Thence as Heaven water deals to Wetshaw head
28 Thence by a Lineal Line to Forgill Gate
29 Thence by Lineal Line down Forgill to Sinder-Gate
30 Thence down Arklebeck to the foot of Harnegill Beck
31 Thence up Farnedale to the Height of Mosedale-Rigg
32 Thence as Heaven water parts to Almond-Cragg to the Edge
End
33 Thence by a Lineal Line to Mett-Thorn-Gate
34 Thence by a Lineal Line to Awme-Pool in Swale
35 Thence down Swale to Stollerton-Stile."
* In the original 'Tann' is erased and the remainder of that line and the
following line inserted.

4. 1735: DRO Catalogue entry "Boundary of the Honour of
Richmond n.d., c. 1900" actually dated March 1910. (DRO D/HH
6/2/244, 2 pages). Transcription by James Iveson of Angram, dated
March 1910; he gives the date of original source as 1735.
    "Copy of the Boundary of the South and Western portion of
Swaledale from Stollerton <u>Stile to Hollow Mill Cross</u> From
Hollow Mill Cross To Stollerton Stile (vice versa).
    From Hollow Mill Cross as Heaven Water deals – to the Grey
Yawd in Cawdburgh and from the Grey Yawd in Cawdburgh as
Heaven Water parts – to the Nine Standards – & from the Nine
Standards as Heaven water parts – to the Harthorne Cragg & from
the Harthorne Cragg as Heaven water deals to Brownbergh Edge

from Brownbergh Edge down the White Gill as Heaven water deals to the ... Tanne (or Tarn perhaps) from the Tanne as Heaven water deals to Taggon – Tanne (or Tarne) & from Taggon Tanne as Heaven water deals to Thomas Gill Head... and... from Thomas Gill Head as Heaven water deals to East Stonesdale Grove Head, & from there, as Heaven water deals to the height of Water Cragg & from there as Heaven water deals to Mosedale Head, & from there as Heaven water deals to Micke Punchard – from there as Heaven water deals to the Height of Pinseat, & from there as Heaven water deals to Waytshaw Head – by lineal line to Forgill gate by lineal line down Forgill to Sindergate and so down the Arkele Beck, to the foot of Carngill Beck and so up Farnedaill to the heights of Mosedale Rigg, as Heaven water parts and so forth to Aldmond Crag & from Aldmond Cragg to the Edge End & from the Edge End by lineal line to Awme Pool in Swale So down Swale to Stollerton Stile.

"South & West Side from Stollerton Stile. From Stollerton Stile to the Head of Codgen (or perhaps Cogden) & so forth towards the South to Brown Seat & forth as Heaven water parts betwixt Swaledale and Wensleydale unto the height of Bolton Greets & so forth as Heaven water parts to the Heights of Windegates & so West as Heaven water parts unto Stonegrave Gill & so forth betwixt Swaledale and Wensleydale as Heaven water parts to Rede Keld & so forth as Heaven water parts to the Height of Shumer Fell – (Shunner fell) & so forth as Heaven water parts to the Head of Middle Sedeck (perhaps Sleddale) and so forth betwixt Swaledale and Malerstang – as Heaven water parts unto Hudeseat Moracle (perhaps Hugh Seat) and so forth as Heaven water parts unto the White Stones in Fels End & so forth as Heaven water deals to Hollow Mill Cross.

"P.S. In copying the Boundary It is found that the names are altered or differently called then unless an Error has been made by the former copyist, and some places that are mentioned cannot be found – namely the Tanne or Taggon Tanne – approximate to Brownber Edge – & some other places. Coppied C March 1910. Previous copyist 1735, 175 years of difference. James.Iveson Angram. Mch. 1910."

The punctuation and underlining are as in the original; repetitions have deliberately been left in for once, to avoid confusion.

5. 1710, 19th June (DRO D/HH 6/2/256, pages 3 and 4 of 4).
"By virtue of an ... annexed for riding the Bounder of the Manner of Healaugh and Meucar in Swaledale from Wynd Gate to Nine Standards wee whose names are hereunder inscribed together with several other persons Did upon Monday the nineteenth day of June 1710 instant ride the same. Notice in writing having been first of all given to the several adjoining lands in their respective Agents who all attended and meet att the said Rideing where these Bounders adjoyned to their respective Maners and Lordships which bounder was then rid or gone in the manner following:
"Viz. Beginning at Wyndgate where we were joyned by John Metcalfe, George Robinson and James Nicholson, Bayliffs and Agents to Thomas Metcalfe Esq., Mr William Thornton, George Kendall, James Metcalfe, Francis Rogers and other Freeholders and Inhabitants in Happy [?] Newbiggin and Cockridge [?] and rid from thence as Heaven Water deals to Tarn Seete from thence as Heaven Water deals to a Hurrock of Stones southward from where the two rodes [= roads] leading from Swaledale to Cockridge [?] meet and upon the East side thence unto the said way from thence above the Head of Oxnopp Gill to Black Hole from thence to the Hurrock on the height of Backstone Edge and soe above Stony Gill Head Dale [?] then as the Heaven Water deals where we were joyned by Mr Alexander Smith, Mr Barnard Smith, Mr Augustine Metcalfe and others Agents or Officers to the Lord Lonsdale from thence by Jock [?] or Soft [?] Cragg to Ogrome Gate [or Seete?] Standard from thence to Lovely Seate Standard or Beacon and all these as Heaven Water deales from thence as Heaven Water deals above the Cliff or Trope Head .... rack Meay [?] from there as the Heaven Water deals by the Standard att the West End of Hood Rigg and soe by the height of the Little Shunner Fell and Mickle Shunner Fell Hurrock and soe as Heaven Water deals by the Hurrock on Knoutberry [?] to the great Hurrock att Heugh Seate where we were joyned by Mr Thomas Carleton, Richard Waller and John Wharton, Agents or Bayliffs to the Earle of Thanett from thence as Heaven Water deals above the Head of Long Gill to the Hurrock of Stones upon Stony Band from thence by Gregory Chappell High Seat and High Pike as the Heaven Water deals to the Grey Stone at the Fells End.

6. 1708 [Title page] "Stops made on the Lord Wharton's officers riding their bounds of Swaildail adjoining to Stainmoore. EAH" [initials of E A Heelis, Agent]. (CROK WD/HOTH) August 18 1708. The Preface, in a different script, reads:

"A Particular of the Bounder Marke between Stainmore and my Lord Wharton's bounder of Swaildale where my steward read to his steward and Tenants my Bounder for they had none, and when they entered within my Bounders my steward stoped them and showed them there mistakes which they rode the 18 August 1708."

The main document relates to a dispute over some 100 acres between Beck Meeting and Benty Batts/Nine Standards, explaining the procedure and reasons for disputes, and it reads as follows:

"First beginning at Tack and Tan, from thence to Cocklake Rigg, from thence directly to Hugh Seat Nab, from thence to a little tarne called Brownber Tarn, from thence directly westward to ye two becks meeting in Whitsondale, all which bounder markes ye said servants and Tennants of ye Lord Wharton agreed to, save Cocklake Rigg, and ye two becks meeting in Whitsondale, the said Lord Wharton's officers and tennants pretending to ride by ye topps of ye hills, and as heaven water delt was their bounder markes, or divides of ye said Earles bounders, to ye bounder markes they so agreed to, but ye said Earles servants then told them that ye bounder markes above were ye onlye ancient true and immemorial bounder marke, goinge from bounder marke as directly to ye next bounder marke, as a line could be drawne, and from ye two becks meeting on Whitsondale, ye said Earle of Thanet's bounder marke was to a hurrock of stones of ye South end of benty batts, from thence to an Hurrock of Stones on ye midle of Benty battes, from thence to a Mare Stone on ye South Side of Nine Standards, but ye said Lord Whartons officers or tennants carryed their bounder flagg on ye ridge or topp of ye hills and did not go by ye said two hurrocks of Stones on benty batts, whereby they included above one hundred acres of waist ground from ye said Earle Thanetts waist grounds (as we believe) to ye said Lord Wharton's waist grounds. And we do further testify that when ye said Lord Whartons bounder flag went by ye said ridges or topps of ye hills and not directly from ye said bounder marke to bounder marke, the said Earles Officers told then they reed wrong and stopped them, or bidd them take notice they stoped them, in places where they could come to ye foot people that carryed ye said bounder flag (but in many places could not come at or meete them on horseback by reason of ye boggs and mosses). And ye said Mr. Hall and Mr. Carleton desired ye Lord Whartons officers and Servants to produce and show their bounder book or Roll, but they said they had none, onely showed a note they pretended they had out of their bounder book, but ye said Mr Carleton produced and red to them ye Earle of Thanet's bounder Roll being according to ye bounder markes above, and told them all ye Earles ancient bounder books or rolls were according to ye bounder markes above, All which we will testifie when required. Witness our hands ye Eighteenth day of August Anno Dni. 1708." [List of Witnesses, divided into five "Tenants" Tho. Carleton, Tho. Munkhouse, John Morland, John Williamson, John Morland, and eight "Neither tennants their [i.e. there] nor intrested" Jo. Hall, Tho. Carleton, Rich. Waller, John Wharton, Anthony Ffothergill, Simon Mayson mke a [?], John Futhergill, and Thomas Ward.

7. 1684: Machell MSS *History of Westmorland* Volume 3 page 95, on paper. CROC.

"The Bounder of Stainmoor ridd by the right honourable Thomas Earl of Thanet Island, Lord Tufton of Tufton, Lord Clifford Westmorland and born [?] Lord of the Honour of Skipton in Craven, and hereditary Sherriffe of the County of Westmorland in his owne person ye 11th and 12th dayes of September in the thirtieth year of the reigne of our Sovraine Lord Charles the Second by the Grace of God of England Scotland France and Ireland King, Defender of the Faith, AD 1684."

This dating recognises The Commonwealth of Oliver Cromwell 1649-58, and Richard Cromwell 1658-59, whereas the dating of the WD/HOTH version below does not.

"1. Beginning at Winton Briggstones.

2. From thence up the sike near the South end of Winton Mill to Fletchers Close Nooke.

3. From thence up Whingill beck to Whingill head.

4. From thence along a little wall called Winton Ring dike to Stainbank head

5. From thence to a Grey Stone near ye East end of Coat garth house

6. From thence along Langrigg Skarr to a Graystone within Hartley yate

7. From thence to Raven Skarr

8. From thence up Hernegill Beck to Hernegill Side

9. Thence to a great stone on Low Grayrigg

10. Thence to a great stone on High Grayrigg

11. Thence up the north end of Green Side by the Mayor potts

12. From thence to an Hurrock of Stones on Bassen/Baxen Fell Side

13. From thence to a meare stone on the South side of the nine Standers

14. From thence to an Hurrock of Stones on ye midle of Benty Batts.

15. From thence to an Hurrock of Stones at the South End of Benty Batts.

16. From thence directly East to the two becks meetinge in Whitsundale.

17. Thence to a litle Tarne called Brownber Tarne

18. From thence directly/North to Hugh Seat Nabb.

19. From thence to Cocklake rigg

20. From thence to Tack and Tann.

21. From thence to Yard Loupe [Lamp?]

22. From thence to Drygill Head

23. From thence to two gray stones on Taylor Rigg

24. From thence to the White Stone in Easgill

25. From thence over Black Sike brigg to Aygill pool foote.

26. From thence to a gray stone in Wharfgill head.

27. From thence to a White Stone in White Banks

28. From thence to Rere Cross

29. From thence to Beldhow Hill

30. From thence to Rise brigg sike

31. From thence to Mickledod

32. From thence to a great ragged stone where Black beck and Bowden [= Balder] beck meet.

33. From thence to the East end of Pinod Hill.

34. From thence to the head of Potters Reede.

35. From thence to the foor of Brardstone graine.

36. From thence to a great stone at ye East end of Dowcragg.

37. From thence to a great hewn stone in the bowght of Dowcragg

38. From thence to the head of Rowton sike.

39. From thence downe Rowton sike to the foote thereof.

40. From thence to an Hurrock of Stones at the East end of Leesett.

41. From thence to the foot of Masten sike where it meetes with Force beckes.

42. Then all alonge up Masten sike to an Hurrock of Stones in the Bought of Mickle Fell.

43. From thence to the head of Birk sike.

44. From thence down Birk sike all alonge till it meetes with Maze beck.

45. From thence up Maze beck till it meetes with Swarth beck.

46. From thence to a Hurrock of Stones on Arneside Rake.

47. From thence to an Hurrock of Stones at ye North end of Litle fell.

48. From thence to the head of Cirygill [Drygill?] sike.

49. From thence downe Cirygill [Drygill?] sike to the head of West Swindale.

50. From thence downe Swindale beck to Swindale foote near Hilton town end.

This Bounder was ridd in the presence of us (the undersigned)"

The texts in the two versions from CROK/WD/HOTH and CROC Machell MSS Volume 3 are virtually identical; the only differences at waypoints 12 and 18 are separated by a forward slash / above.

Appendix D

Man-made mountain tops

The west and north of the British Isles contain many examples where man has extensively and impressively modified the tops of hills and mountains to suit his purposes down through the ages before recorded history. Perhaps the best known and researched example is Maiden Castle in Dorset, but there are many others in the relevant archaeological literature. Not all these impressive features are on the the tops of hills; in the case of Silbury Hill in Wiltshire the hill is entirely man-made but set in otherwise fairly flat terrain. But in the present case, we are concerned with hill-tops, and specifically with the question: would an extensively modified hill-crest be unique?

Two researchers working at their own expense in South Wales for decades have produced some remarkable finds. Their work is described in some detail in Adrian Gilbert's popular account *The Holy Kingdom* (Corgi Books, 1998) which also gives much of the background to the problems they have had in securing recognition. It makes for very interesting reading, and although we cannot take it that the author is entirely disinterested (he has after all written a book that is for sale to the general public), it is not unreasonable to assume that an honest and accurate description is being presented by an otherwise unbiased observer. It tells an astonishing and informative story which deserves to be more widely known.

The researchers Alan Wilson and Baram Blackett have been unable to find a publisher for their many books, which were therefore initially self-published, and they have been obliged by the events described by Gilbert to leave their native South Wales and re-settle in Newcastle-upon-Tyne. Some of their results have latterly been published by Grant Berkley and the following quotes are taken from *The search for the Ark of the Covenant* (Berkley, 2007). On page 353:

> "A strange and little publicized excavation on a hill in the North of England had revealed an underground chamber that was reached through a cleverly constructed vertical shaft that dog-legged slightly near the surface. The entry was disguised and filled with small stones. The shaft led downwards into a chamber, and in this

chamber there was a large ledge well above floor level. On this ledge were the remains of whoever the important person was – probably a British King – who had been buried there in antiquity. Another shaft cut low down in the floor of this burial chamber led downwards and outwards and emerged lower down the hillside in a very neatly arranged drainage system. The drain reached the surface as a hole filled with small stones that was in the shape of a bowl shaped man-made pit. The system encouraged rainwater to percolate rapidly into the bottom of the chamber, where it was then led away quickly but in a controlled manner through the drain."

The researchers had already identified at least two other such sites in South Wales which they had described in some detail earlier in the book. On page 235 they describe having located the site at Tywyn-y-Glo (meaning 'the Mound of Fire' or 'the Mound of Brightness') above Fan Haulog ('shining brightness') Farm near Ynysybyl ('the enclosure of the ark,' not Ynysybwl) in the Rhondda Valley; they continue on page 356:

"... there were no less than five such drains on the north slope of the hill. It was therefore plainly obvious that a huge effort had been made in antiquity to construct a very large drainage system to draw off water that might penetrate the probable chamber under the surface at the top of the hill. The presence of a standing stone surrounded by flat pavement like stones set into the ground around it to ensure stability marked the exact place."

My point here is that these writers are describing physical features at a known place, in other words they mention physical facts so that what they claim to have found can be verified or disproved; either these drains and stones exist or they do not. They would not be the first inconvenient facts encountered by archaeology; and if they are not facts, then it should be a simple matter for competent experts to expose the deception and challenge the perpetrators to public debate. So far as I know, this has not yet happened; far from it, in fact.

I do not know – and the author does not reveal – the location of the "little known excavation in the North of England" that is being described in the first quotation above. Given the nature of the find and the events recounted elsewhere in Grant Berkley's book and by Gilbert, that is undertandable and hardly surprising.

So we have here at least two examples of man-made mountain tops, sites that have been extensively modified by man's activities. While I am not claiming that the features tentatively identified from aerial photography of the Nine Standards are as dramatic as the drainage systems described above, such features do merit examination on the ground, and we shall not know what those feature really are until some serious effort is made to establish the physical and incontrovertible facts about the site.

Appendix E

Perambulations are not entirely a thing of the distant past. As already noted above, they should in theory have become redundant with the creation of the Ordnance Survey's maps in the late 19th century as the authoritative basis for all boundary locations. But in practice disputes continued – and indeed continue – over small and relatively insignificant areas in the more remote extremities of this land. In addition, there has happily been a recent trend for local groups to maintain or revive traditions that in the past generated community spirit and provided an opportunity to express local solidarity in the face of administrative indifference. Today, such excursions are often simply an excuse to go out with friends and acquaintances, to get some exercise, walk the dogs and have an enjoyable outing on the fell tops, while of course reassuring themselves that the perfidious neighbours have not encroached on the jealously protected community lands...

Plates 28 and 29 (pages 139 and 149) give some idea of what these ceremonies were like. The first shows the group of about 70 people, and three horses, assembled at Watergate Bottom or 'Watter Yat' beside the River Eden on 4 July 1906 to walk the boundary of the township of Mallerstang within the parish of Kirkby Stephen. Mary Thompson (1965) gives a detailed account of the proceedings as reported to her by Matthew Robinson of Nateby who had taken part as a boy of twelve years on his horse Blossom (later borrowed by a certain small and fat gentleman who, unable to manage the arduous walking involved, offered to buy the horse for £30, a huge sum at that time). The second shows a smaller, but no less enthusiastic or determined, group assembled under the same – now apparently leafless – tree at Watter Yat on 24 June 2006 to celebrate the Centenary of the 1906 perambulation, under the inspired leadership of Dr John Hamilton of the Thrang in Mallerstang, current Chairman of the Mallerstang Parish Meeting, and complete with a designated EU Monitor! No horses, though. A full account of the proceedings and some other pictures are given on the excellent Mallerstang Parish Meeting website at www.mallerstang.com/parishmeeting.htm

I am indebted to John Hamilton both for sending me copies of these two photographs and for his permission to use them in this book.

Bibliography

Anderson, Alan O. 1908, *Scottish Annals from English Chroniclers; AD 500–1286.*

Atkinson, John Christopher, 1889, *Cartularium abbathiae de Rievalle ordinis Cisterciensis fundate anno MCXXXII or Cartulary of the Cistercian Abbey of Rievaulx, founded in the year 1132.*Volume 83, Surtees Society.

Berkley, Grant, 2007, *The Discovery of the Ark of the Covenant; based on the works of Baram Blackett and Alan Wilson.* Trafford Publishing, Victoria BC, Canada.

Binding, C J and Wilson L J, 2004, *Ritual protection marks in Goatchurch Cavern, Burrington Combe, North Somerset,* University of Bristol Spelaeological Society, Volume 23, Number 2, ISSN 0373-7527. For summary of main points visit: www.apotropaios.co.uk/goatchurch_cavern_marks.htm

Birkbeck, Douglas, 2000, *A History of Kirkby Stephen*, Cito Press, Soulby, Kirkby Stephen.

Bodleian Library Oxford, undated. Finding Aid: *Collections of Nathaniel Johnston and Richard Frank,* Bodleian Library website.

Bower, Walter, 1722, Scotichronicon of John Fordun – see Fordun entry below.

Braithwaite, John Waistell, 1884, *Guide to Kirkby Stephen, Appleby, Brough, Warcop, Ravenstonedale and Mallerstang including a map etc.* JWB & Sons, Kirkby Stephen.

Braithwaite, John Waistell, 1924, *Guide to Kirkby Stephen, Appleby, Brough, Warcop, Ravenstonedale and Mallerstang including a map etc*, Revised Edition, JWB & Sons, Kirkby Stephen.

Burton, John, 1758, *Monasticon Eboracense; and the ecclesiastical history of Yorkshire*

Cherry, J and Cherry, P J, 1987, *Prehistoric Habitation Sites on the Limestone Uplands of Eastern Cumbria,* Cumberland and Westmorland Antiquarian and Archaeological Society, Research Series, Volume II, Titus Wilson, Kendal.

Cherry, J and Cherry, P J, 2002, *Coastline and Upland in Cumbrian Pre-history; A Retrospective,* Transactions of the Cumberland and Westmorland Antiquarian and Archaeological Society, 3rd series,

Volume II, Article 1, Titus Wilson, Kendal.

Clappinson, Mary and Rogers, T D, 1991, *Summary Catalogue of Post-Medieval Western Manuscripts in the Bodleian Library Oxford, Acquisitions 1916-1975 (SC 37300-55936)*, Volume II (SC46394-55936), Clarendon Press, Oxford.

Clare, Tom, 1979, *Rayset Pike Long Cairn in the Machell MSS*, TCWAAS, Series Two, lxxix, 144.

Clarkson, Christopher, 1821, *History of Richmond in the County of York, including a description of the Castle, Friary, Easeby Abbey, and other remains of antiquity in the neighbourhood*, Printed for the author, Richmond.

Clay, C T, 1914, *Early Yorkshire Charters; being a collection of documents anterior to the thirteenth century made from public records, monastic chartularies, Roger Dodsworth's manuscripts and other available sources*, Six volumes, Yorkshire Archaeological Society. Based on the manuscripts of Wm. Farrer and edited by Charles Travis Clay. Ballantyne, Hanson, 1914. See also 'Farrer' entry below.

Cooper, Edmund, 1948, *Muker; the Story of a Yorkshire Parish*, Dalesman Publishing Company.

Cooper, Edmund, 1973, *A history of Swaledale*, Dalesman Books, Clapham.

Cooper, William, 2002, The *Brut y Bryttaniat* or *The Chronicle of the Early Britons*, formerly called the *Brut Tysilio*, Tysilio's Chronicle and known as *The Chronicle of the Kings of Britain*, Jesus College shelfmark MS LXI. Downloadable at: http://www.annomundi.com/ history/chronicle_of_the_early_britons.htm Note that the underlines in the last part of the web address are not hyphens, but underscores like this: chronicle_of_the_early_britons.htm

Cox, B, 1976, *The place-names of the earliest English records.* In *Journal of the English Place Name Society*, 8, pp.12-66.

Curwen, John F, 1932, *The Later Records relating to North Westmorland, or the Barony of Appleby.* Record Series, 8. Cumberland and Westmorland Antiquarian and Archaeological Society, Titus Wilson, Kendal.

Davis, G C R, 1958, *Medieval Cartularies of Great Britain; a short catalogue*, Longmans, London.

Dugdale, Sir William, 1693, *Monasticon Anglicanum: or a history of the ancient abbies... in England and Wales.* English version, 6 volumes in 8 parts, 1817-30. Ed. J Caley, H Ellis and the Rev. B

Bandinel. London.

Ekwall, E, 1960, *The Concise Oxford Dictionary of English Place-names,* 4th Edition. Oxford.

Ellwood, T, 1895, *Lakeland and Iceland comprising: A glossary of words in the dialect of Cumberland and Westmorland and North Lancashire, and The Landnama Book of Iceland,* 1995 reprint by Llanerch Publishers, Felin Fach.

Farrer, William, 1914, *Early Yorkshire Charters; being a collection of documents anterior to the thirteenth century made from public records, monastic chartularies, Roger Dodsworth's manuscripts and other available sources,* six volumes, Yorkshire Archaeological Society. Based on the manuscripts of Wm. Farrer and edited by Charles Travis Clay, Ballantyne, Hanson, 1914.

Faull, M, 1974, *Roman and Anglian Settlement Patterns in Yorkshire*, in *Northern History*, 9, pp. 1-25.

Fell, C I, 1940, *Bronze Age connections between the Lake District and Ireland,* Cumberland and Westmorland Antiquarian and Archaeological Society, Series 2, Volume XI, pp. 118-130, Titus Wilson, Kendal.

Fieldhouse, Roger and Jennings, Bernard, 1977, *A History of Richmond and Swaledale*, Chichester, Phillimore.

Fleming, A, 1994, *Swadal, Swar (and Erechwydd?): early medieval polities in Upper Swaledale* in *Landscape History.* Journal of the Society for Landscape Studies, Volume 16, 1994.

Fleming, A, 1998, *Swaledale: Valley of the Wild River.*

de Fordun, Johannes, 1722, *Scotichronicon with supplement and continuation* by W. Bower.

Fox, Sir Cyril, 1938, *The Personality of Britain: its influence on inhabitant and invader in prehistoric and early historic times,* National Museum of Wales and Press Board of Wales, Cardiff.

Gale, Roger, 1722, *Registrum Honoris de Richmond: Exhibens Terrarum et Villarum Quae Quondam Fuerunt Edwini Comitis Infra Richmondshire Descriptionem...* 'Register of the Honour of Richmond,' R.Gosling, London.

Gelling, Margaret, 1978, *Signposts to the Past*, London.

Gilbert, Adrian; Wilson, Alan; and Blackett, Baram, 1998. *The Holy Kingdom,* Corgi Books, London.

Gough, Richard, 1768 and 1780 editions, *British Topography.*

Hamilton, John, 1993, *Mallerstang Dale*, Broadcast Books.

Hardy, Stuart, 2003, *The Search for the Nine Maidens,* Luath Press.

Harrison, Marshall-General George Henry de Strabolgie Neville Plantagenet, 1779, *The History of Yorkshire and Yorkshire Families.*

Harrison, William, 1577, *An historical description of the islande of Britayne, etc.* in R Holinshed, *The First volume of the Chronicles of England, Scotlande and Irelande,* London.

Hartley, Marie and Ingilby, Joan, 1956, *The Yorkshire Dales,* J M Dent, London.

Hartley, Marie and Ingilby, Joan, 1986, *Dales Memories*, Dalesman Books.

Higham, N, 1986, *The Northern Country to AD 1000*, London.

Higham, N, 1993, *The Kingdom of Northumbria*, Stroud.

Hinson, Ron and Lucie with J L Barker, 1968 (reprinted from 1956), *Swaledale from Source to Richmond: A Visitors' Guide,* Dalesman Press.

Hogg, A H A, 1946, *Llwyfenydd* in 'Antiquity', Volume XX, pp. 210-211.

Holinshed, 1577, *The First volume of the Chronicles of England, Scotlande and Irelande,* London.

Hunter, Joseph, 1838, *Three catalogues describing the contents of the Red Book of the Exchequer, of the Dodsworth mss. in the Bodleian Library, and of the MSS* (the third is Roger Dodsworth mss. in the library of the Hon. Society of Lincoln's Inn.

Jackson, K J, 1970, *Romano-British names in the Antonine Itinerary.* in Rivet, A L F, *The British Section of the Antonine Itinerary* in *Britannia*, 1; Appendix II p.68-82.

Latham, R E with Howlett, D R, 1986, *Dictionary of medieval Latin from British sources,* Oxford University Press for the British Academy.

Latham, R E, 1965, *Revised Medieval Latin Word List from British and Irish sources, with supplement*, Oxford University Press for the British Academy.

Le Patourel, H E J; Long, M H and Pickles, M F, 1993, *Yorkshire Boundaries,* Yorkshire Archaeological Society, Leeds.

Machell, Thomas, 1695? *History of Westmorland.* This is in six undated manuscript volumes in the archive of the Dean and Chapter of Carlisle Cathedral, accessed via CROC. Machell lived 1647-1698.

Mackenzie, D A, 1935, *Scottish Folklore and Folklife*, Blackie, London and Glasgow.

Nicholls, Rev. W, 1883, *The History and Traditions of Mallerstang Forest and Pendragon Castle.*

Nicolson, Joseph and Burn, Richard, 1777, *The History and Antiquities of the Counties of Westmorland and Cumberland,* W Strahan and T Cadell, London.

Oppenheimer, Stephen, 2006, *The Origins of the British,* Robinson, London.

Oxford Archaeology North, 2005, *Nine Standards, Kirkby Stephen, Cumbria.* Archaeological Desk-Based Assessment Report, East Cumbria Countryside Project.

Oxford English Dictionary, 1979, micrographically produced, 10 volumes in two, Clarendon Press, Oxford.

Page, William, 1923, *A History of Yorkshire North Riding,* The Victoria History of the Counties of England, 2 volumes; Volume 1 1914, Volume 2 1923, Roan.

Payton, Philip, 2004, *Cornwall: A History,* Cornwall Editions Ltd.

Phythian-Adams, Charles, 1996, *The Land of the Cambrians; a study in British provincial origins, AD 400-1120,* Scolar Press, Aldershot.

Pontefract, Ella with Hartley, Marie, 1944 (5th Edition), *Swaledale,* J M Dent and Sons, London.

Pryor, Francis, 2003, *Britain BC: Life in Britain and Ireland before the Romans,* Harper Collins.

Renfrew, Colin, 1987, *Archaeology and Language: The Puzzle of Indo-European Origins*, Penguin Harmondsworth.

Roberston, Dawn and Koronka, Peter, 1992, *Secrets and Legends of Old Westmorland*, Hayloft Publishing Ltd, Kirkby Stephen, and Cumbria County Council Library Service.

Royal Commission on Historical Monuments, 1936, *An Inventory of the Historical Monuments in Westmorland,* HMSO, London.

Ryley, William, 1661, *Placita Parliamentaria*, 'Pleadings in Parliament.'

Simpson, W. Douglas, 1940, *St. Ninian and Christian origins in Scotland.*

Simpson, John A and Weiner, E S C, 1989, *Oxford English Dictionary* in 20 volumes, Clarendon Press, Oxford.

Smith, Albert Hugh, 1967, *The Place Names of Westmorland, parts 1 and 2,* English Place Name Society, Volume XLII, Cambridge University Press.

Smith, Albert Hugh, 1928, *The Place Names of the North Riding of*

Yorkshire, English Place Name Society, Volume V, Cambridge University Press.

Stenton, Sir Frank, 1971, *Anglo-Saxon England* Third Edition in *The Oxford History of England,* Clarendon Press, Oxford.

Stevens, John, d. 1726, *The history of the antient abbeys... Being two additional volumes to Sir William Dugdale's Monasticon Anglicanum,* London.

Sullivan, Jeremiah, *Cumberland and Westmorland, Ancient and Modern, the people, dialect, superstitions and customs,* 1857.

Surtees Society, *Cartulary of Rievaulx,* Volume 83, see J C Atkinson

Swailes, Anne and Alec, 1985, *Kirkby Stephen,* Titus Wilson, Kendal.

Sykes, Bryan, 2001, *The Seven Daughters of Eve,* Bantam, London.

Sykes, Bryan, 2003, *Adam's Curse: A Future Without Men,* Bantam, London.

Tanner, Thomas, 1744, '*Notitia Monastica,* or an account of all the abbies, priories, and houses of friers, heretofore in England and Wales and also of the colleges and hospitals founded before AD 1540, John Tanner, London.

Thompson, Mary Mabel, 1965, *A Westmorland dale,* James Whitehead, Appleby.

Thomson R L, 1964, *Celtic place-names in Yorkshire,* Trans. Yorkshire Dialect Society II. pt. 64, p.41-55.

Trice Martin, Charles, 1892, *The Record Interpreter,* Second Edition facsimile Phillimore, 1982 - no that date's not a typo!

Waddell, L A, 1924, *The Phoenician Origin of Britons, Scots and Anglo-Saxons: Discovered by Phoenician and Sumerian Inscriptions in Britain, by Pre-Roman Briton Coins and a Mass of New History,* Williams and Norgate, London.

Wainwright, Alfred, 1973, *A Coast to Coast Walk,* Westmorland Gazette, Kendal

Wainwright, Alfred, 1980, *An Eden Sketchbook* Westmorland Gazette, Kendal

Walker, S H, 2007, 'The Nine Standards' in *Landscape and Arts Network online Journal,* Number 41, June 2007.

Webster, Robert Arthur, 1969, *The Romano-British settlements of Westmorland: a study in cultural ecology,* unpublished PhD thesis, R1612, University of Reading.

Whelan, William, 1860, *History and Topography of Cumberland and Westmorland,* Whittaker, London.

Whitaker, Thomas Dunham, 1823, *An History of Richmondshire, in the north Riding of the county of Yorkshire...* printed for Longman, Hurst, Rees, Orme and Browne, London.

Williams, Sir Ifor, 1975, *The Poems of Taliesin*, Dublin.

Winchester, Angus J L, 2000, *Discovering Parish Boundaries,* Shire Publications, Princes Risborough.

Correspondence held at the Historic Environment Records office at Kendal County Offices, Cumbria:

1. Letter from Tom Clare to Alec Swailes dated 21 March 1984 ref. TC/AM/S1513

2. Letter from Alec Swailes to Tom Clare dated 23 March 1984,

3. Letter from Edmund Cooper to Alec Swailes dated 24 May 1974, and

4. Alec Swailes' manuscript copy, dated 24 May 1974 and entitled *Early References to Nine Standards – from Edmund Cooper*, of Cooper's manuscript copy of the document in Lawrence Barker's Papers by Cornelius Fryer, evidently a translation into English from an original presumed to have been in Latin.

Permissions

Quotations from the Hanby Holmes Archives are made by permission of Durham County Record Office, and are referred to in the text as DRO/HH followed by the specific reference number. Plates 9 and 14 are reproduced by permission of the owners of those documents, obtained on the author's behalf by the Durham County Archivist Liz Bregazzi. The documents were made available to the author at the Durham County Record Office by Jennifer Gill, MA, County Archivist and her staff.

Quotations from the Lonsdale archive are made by permission of Jim Lowther on behalf of the Lowther Estate Trustees. The manuscripts were made available to the author at the offices of the Carlisle County Record Office by the Assistant County Archivist David Bowcock and his staff.

Quotations from the Machell manuscripts are made by permission of the Canon Librarian D. H. Jenkins, The Abbey, Carlisle. The manuscripts are the property of the Dean and Chapter of the Cathedral, and were made available to the author at the offices of the Carlisle Country Record Office by Assistant County Archivist David Bowcock and his staff.

Quotations and reproductions as plates 8, 10 and 11 of material from the Hothfield archive are made by permission of the Right Honourable Lord Hothfield, Drybeck, Appleby-in-Westmorland. The material was made available to the author at the County Record Office Kendal by Assistant County Archivist Peter Eyre and his staff.

Quotations and reproductions of the Cornelius Fryer paper as plates 12 and 13 are made by permission of the owner, Lawrence Barker of Healaugh in Swaledale, who made the material available to the author.

Plates 1 and 19 are the copyright of GetMapping, and the original image was purchased with the right to reproduce up to ten copies in publications.

Some of the photographs I have directly from Simon Ledingham, others I got on a DVD from Barry Stacey at the Kirkby Stephen Tourist Information Centre, but I know they are the work of Simon Ledingham, hence the dual attribution.